FROMMER'S
LAS VEGAS
MARY RAKAUSKAS

D1487887

1989–1990

Published by Prentice Hall Trade Division
A Division of Simon & Schuster, Inc.
Gulf + Western Building
One Gulf + Western Plaza
New York, New York 10023

ISBN 0-13-047614-5
ISSN 0899-3262

Manufactured in the United States of America
Designed by Levavi & Levavi, Inc.

*Although every effort was made to ensure the accuracy
of price information appearing in this book,
it should be kept in mind that prices
can and do fluctuate in the course of time.*

CONTENTS

MAPS

To my gamboling cronies—
Shirley and Marie

INFLATION ALERT: I don't have to tell you that costs will rise regardless of the level of inflation. For that reason it is quite possible that prices may be slightly higher at a given establishment when you read this book than they were at the time this information was collected. Be that as it may, I feel sure these selections will still represent the best travel bargains in Las Vegas and environs.

A DISCLAIMER: Although every effort was made to ensure the accuracy of the prices and travel information appearing in this book, it should be kept in mind that prices do fluctuate in the course of time, and that information does change under the impact of the varied and volatile factors that affect the travel industry.

INTRODUCTION

LAS VEGAS: A TOP AMERICAN RESORT

□ □ □

Las Vegas is a winning resort city. It's a desert wonderland, this top American vacation destination.

Las Vegas has busted Hollywood's hand as the world's entertainment capital. You can see more name stars glowing on-stage every night than MGM had on its movie lot during its entire history.

Some say Las Vegas is an architectural disaster, housing a world of perpetual motion. Others say Las Vegas personifies the American spirit—loud, brash, aggressive—a place where hope springs eternal to overcome the odds and beat the system (how else to explain Las Vegas's $2-billion-a-year gross income?). Las Vegas is gambling. Stakes start as a paltry nickel in downtown slots, and you can go up to $5,000 on a single bet at gambling tables. One anonymous roller known only as "Crawford" flew off in his own private plane after raking in $800,000 in winnings during one eight-hour spree. Some say he breezed in from the Oklahoma oil fields. He tipped cocktail girls with $500 chips, tossed down Bloody Marys throughout his red-hot streak, and had the whole town talking before he left.

In Las Vegas, craps and poker have been elevated from smoky back rooms to chandeliered and paneled casinos. Free drinks and cigarettes are courtesies extended to all rollers, but dedicated gamblers with weighty bankrolls are usually invited to posh private layouts. At those inner sanctums, full meals are among the wall-to-wall freebies.

When Bingo was rediscovered as a crowd pleaser, several hotels began to install 1,000-seat parlors. Now players lay down $1 or $2 per card to compete for cash prizes as large as $25,000 in some cases. Bingo is big business. So are blackjack and baccarat and roulette and keno.

Although these are reasons why more than 12 million visitors invade Las Vegas every year, the city has other magnetic appeals.

Where else but in Las Vegas can you play tennis on indoor courts at 4 or 5 a.m.? At the Tropicana Hotel's courts you can relax in a plushly carpeted gallery to watch others play while the bar serves whatever you wish. Las Vegas has more tennis courts open to public play than any city in the world, and it has well-known tennis pros giving instruction.

Golfers get their strokes in Vegas too. No fewer than ten championship courses are open to play. PGA and LPGA tournaments are held here.

Where else but in Las Vegas can you order hefty ranchhand breakfasts at 7, 11, or 18 hours after the usual breakfast time? Clocks don't clock such things in Las Vegas, where time can be ignored by vacationers—and usually is. "When you're having a ball," the Vegas philosophy goes, "who cares what time it is?" And you certainly can't tell the time of day inside a casino.

Where else but in Las Vegas can you dine while watching trapeze artists perform daredevil stunts or bicycling acrobats throw balloons to the kids? Carnival goings-on and breathtaking circus acts for both adults and children are staged at the peppermint-striped Big Top and hotel known as Circus Circus.

Las Vegas is built entirely for fun. It takes the ordinary and makes it extraordinary. It takes the extraordinary, adds imagination and dash, and turns it into a happening to beguile and amuse. Nothing is small, unless it's *the world's smallest.* Big is bigger. A hamburger is a "prime two-pound beefer." A hot dog is "a yard long." A disco is "where the stars all go to unwind." And an insignificant hole-in-the-wall dress shop will purport to have "the world's greatest collection of original designs."

If you stand on the Strip and watch traffic move bumper-to-bumper through the city, you'll see license plates from everywhere. Local taxis with names arranged in dice designs, sleek Porsches and Maseratis, recreation vehicles, pickup trucks, Hertz and Brooks rental cars, sand buggies, motorcycles and scooters—a wheeling world flashes by in a constant flood.

Budget-conscious tourists, Arabian sheiks, students on a fling, families detouring from the nearby great national parks, showbiz and rancher tycoons, Japanese businessmen, politicians, retired pensioners, urbane globetrotters, first-time travelers, and dedicated gamblers—they all find their way to Las Vegas. Some stay to live in the vivid city, thrilled with the always-something-to-do pace.

There's a lot to appeal to everyone in the Las Vegas desert playground. This guide, hopefully, will lead you to the things you enjoy most. It's a cow town grown up, a boom town still booming, with an easy-to-take Out West welcome. You'll discover more bargains in beautiful hotel rooms, more fine places to wine and dine, more entertainment in Las Vegas than in any other resort.

Because there are so many outstanding places at which to stay and things to see and do, I've covered them *selectively*—to keep this book from reaching encyclopedic length. I've personally checked each recommendation, and only places I consider worthy are included.

Although I've also stated rates and prices, please bear in mind that they're subject to change at any time. Usually they'll be fairly close to ranges quoted, if past experience holds true.

But change is inevitable in Las Vegas. And that's what makes it one helluva town. It's the newest. It's the brightest, the grandest, the brashest, the most outlandish. There's absolutely no other place like Las Vegas, Nevada!

NEVADA THEN: Las Vegas always has been a place to make a lot of money. But the Indians, who were here first, and the Mormons, who arrived 30 strong in 1855 to try their hand at farming, didn't fare as well as others. Those Mormons were shortly driven out by bands of Piute, who were in turn driven out; today the Piute Indians are but a mini-minority group in Nevada's overall population.

When prospectors on their way to or from the California gold rush in the 1880s stopped off in Nevada, many hit pay dirt in gold and silver. Actually, the first Nevada ore strike was in Pioche in 1870. (The town is 175 miles northeast of Las Vegas.) Diggings soon spread to other areas, and the search for the precious metals lasted through the early 1900s.

Rich ore veins eventually petered out, leaving sorry ghost towns scattered throughout the high and low desert wilderness that makes up much of Nevada. The landscape near them is pockmarked with abandoned mine shafts. Former mining centers at Searchlight, Goodsprings, Eldorado Canyon, Virginia City, and

Rhyolite are among the many ghost towns you may visit. (Goodsprings is closest to Las Vegas—35 miles, about an hour's drive—but it isn't much to rave about, unless you stop for a drink or two at the metal-lined-and-sheathed Pioneer Saloon. I'll deal with ghost towns in Chapter IX.)

In 1905 the Union Pacific Railroad built a division point depot here, and that's when a parched and dusty tent town became the city of Las Vegas. Land speculation began then and climaxed in a two-day auction when 1,200 residential sites were sold for $265,000. The boom has been going on ever since. The future of Nevada's towns and cities in the early 1900s was entirely dependent on the iron horse. If the railroads came, the towns could survive; without the railroads, most were doomed to fade and fail.

Although gold and silver were dug until ore became so low-grade that it no longer attracted commercial mining operators, Nevada is still called the Silver State. It continues to hold its mining lure as one of the world's prime sources for semiprecious gems. Turquoise and fire opal are the two best-known gem rocks in the area, and there are many others.

NEVADA NOW: Nevada grew faster in the 1970s than any other state in the Union. More than 58% of the state's population (over 567,000) lives in Clark County, where Las Vegas is located, and assessed valuation of property in the county passed the $6-billion mark during 1984. The population rise continues. Clark County is among the top five fastest-growing areas in the U.S.A.

Nevada ranks second only to Alaska in land owned by the federal government. Some 47 million acres of the state are administered by the Bureau of Land Management. That's roughly two-thirds of Nevada! Much of it is devoted to park and recreation areas, and Lake Mead alone has a shoreline of 550 miles and covers 163,000 acres. Distances out here, where the land is big and sparsely populated, are measured more in hours driven than in miles.

On lands privately owned, livestock production is the major preoccupation. Bing Crosby used to have a Nevada ranch, and Wayne Newton still does. Howard Hughes tried ranching at first, near Blue Diamond, northeast of Las Vegas, but problems associated with heavy poaching reportedly cost him $166,000 a year before he sold out.

After the slowdown in gold and silver mining, the next desert boom came with the construction of Hoover Dam in the 1930s. The dam was a shot in the arm for Las Vegas during the Depres-

LAS VEGAS AND ENVIRONS

sion, while the rest of the country was salving its poorness with such tunes as "Pennies from Heaven" and "I Found a Million Dollar Baby in the Five and Ten Cent Store." More than pennies were being made—and spent—in prospering Las Vegas.

Gambling, of course, always was popular among the freewheelers in this laissez-faire western state. But it went through many vicissitudes before it finally was legalized in 1931.

Some say that Clark Gable's first wife, Rhea, helped put Las Vegas on the map of national consciousness when she set up housekeeping here to get her divorce and lost as much as $12,000 in one sitting at the roulette tables. Gossip columnists sharpened their pencils and did their best. The publicity was hairy but effective.

Still others say that the real Vegas boom started with cross-countrying GIs and their spouses and camp followers during World War II. Nick the Greek, the legendary gambler, also attracted a great deal of attention to the Nevada oasis. Certainly, personnel from the Nevada Test Site, from the Nuclear Rocket Development Station, and from several military bases (including huge Nellis Air Force Base, eight miles northeast of Las Vegas) contribute to the current economy as well as to the vast and scary blots of Yucca Flat, Jackson Flat, and Frenchman Flat, designated on the map as *Danger Zones* (where nuclear bombs have been tested).

Without a doubt, each of these elements has helped to make Las Vegas the boom town that it continues to be. Anyhow, it's the fun-in-the-sun mecca for millions of visitors and vacationers each year.

OFF-OFF-BROADWAY, NEVADA: According to *Nevada*
magazine, blockbuster entertainment first made a stand in Nevada not in Las Vegas, but in the tiny town of Elko (pop. 3,800). There, Newt Crumley's Commercial Hotel paid jazzman Ted Lewis a whopping $12,000—that was way back in 1941—to serenade the cowboys and passing tourists. Business picked up so fast that other then-contemporary stars such as Chico Marx, Paul Whiteman, and Ray Noble's orchestra were successively booked.

The experiment made a big impression on neighboring hotels, but wartime travel restrictions and gasoline shortages brought it to an end, and it was 1945 before anything comparable to it was attempted. Then Bugsy Siegel opened the "Fabulous Flamingo" with a $25,000 booking of Xavier Cugat plus Abbott and Costello.

Competition turned into something fierce . . . and financial.

Entertainers who were drawing "only" $20,000 either were on the skids or their agents were dolts. Betty Hutton reportedly drew $100,000 for a brief stint at the Desert Inn. Million-dollar contracts have been reported since, and nobody knows exactly how much star luminaries toted home the last time they were out. But some years ago Neil Diamond earned $650,000 (now a low-scale amount) for a four-night inaugural stint as headliner at the Aladdin's Theatre for the Performing Arts.

In 1955 the Royal Nevadan imported the Broadway production of *Guys and Dolls,* beginning a trend that continues to this day. For a while, the policy was boosted by Broadway's David Merrick, who became a partner briefly at the Riviera. One hit was *Mame,* featuring the very talented star, Juliet Prowse.

For the Stardust, over 25 years ago veteran booking agent Frank Sennes imported Paris's lavish Lido extravaganza. This, too, started a trend. Thematically, many extravaganzas mirror each other, but they also try to outdo each other with technical wizardry, and the results are nothing short of amazing. With the rising cost of superstar entertainment, more and more hotels are adopting the less-expensive "spectacular" format.

At this writing we're back to the big-star attractions and TV performers—Bill Cosby, Sarah Vaughan, Julio Iglesias at Caesars Palace; Eddie Murphy at the Las Vegas Hilton; Englebert Humperdinck and the perennial Wayne Newton at Bally's–Las Vegas; Dolly Parton and Kenny Rogers at the Golden Nugget.

Vegans call Las Vegas the Entertainment Capital of the World. Judged by the talent on hand on any one day, and by salaries paid—a year's entertainment bill on the Strip has topped $200 million—there's justification for the claim. But there are always worriers. Some say that there may not always be enough top-caliber talent to go around.

If sell-out performances by Wayne Newton, Sammy Davis, Jr., Liza Minnelli, Frank Sinatra, Robert Goulet, and Paul Anka are any indication, the worriers are wasting their time. The Nashville Sound has brought a whole new breed of entertainer to Las Vegas. Artists like Dolly Parton and the Gatlin Brothers continue to pack them in.

For a brief and flashy while a couple of years back, Las Vegas attempted to outdo *The Dirtiest Show in Town.* Sex was touted and sometimes spoofed tastefully, but more often it was strictly prurient. Local critics bellowed "Vulgar!" The producers of hard-core dirt had miscalculated their audiences. Too many people found the whole naked scene too boring—or more to the point, too unentertaining—and they shunned the more blatant shows.

Whereupon the trend switched back for the most part, though there are still big-name shows "for mature audiences."

SEVEN COME ELEVEN: The name of the game in Las Vegas is gambling. You can't ignore it, and it's almost impossible to avoid constant confrontation with the chance to take a chance—and another and another.

One-armed bandits crowd your route through the airport terminal, and through supermarkets and drugstores; the little white ball whirls around countless roulette wheels in casinos everywhere, and stakes from 25¢ (though few) to over $10,000 are laid on the line at the craps tables.

Millions of dollars allegedly were skimmed out of casinos by some tout-trained early operators, but that was before the Nevada Gaming Control Board gained such strong authority over their operating procedures. Everybody agrees that today the operations are almost boringly honest and legitimate. The entry of the big corporations (individual investors could no longer come up with the financing) into hotel and casino management has made a big difference, with the death or retirement of some of the oldtime operators speeding the process along. A large number of Las Vegas casinos are operated by corporations rather than by individuals or partnerships.

The Las Vegas boom looks as if it will never end. Major hotels are constantly expanding, and new ones are always popping up. A subsidiary "Strip," though not yet as successful as the original, came into being along Convention Center Drive with the opening of Kirk Kerkorian's International Hotel (now the Las Vegas Hilton) and Howard Hughes's Landmark.

Gaming Control Board regulations used to prohibit people with outside gambling interests from owning casinos in Nevada. But several years ago regulations were relaxed, and a new influx of investment money has been pouring into the state in corporate helpings. It's impossible to stay very long in Las Vegas without hearing about this—and about how the hometown ways are being displaced by big business.

WHO OWNS LAS VEGAS?: Ownership in Las Vegas is so intermeshed with corporate investment that it's almost impossible to determine exactly where the power lies. Big stockholders often control corporate decision-making because of their immense investments, which are seldom known to the public. Las Vegas fits into the American free-enterprise complex in other strangely involved ways. The little old lady sitting next to you in a keno parlor, for instance, might conceivably own a hefty corner of Las Vegas because she has a block of stock, or a chunk of money in a Minneapolis bank. The paradox is that she may not know that her investment money is being used in Las Vegas.

In spite of the convolutions of corporate finance, certain individuals (or their estates) stand out. Howard Hughes can't be ignored. Neither can Del Webb, Kirk Kerkorian, Bill Harrah, Benny Binion, Jackie Gaughan, and others. The monumental holdings of some of these individuals are staggering.

Howard Hughes

Howard Hughes, as one of the world's richest men, held center stage as a dashing figure all his life. As a pioneer pilot on world flights, he was an adventurer. As escort to leading ladies in Hollywood, he was handsome, "an admirable and eligible contender" for the affections of some of the most famous stars. As a movie mogul, he made Jane Russell and her bust measurements famous. And besides, he was a millionaire when millionaires were uncommon, a guy with personality and charm who had everything going for him. Before he beat his retreat, he was a giant, a hero. He was Hughes Aircraft. He was also the financing force behind one of the most abysmal failures in the aircraft industry—the Spruce Goose. Even years after his death, he is still one of the world's most talked-about, or speculated-about, men.

His Las Vegas holdings have included the Sands, Castaways, Frontier, Desert Inn, and Landmark hotels. The Silver Slipper was another of his properties. Add Harold's Club (in Reno) to the line-up and considerable acreage adjoining McCarran Airport, options on about 500 old silver- and gold-mining claims in Nevada, as well as the immense Krupp ranch, where it is believed he lived part of the time.

Perhaps we'll never know the real Howard Hughes story. Clifford Irving's publishing hoax almost succeeded, partly because people were so curious about this mysterious millionaire. But when Irving and his wife went to jail, the public still knew nothing of Howard Hughes.

One of the most interesting portraits of Hughes to emerge since his death is James Phelan's *The Hidden Years*. Phelan, a journalist, had been keeping tabs on Hughes for about 20 years. When Hughes died, he began to gather information from employees who had worked for Hughes, as well as from other sources. His compelling portrait describes one of the world's richest men who died in a pitifully wretched condition—almost deaf, starving, one leg atrophied, his body covered with bedsores. But even Phelan can only speculate why Hughes cut himself off from the world and allowed himself to degenerate to such a lowly state.

Kirk Kerkorian

Another name to reckon with in Las Vegas is Kirk Kerkorian, the publicity-shy entrepreneur. Kerkorian made a big splash in Las Vegas when he bought the Flamingo, but he was already well on his way with wheelings and dealings that included the purchase and eventual sale of the land on which Caesars Palace was built. Later he built the 1,500-room International Hotel (now the Las Vegas Hilton), Nevada's largest resort hotel.

For a while it appeared that Kerkorian might be tiring of Las Vegas involvements. He sold the Flamingo and the International to Hilton Hotels. At first it was reported that he would keep his gambling concessions in the hotels. But, no, Hilton bought those too.

It's clear now that Kerkorian never did drop out of the Vegas scene. He did sell his personal interest in the Bonanza Casino, but he sold it to MGM, and MGM built the MGM (now Bally's) Grand Hotel. Among his recent interests have been the Sands Hotel and the Desert Inn. Small wonder that watching the moves of Vegas high financiers is like watching a billiard game: one shot, and the balls veer off in every direction.

Kerkorian is difficult to see, the bane of every reporter and gossip columnist in Las Vegas. One fortunate journalist, Susan Gould, after weeks of negotiation, was granted an interview with Kerkorian for a magazine. Some interview! Most of Susan's time with Kerkorian was spent on the tennis court, she revealed, where Kerkorian liked to work out with his attorney. Whenever Susan asked a question, Kerkorian, virtually wordless, nodded to his attorney to answer.

Still, Mr. Kerkorian is said to be a likeable man, and he's a Vegas name to remember.

Born in Fresno, California, the son of an immigrant turkey farmer, Kerkorian made his money from a charter air service. He moved into Las Vegas with the purchase of the Flamingo for $12.5 million, a nice little deal, and made a pile (500% profit) on the sale of his land for Caesars Palace.

Del Webb

Also among the major hotel impresarios in Las Vegas was Del Webb, who died at 74 in July 1974. If there was ever to be a "Mr. Las Vegas," Webb was it, *nolo contendere!*

Son of a Fresno contractor, he began his working life as a carpenter in Phoenix, Arizona, his first job being to finish building a friend's grocery store. From this unpromising beginning Webb built up a nationally known construction firm, which, during World War II, was awarded numerous government contracts—airfields, hospitals, training bases, and prisoner-of-war camps. Inevitably his firm became associated with Hughes Aircraft—two giants together—and completed such projects as a radar system manufacturing plant and nuclear research laboratories.

By the end of the war Webb began to look into Las Vegas and contracted to build the first of the new-style hotels—the Flamingo, formerly owned by Kerkorian. About the same time Webb (who always prefaced the name of his properties with the prefix "Del Webb's . . .") became a co-owner of the New York Yankees, along with Dan Topping, retaining his interest until 1965, when he sold out to CBS. Some of his other interests were oil exploration and partnership in a movie company with Bing Crosby.

Webb's company specialized in constructing retirement communities, shopping centers, and resort hotels. He sold his Silverbird Hotel to Caesars World in July 1972. Impressively tall, Webb always wore a hat. With his death, the old order diminished. But his name lives on.

Bill Harrah

Big-time operators in Nevada can't be mentioned without including Reno's late Bill Harrah. His personal income was supposed to have passed the $40-million-a-year mark, and an authority at the Gaming Control Board once said that "he's the second man on the totem pole in Nevada, close to Howard Hughes in total value of holdings."

BIG-TIME GAMBLERS: Las Vegas has had its share of colorful characters, and most of them have been gamblers. The most colorful of the gamblers was certainly—

Nick the Greek

King of Gamblers from 1928 to 1949—and the man who may have done the most to put Las Vegas and its casino games on the map—was the legendary Nick the Greek (his real name: Nicholas Dandolos). In his time the famous gambler-philosopher won and lost more than $50 million, and he died poor. But at one time the Las Vegas Chamber of Commerce had more inquiries about the Greek than they had about another phenomenon, Boulder Dam.

Nick the Greek refused ownership of Las Vegas land in payment for gambling debts owed to him. He also spurned offers of other ventures, including hotel partnerships, that would have made him financially independent. (His name attracted business.) Nick preferred to gamble for his fortunes, claiming that he'd rather pay and lose. Raking in house percentages, he said, would have robbed him of the thrill of betting, even though he knew, eventually, that he would be among the victims of the house percentages, a loser.

Ed Sullivan and other celebrities attended Nick's funeral on December 30, 1966. Among his pallbearers and honorary pallbearers were Kirk Kerkorian, three of the Binions (owners of the Horseshoe), Jackie Gaughan, and the governor and the governor-elect of the state of Nevada.

(Jimmy the Greek, Las Vegas's professional odds maker, and colorful in his own right, bears no relation to the late great Nick.)

Amarillo Slim

"Amarillo Slim" Preston was among the elite of big-time poker. At the third World Series of Poker at Binion's Horseshoe Casino in May 1972, Thomas Austin Preston, Jr., a Texan with a slow drawl, loped off with $60,000. (Eight players had started in the poker series five days earlier, each with $10,000 in the pot, but one player dropped out with $20,000.)

Preston played in Europe and Australia, "wherever there's a big one." Before turning professionally to poker, Preston was a professional billiards player.

When he won the series, Amarillo Slim's final opponent in the game was Walter Clyde "Pug" Pearson. (What would gamblers do without nicknames?) Another player in the match, Adrian "Texas Dolly" Doyle, withdrew from the game after four days because of fatigue, nausea, and dizziness.

At one high point during the series, Slim's eye was taken by a blonde waitress with a small tattoo on her thigh. "Lordy me!" purred Slim. "What a purty sight!" He ordered a cup of java from the girl, but added that he'd like to talk about that tattoo "later."

Ken Uston

The newest of the Vegas glamorous gambler legends is Harvard Business School graduate Ken Uston, the head of a card-counting ring that is the bane of casino officials. After a few disillusioning years in the business world ("I'd been earning $2,700 a month in this straitlaced job that was boring as hell," said Uston), he became intrigued by cards. In his first six months, working with partners, he won about $150,000. He won $27,600 in 45 minutes one day at the Fremont Hotel. He and his cronies have officially been declared persona non grata in Vegas ("inimical to the interests of the state of Nevada") for several years now, and Uston has retaliated with discrimination suits. Meanwhile he still gambles occasionally with the aid of makeup and disguises. He also has trained a team of counters, some of whom play with his money and give him a cut. And he's been gambling in Atlantic City, where casinos tried to bar him but were unsuccessful. They're currently planning new ways to foil card counters with extra shuffling and more decks. Though he claims that "anyone with an IQ of 110 who passed high school algebra can be a counter" (a promotion for his book, *I Won Three Million at Blackjack*), Uston is a Phi Beta Kappa with a degree in economics.

CHAPTER I

LAS VEGAS: GETTING DOWN TO BASICS

□ □ □

Las Vegas is an oasis in a sparse and arid desert, the biggest city in the state of Nevada. It's located in the southernmost precincts of a wide, pancake-flat valley known as Las Vegas Valley, hemmed in by treeless mountains. They reach a height of 11,912 feet and glow in the distance with changing earthen hues at sunrise, as low mists burn off in a dance of rainbows. Dramatic and lovely.

The city is 2,162 feet above sea level and hugs close to the California and Arizona borders. Las Vegas is closer to Los Angeles, California (298 miles southwest), to Phoenix, Arizona (294 miles southeast), and to Salt Lake City, Utah (442 miles northeast), than it is to Nevada's second-largest city, Reno (448 miles northwest). San Francisco is 620 miles to the west and slightly north.

Las Vegas got its name in the 16th century, when the Spanish Trail was hewn to link Santa Fe with the missions of California. Spaniards called the region Las Vegas, meaning "the meadows," for the grassy fields that abounded here because of natural springs. Very little of the architecture in Las Vegas relates to its Spanish heritage, however, which is surprising when you compare the city with many in Florida and California.

ANYTHING FOR MONEY

You'll find practically none of the legacies of the past in Las Vegas. It's a contemporary place, where the look is Now—or, at least, barely yesterday. It's ablaze at night with miles of neon twisting around hotels and garishly touted little chapels doing an any-hour business in weddings, formalities completed in a fast 15 minutes ("Payroll Checks and Personal Checks Accepted").

You can't wander through the gambling casinos of Las Vegas for long before you notice the clocks—or, more significantly, the lack of clocks. Because you're here to gamble, aren't you (aren't you?), and why do you need to be distracted by knowing what time it is? Windows in the casinos are practically nonexistent too. The 29th-floor casino at the Landmark Hotel, where day and night views of the Strip and surrounding desert were a happy distraction, didn't work out. Gamblers, apparently, would rather not know what time it is.

Gambling is the *raison d'être* for this town, and its pervasive presence will tempt you everywhere, from the provocatively mini-skirted keno girls who help you to play the game while you're eating breakfast in the coffeeshop, to the system of establishing credit and cashing checks or changing bills in the casinos rather than at the hotel cashier's desk. There's always the possibility that you'll spend some on the way out.

At one time Las Vegas hotel people were in a dither about whether or not to allow television sets in rooms (they ultimately did). But over the years it's been realized that more distractions simply keep customers in town longer. Odds are *always* in favor of the house—that's what the gambling business is all about—and there's no way the house can lose in the long run, as long as you stay and enjoy yourself.

One of the things that most helped the mobility of visitors to Las Vegas in recent years has been the wide adoption of the European Plan. Meals seldom are included in hotel tariffs now, and you can dine anywhere you wish. So you can hit one place for an early lounge show, another for a dinner show, another for a midnight show, yet another for gambling and imbibing and more lounge entertainment, and then go back to your hotel for more of the same. After-midnight buffets and chuck wagons are common, entertainers do their thing to as late as 5 a.m., and big, low-priced breakfasts are served at any hour of the day or night.

Some of the hotels have added so many wining and dining services that, although gambling once accounted for 90% of their income, it's now closer to 50%. That doesn't worry too many hotel people. For Las Vegas's visitors have been leaving behind a fortune in gambling losses. (Gross taxable revenue from gambling was a staggering $2.1 billion in 1985.)

Maybe this has nothing to do with the considerable fortunes spent in Las Vegas . . . but a downtown souvenir shop that used to offer newspaper headlines bearing your name coupled with some catchy phrases, such as "_____Wanted Dead or Alive" or "_____Weds Vegas Showgirl," eliminated the headline that read "_____Breaks Bank in Las Vegas." I've never known anyone who has, but you'll always hear about how somebody just missed it.

TRAVELING AROUND LAS VEGAS

THE LAYOUT: Las Vegas doesn't seem large, unless you're trying to cover it in the midday sun, on foot. The sections of town of most interest to you as a tourist are contained in a fairly compact triangle.

The Strip (its real name is Las Vegas Boulevard South) comes in from the southwest and heads northeast, intersecting with Fremont Street in the downtown Casino Center area. As Fremont runs southeast (becoming Boulder Highway), these two major streets form two sides of a triangle, each about six miles in length. And inside this triangle (bounded on the south end by Hacienda Avenue) are the airport and nearly all the major hotels, casinos, golf courses, shopping centers—what have you.

GETTING AROUND: You can walk from the southernmost hotel on the Strip (the Hacienda) to the northernmost (the Sahara), but it's a considerable hike. At night, when the sun is down, it can be enjoyable if you have lots of time; during the day, the farther you walk, the hotter it seems to get. And if you wish to go downtown to the spread of hotels on Fremont Street, add another three miles or so, and several hours.

The following are some good alternatives to foot power.

Public Transportation

The **Strip Bus** goes from the Hacienda Hotel at the southernmost end of the Strip, stopping at all the major hotels, and turns into the Casino Center. If you get off at Fremont, you can pick up a bus back to the Strip at the corner of Fremont and Third. Bus fares are a uniform $1, exact change only. If you plan on using the bus several times, purchase a ten-ride commuter card from the driver

LAS VEGAS
AT A GLANCE

for $6.65. Buses run about every 15 minutes from 6 a.m. to 12:45 a.m., every half hour from 12:45 a.m. to 2:45 a.m., and every half hour from 2:45 a.m. to 6 a.m.

For further transit information, phone 384-3540.

Taxis

The easiest, most leisurely approach to transportation in Las Vegas is the taxi. Cabs charge $1.70 for the first fraction of a mile and 20¢ for each additional one-seventh mile—that is, $1.40 for each additional mile. Roughly speaking, a taxi ride between Strip hotels and downtown will be about $10. That's not cheap, but by using a cab you avoid the bother of parking and the cost of tipping for valet service. And you can save money by sharing the fare with someone interested in trying his or her luck at the same place down the road as you.

There are plenty of taxis, particularly at the entrances of the larger hotels. If you want to arrange for a taxi at a particular time, any one of the following companies will provide the service: **Desert Cab Company** (tel. 736-1702), **Whittlesea Blue Cab** (tel. 384-6111), or **Yellow and Checker Cab Companies** (tel. 873-2227).

As I've also mentioned under the "ABCs of Las Vegas" section, below, the limousine from the airport to Strip hotels costs $3 per person, $4.50 to downtown Las Vegas.

Car Rentals

Plan ahead. If you intend to rent a car during your vacation, before you leave home check your policy or call your insurance agent to determine the limits of your coverage. Does your insurance cover theft, vandalism, or collision damage to the rented car? Does your credit card cover these risks if you use it for the rental? If not, you may want to pay the added cost for the collision-damage, theft, and vandalism waiver. As of this writing, most rental firms make customers liable for damage up to the total value of the car. The waiver currently averages $10 to $12 per day.

If you rent from one of the well-established companies, large or small, the odds are that the car won't be a clunker. Check the cost, daily or weekly, and the charge for mileage as well as optional insurance and taxes. And since not all rental companies are located at the airport, ask about pickup and delivery—you may need to take a taxi from the terminal.

If you plan to pick up the car at one location and return it to another, ask about the drop-off charge, if any. And if you rent the car at a weekly rate and decide to return it early, you may be charged at the much higher daily rate. Ask!

And before you drive away, check the registration—make certain it's still in effect. Finally, find out if the company has a phone number for emergency road service.

MILES TO/FROM LAS VEGAS (to the nearest 5 miles)

Bakersfield	285 miles	Palm Springs	275 miles
Barstow	155	Reno	440
Bishop	275	Sacramento	595
Fresno	385	San Bernardino	225
Hoover Dam/Lake Mead	30	San Diego	340
Lake Tahoe	445	San Francisco	620
Laughlin	100	San Luis Obispo	417
		Santa Barbara	345

Quite a few of the major companies—Hertz, Avis, Budget, and Nationwide—have offices at the airport and/or along the Strip. An alternative to the majors is **Brooks Rent-a-Car,** 3039 Las Vegas Blvd. South at Convention Center Drive (tel. 735-3344, or toll free 800/634-6721). Rates for all sorts of cars—they try to maintain the lowest in Las Vegas—start at $13.99 a day, plus 25¢ a mile, or $25.09 per day with unlimited mileage. Weekly rates begin at $129.99, with 700 miles free; thereafter, the mileage charge is 25¢ per mile.

THE WEATHER AND WHAT TO WEAR

As a western town, Las Vegas is casual. You won't see as many cowboys in high-heeled boots and Levis as you might have a few years back, but dress in Las Vegas runs the gamut of resort informality. Sports clothes are predominant during the summer—with open shirts, washable cottons, that sort of informality—when the temperature climbs over the 100° mark. Only the more elegant restaurants suggest that anything as formal as a tie and jacket be worn by men. In spring, fall, and winter, suits and woolens are comfortable, especially at night, although it's often warm enough for light cottons during the day.

A 19-year average showed bright sunshine 85% of the time.

Keep in mind that Las Vegas is in the desert. Humidity averages a low 22%. That's dry! And because it's a desert place, plan on daytime-nighttime variations of 20° or more. When it's hot, it's very hot, but night chill can set in quickly. Women sometimes wear furs at night over light dresses.

Another fact about desert vacationing must be considered— dehydration! If you come from an area where the climate is humid, you'll shortly begin to notice that your lips, nostrils, and mouth become drier after the first couple of days. It's natural in the desert, where you also perspire more freely (quick, the cologne!).

Definitely, you should consume more liquids—about eight glasses of water, orange juice, lemonade, whatever, is the minimum liquid intake you'll need daily. That amount of liquid won't distress you in the least, either, because you'll have a powerful thirst. Avoid taking at least this amount of liquid and you'll undoubtedly experience discomfort with cracked lips and other such problems. Big glasses of ice water are served in most dining places the moment you sit down, and don't be afraid to ask for more. Waiters and waitresses are used to the request; they get thirsty in Las Vegas too.

A CLOSER LOOK AT THE WEATHER
(in degrees Fahrenheit)

	High	Average	Low
January	55	44	33
February	62	50	39
March	69	57	44
April	79	66	53
May	88	74	60
June	99	84	68
July	105	91	76
August	103	88	74
September	96	81	65
October	82	67	53
November	67	54	41
December	58	47	36

TRIPS TO THE ALTAR

Because of the liberality of marriage laws—no blood tests, no waiting periods, no fuss—Nevada always has been popular with couples in a hurry.

More than 500 persons in the state are licensed to perform marriages. Until a few years ago, pastors of churches with congregations of five or more were qualified for the sanctifying trade. This has given rise to a special class of ministers known as Marryin' Sams or Lady Marryin' Sams, who operate out of a lineup of 20 or so quaintly named chapels along the Strip alone. Recently the legislature concluded that these gentlemen and gentlewomen have proliferated too fast, and a law has been passed stating that the performing of marriage ceremonies must be incidental to the pastor's main duties.

Probably the most famous of these marrying institutions is **The Little White Chapel.** As you'll see on the sign out front, Joan Collins was married there (to Peter Holm, in case you've forgotten). While the cost of the ceremony was not publicized by the chapel's owner, Charlette Richards Sturgeon, the after-cost of the wedding received considerable coverage. Not to worry, however: The Little White Chapel will attend to marrying even the likes of thee and me, for a reasonable fee.

Marryin' Sams have a lucrative thing going. It's been estimated that they divide up about 56,000 marriages a year, with an average take of about $200 per couple. That includes $75 for the chapel, a bit for the minister, $20 each for witnesses, and a variety of optional extras like corsages, photographs, recordings of the ceremony, recorded or live organ music, and all that. A cheapie no-frills hitching can cost as little as $100, sometimes less on a slow day.

Taxi drivers still compete at the airport for couples obviously in a marrying mood, hoping for and usually getting a tip from the chapel as well as some generous handouts from the couples, plus "a little extra" for witnessing the event.

Some Vegans are distressed that certain chapels make a mockery of marriage. A number of them have little to do with houses of worship; they're little rooms to get married in, and that's it.

Marryin' Sams were outraged years ago when one of the hotels began to sponsor weddings performed onstage (couples were awarded free honeymoons in Hawaii) during the Don Ho show. They labeled it as unfair competition and vowed to work to stop the spread of this undignified practice.

Even if you go to a wedding chapel, by the way, you must have a marriage license. The county exacts its bounty. A license costs $27, and you must apply between 8 a.m. and midnight, Monday through Thursday, at the **Clark County Marriage License Bureau,** 200 S. Third St. (tel. 455-3156, 455-4415 after 5 p.m. and on weekends and holidays). If you can't fit the regular hours into your schedule, the bureau stays open continuously from 8 a.m.

Friday until midnight Sunday. The Courthouse, 200 S. Third St. (tel. 455-4011), also doles out information on requirements for divorces—which are fairly easy to obtain, providing that residence requirements are observed.

This neat little supermarket for tying and untying matrimonial knots is very big in Reno, but the same liberal laws are equally effective in Las Vegas, where you can get married in a helicopter, under water, or just plain on the ground.

THE ABCs OF LAS VEGAS

Here's an alphabetical guide to certain basic information (and some not so basic) intended to help make your trip as enjoyable and frustration-free as possible.

AIRLINES: Nonstop flights connect Las Vegas with a number of cities in California: Bakersfield (Delta Air Lines); Burbank (America West, US Air); Fresno (Delta Air Lines); Long Beach (America West); Los Angeles (American Airlines, America West, Delta Air Lines, Eastern Airlines, US Air); Ontario (America West, Sunworld International); Orange County (America West, Southwest Airlines, US Air); San Francisco (America West, United Airlines, US Air); San Jose (America West, Delta Air Lines, US Air), Santa Barbara (Delta Air Lines); Santa Maria (American Airlines). Major carriers also offer nonstop service from New York City airports: Continental flies direct from Newark, and American West flies direct from JFK.

AIRPORT: The $7.50 surcharge on your ticket to Las Vegas pays for the city's main airport, ultramodern McCarran International, where you can begin gambling at the slots as soon as you disembark.

It takes about 15 minutes and $7 to $9 to get to the middle of the Strip by taxi. In addition to the base fare of $1.70 for the first one-seventh mile and 20¢ for each additional one-seventh mile, there is also a 20¢ tax per group for pickups at the airport and a 20¢ charge for each passenger over three. The limousine (or minibus) from the airport to Strip hotels costs $3 per person; it's $4.50 per person to downtown Las Vegas.

AREA CODE: The area code for Las Vegas—in fact, for all of Nevada—is 702.

BABYSITTERS: If you're staying at one of the large hotels on the Strip or downtown, the concierge can make arrangements for you or recommend organizations to call. Two sitter agencies are listed in Chapter VIII.

The Las Vegas Hilton has a unique Youth Hotel within the premises for children aged 3 through 18. However, you must be a guest at the hotel to take advantage of the facilities. See details in the Hilton entry in the "Top Hotels" section, Chapter II.

BANKS: As with most cities, banks are generally open from 10 a.m. to 3 p.m. However, if you need to cash a check, your hotel may be your best resource, depending on the amount involved. See also the "Cash and Credit" entry, below.

BUSES: The Greyhound Trailways depots are on 200 South Main St. (tel. 382-2640) and in the Flamingo Hotel, 3555 Las Vegas Blvd. (tel. 733-3111).

CASH AND CREDIT: You can readily cash traveler's checks at the cashier's cage in the casinos. If you intend to gamble, cash the checks first—they're not negotiable at the tables.

Establishing credit for a short-term stay in Las Vegas is accomplished more often through the casinos than through the banks. Bring credit cards, driver's license, and other identification and you can usually be "cleared" within 24 hours to cash personal checks, etc., up to the limit you've arranged with the casino. Once you've established credit with a casino, it remains in effect for repeat visits to the city. It's also possible to write to a casino in advance and establish credit before you arrive.

CASINO PROTOCOL: You can wear, or not wear, almost anything at a casino. And at a craps table you can whoop and holler to your heart's content. Smoking is permitted at the majority of tables, but you may now notice some nonsmoking tables. There is one strict prohibition in all casinos—no cameras are allowed.

CHARGE CARDS: All major credit cards are generally accepted in lieu of cash at hotels, restaurants, shopping and sports facilities in this town. However, it's always wise to check ahead if you're considering an exceptionally large purchase.

CHIPS: Casino chips were once as good as cash anywhere in Las Vegas. Nowadays they are accepted only in the casinos where they're issued—and in church; some people still drop them into collection boxes, an old Las Vegas tradition. Reason for the change in use as currency: a rash of counterfeit chips began to show up. So cash in your chips before you leave any casino, unless you're planning to return there.

CRIME: In any city where as much money changes hands as in Las Vegas, you will also find crime. To avoid an unhappy incident, use discretion and common sense. If you're carrying a handbag, don't, for example, put it on the ledge just beneath the craps table where players rest their drinks. It's out of view and a tempting target. Always keep your handbag close to you and in plain sight.

DENTISTS AND DOCTORS: Hotels usually have a list of dentists and doctors, should you need one; in addition, they are listed in the Centel Yellow Pages. For dentist referrals, call the **Clark County Dental Society** (tel. 435-7767): for a doctor, call the **Clark County Medical Society** (tel. 739-9989).

DRIVING: Any trip to Las Vegas from California involves desert driving. Take basic precautions at all times, but especially during the summer. Before leaving, check your tires, water, and oil. Take about five gallons of water in a clean container so that it can be used for drinking or for the radiator. Pay attention to those road signs suggesting when to turn off your car's air conditioner. Slow but continuous climbs through the mountains can cause overheating before you notice it on your gauge. And don't push your luck with gas. It may be 35 miles, or more, between gas stations, so fill up before you begin to run low.

If your car overheats, *do not* remove the radiator cap until the engine has cooled, and then only very slowly. Add water to within an inch of the top of the radiator.

FESTIVALS AND EVENTS: The best and most comprehensive source for this information is the **Las Vegas Chamber of Commerce,** 2301 E. Sahara Ave., Las Vegas 89104 (tel. 457-4664), open weekdays from 8 a.m. to 5 p.m. You can send a request for a list of the annual events, enclosing a stamped, self-addressed envelope.

You'll also find weekly information in the Friday edition of the *Las Vegas Review-Journal* and in *Today in Las Vegas;* see "Information" entry, below.

HOSPITALS: A 24-hour emergency service with outpatient and trauma-care facilities is available at **Southern Nevada Memorial Hospital,** 1800 W. Charleston Blvd., at Shadow Lane (tel.

383-2000); the emergency room entrance is on Rose Street. **Humana Hospital Sunrise,** 3186 Maryland Pkwy., near Desert Inn Road (tel. 731-8000), the largest proprietary hospital west of the Mississippi, also has emergency facilities.

Note: Southern Nevada Memorial has a **Poison Information Center** (tel. 385-1277) open around the clock.

INFORMATION: For brochures, maps, information on accommodations, etc., stop at the Las Vegas Chamber of Commerce—a very helpful center for visitors. Their address, phone number, and hours are given above in the "Festivals and Events" entry. For Nevada tourism information, including that for Las Vegas, call toll free 800/638-2328 (a 24-hour line). For Las Vegas reservations and show information, call 800/423-4745.

One of the best sources of information on what's doing in Las Vegas is *Today in Las Vegas*—a free weekly publication you'll find at almost any bell desk in a large hotel, as well as at the airport. It includes up-to-the-minute reviews and listings of all shows and events, as well as the performance times.

INSOMNIACS: Not a problem in Las Vegas—everything moves around the clock. You need never know what time it is, whether it's day or night, or what the weather's like outside.

LIQUOR LAWS: There are no restrictions on the hours when liquor can be sold or served, but you must be 21 to imbibe legally in town.

NEWSPAPERS: The *Las Vegas Sun* is the town's morning paper. The Friday edition of the afternoon paper, the *Las Vegas Review-Journal,* offers a rundown of the shows in town, as well as an overview of most other forms of entertainment, restaurants, and happenings in nearby resorts.

PETS: Hotels and motels generally will not accept pets. If you're traveling with Bowser, or Boneypart the cat, ask before making the reservations. Motel 6 does accept a pet (within reason), but will not permit the animal to be left unattended.

If you travel via RV, motor home, or with trailer or van, and take pets with you, an ideal location next to the Strip is the Circusland RV Park, adjacent to the Circus Circus Hotel and Casino. Circusland has family and pet sections with dog runs.

POLICE: For emergency help, dial 911. The nonemergency Police Department number is 385-1111; that for the Nevada Highway Patrol is 385-0311.

RELIGIOUS SERVICES: The Las Vegas area has hundreds of churches and synagogues (at last count about 380), representing virtually every denomination. It's been said that on a per-capita basis there are more houses of worship in Las Vegas than in any other metropolitan area in the nation, and we all know what everyone's praying for. The breakdown: 49% Protestant, 24% Roman Catholic, 23% Mormon, 3% Jewish.

The houses of worship listed below are located along the Strip and downtown (for other denominations and locations, consult the Centel Yellow Pages): **First Baptist,** 300 S. Ninth St., at Bridger Ave., downtown (tel. 382-6177); **First Southern Baptist,** 700 E. St. Louis Ave., on the Strip (tel. 732-3100); **Guardian Angel Cathedral** (Roman Catholic), 302 E. Desert Inn Rd., on the Strip (tel. 735-5241); **Joan of Arc** (Roman Catholic), 315 S. Casino Center Blvd., downtown (tel. 382-9909); **Reformation Lutheran,** 1580 E. St. Louis Ave., near the Strip (tel. 732-2052); **First United Methodist,** 231 S. Third St., downtown (tel. 382-9939); **Temple Beth Sholom,** 1600 E. Oakey Blvd., near the Strip (tel. 384-5070).

STORE HOURS: Stores are usually open from 10 a.m. to 9 p.m. Monday through Friday, to 6 p.m. Saturday, 11 a.m. to 5 p.m. Sunday.

TAXES: Sales tax in Las Vegas is 6%.

TIPPING: Those over 21 undoubtedly already know about tipping the usual 15% in restaurants. However, when you're at a table in a casino, be it craps, blackjack, roulette, baccarat, or whatever, a cocktail waitress will be around to ask if you want anything to drink. There is no charge for the drink, hard or soft, but it is appropriate for you to tip (or "toke") the waitress—$1 (or a comparable chip) is about right, more if you wish.

At the gaming tables, it's perfectly acceptable to tip the dealer or croupier in proportion to the service you've been getting and the size of your winnings.

When checking into a hotel with several bags, a tip of $5 is par for the course.

Valet parking is a great convenience at any of the Las Vegas hotels. A tip of $1 is appropriate, and it's not much to pay for the service.

When you leave the hotel, a tip of $1 per day for the period of your stay, left with the maid or in the room, is a most reasonable amount and will be appreciated.

If you want a better-than-average seat at any one of the shows, tip the maître d'. The usual donation is $5, but if it's a "big name" show, you might up the ante to $20 for the seating *you* want, though the top of the range is optional.

TRAINS: The **Amtrak** station is on One North Main St., at Union Plaza (tel. 386-6896, or toll free 800/872-7245).

USEFUL NUMBERS: You can obtain **weather information** for Las Vegas at 736-6404, **information on highway conditions** at 385-0181, **the time of day** at 118 (a three-digit number, similar to directory information, 411).

WHERE TO STAY IN LAS VEGAS

□ □ □

A statistician could be kept busy full time just turning out figures on accommodations in Las Vegas. At last count, the city had over 37,000 hotel rooms, and motel rooms added another 19,000. Because most rooms in Las Vegas are doubles, that's enough space to sleep every resident in a small city—plus a town or two!

Still, new accommodations are forever being built. A few hundred additional rooms are under construction at this writing, and more are on the planning boards—with money already allocated to begin work.

The builders apparently know what they're doing. On busy weekends, you'll see *Sold Out* and *No Vacancy* signs all over town. So the city keeps booming, and mushrooming, up and out, straining to keep up with demands.

If it takes a data-processing machine to keep up with new hotel projects, you can imagine what it's like in personnel departments. Some hotels have 2,000 or more employees. Every time a new hotel opens, there's a scramble for top jobs, which makes tidal waves in other hotels, casinos, restaurants, beauty parlors, boutiques, and in every service that fits into hotels. But even though job-hopping in Vegas sometimes reaches frantic proportions, tough competition keeps people on their toes. Service is amazingly good.

The long litany of remodeling and expansion projects is recorded in local news media with almost boring monotony. Recently completed are expansions at the Four Queens, Circus

Circus, Union Plaza, Riviera, Sahara, Fitzgerald's, Landmark, and Mint.

THE THREE LOCATIONS: As a tourist in Las Vegas, you'll be concerned mostly with hotels in three locations—along the **Strip,** in the **downtown** area on Fremont Street, and in a sort of amendment to the Strip along **Convention Center Drive.** Centers of activity on the Strip and on Fremont Street intersect, and Convention Center Drive runs into the Strip between the Riviera Hotel and the Desert Inn, almost directly opposite the Stardust. It's difficult to get lost in Las Vegas, and there's no such thing as being far away.

Generally, prices along the Strip are higher than those downtown. But the rule gets twisted often. You'll find bargains on the Strip too. Some visitors also characterize the Strip as formal, dressy, straitlaced (a perspective, I suspect, that results from a visit to Caesars Palace or the Las Vegas Hilton). Downtown, they say, they have an opportunity to rub elbows and talk with more people because of the small-town friendliness in such hostelries as the El Cortez and the Golden Nugget. But a similar downtown ambience can be found at the Hacienda at the southern extremity of the Strip and at the Stardust in the center of the Strip, and the downtown Golden Nugget and Union Plaza are more elegant, in the style of the bigger Strip hotels. So don't accept any of the rules as hard and fast. The exceptions are many.

Most of the Fremont Street crowd is casual indeed, dressed more for shopping than for gambling. Same goes for the downtown casino and hotel habitués—a far cry from the black-tie sedateness of the classic European casinos. Although gambling in the more elegant and grandly chandeliered hotel casinos along the Strip isn't quite so shirtsleeve (understated garb and jackets and ties tend to be more common, especially during the cooler spring, fall, and winter months), there's no rule that states that you can't wear just about what you please in the casino, in the hotel, even at the show.

The Strip is nearest to the McCarran International Airport, where you'll debark from your flight. From there, you should anticipate about $10 in taxi fare to most Strip locations, though many hotels provide complimentary limousine service to the airport. The airport limousine (tel. 739-7990) to the Strip hotels costs $3; to downtown, it's $4.50.

CAUTION: You're taking a chance if you arrive in Las Vegas without a reservation. The airlines alone carried 11 million passengers into the city last year, and the largest numbers arrive on weekends. Besides this, considerable traffic floods the highways from Los Angeles, 289 miles away, and from lots of other points within closer range. And for several years, Vegas hotels have been developing and extending their convention arrangements, making the city one of the top convention cities in the United States. So hotel space gets tight, very tight, especially on crowded weekends, when getting a room without reservations may be a big gamble.

PACKAGE PLANS FOR SAVINGS: If you're planning only a short stay in Las Vegas, look into the hotel package plans. They grant considerable price reductions. Dining, cocktails, big shows, and other extras are built into the offerings. Some are for golfers too, and provide opportunities to play more than one good golf course, usually with greens fees and other costs included. I've described some of these plans under the hotels in the upcoming listings. Inquire when you reserve a room whether packages are available.

Hotels, however, generally maintain an excellent record in meeting the needs of the fantastic weekend invasion of visitors. Most stick fastidiously to their published rates, and will provide you with reasonably priced accommodations whenever possible.

On the other hand, a number of motels (fortunately, a small number) *do not* have available rate sheets, and many of these are known to jack up prices to the level of highway banditry on busy weekends. It's not uncommon for unwary visitors to pay $50 or more for a motel room for the night, when they should be getting a lot more for a lot less.

So protect yourself by comparing prices and making a reservation in advance at one of the hostelries recommended in this book. Of course, if you should arrive without an advance reservation, avoid those places that won't show you a rate sheet. When prices climb very much above the ones listed here, you can be assured that there's something awry.

A NOTE ABOUT LISTINGS: To sectionalize this chapter in easy-to-follow form, I have covered deluxe accommodations first, followed them with rooms in the moderate-price range, and then with those in the budget-price category. In each section, hotels on and near the Strip precede downtown locations. Motels are listed at the chapter's end.

Also, since in Vegas the hotel/casino complex is not just a place to stay but the reason for coming, many tourists barely leave their hotels. Which is just the way the hotels want it; each offers a full complement of dining choices, nightlife, gambling, etc. Though I have a restaurant section coming up, so many excellent restaurants are right in the hotels that I'm going to list many notable ones here. Nightlife options, however, will all be dealt with in a separate chapter.

THE TOP HOTELS

As we go to press, construction of the **Golden Nugget on The Strip** has not yet been completed. This spectacular hotel is being built on 88 acres of county property, adjacent to Caesars Palace.

Whether you plan to stay there or not, it's got to be the place to see and an extraordinary place to dine. Steve Wynn's remarkably successful touch with the Golden Nugget downtown will undoubtedly make this new Strip hotel a winner.

The Golden Nugget on The Strip will have 3,000 to 3,600 rooms, a showroom, and seven restaurants—one Japanese, done like a teahouse, set on a mountaintop; one Chinese, very exotic, much like Shanghai in the '30s; one continental; one steakhouse; and, the crowning glory, a seafood restaurant with Hawaiian decor, rather like an old whaling village of the type once found on Maui. There will also be two 24-hour coffeeshops for late-night snackers.

The hotel will be in a Y configuration on top of the casino so that you can enter the arena at various points.

There will be a unique swimming area—designed to provide fun as well as exercise. You can swim among islands, grottos, even in and out of lagoons. For tennis buffs, several courts will be lit for night play.

For the exact date of the opening of the hotel, I suggest that you contact your local travel agent.

BALLY'S–LAS VEGAS: 3645 Las Vegas Blvd. South, Las Vegas, NV 89109 (tel. 702/739-4111, or toll free 800/634-3434, 800/634-6363 in California, Arizona, Idaho, Oregon, and Utah).

Not only is it completely rebuilt since the disastrous 1980 fire that destroyed much of the hotel and all of the casino, Bally's–Las Vegas is bigger than ever with 800 additional rooms.

Many hotels claim to be resorts, but this one fully qualifies as a complete and self-contained resort. It has a 75,000-square-foot shopping arcade, day and night activities galore, gambling, two major showrooms, movies, complete health-club facilities for men and women, a youth center, a therapeutic pool, two swimming pools (one Olympic size), ten night-lit tennis courts (no charge for guests), six restaurants and snackbars, numerous cocktail bars—the works. Not to mention golf privileges for guests at the Dunes' 18-hole course, just across the street. It's a spacious spa, a singular world under one roof. And returning for a moment to the subject of fire, this property (and every Vegas hotel—they've all learned a lesson) has now installed the best available multi-million-dollar system to detect and control fires.

Although Bally's (even before rebuilding) cost a lot more than $100 million, the public relations staff sticks with that "modest" figure. "The figure is easiest to remember," they say. But everything at Bally's is on a colossal scale. They transported over 800 tons of marble from Italy just for the fountain at the front entrance; their furniture order was the largest ever placed for one hotel; for two years, sculptors in three Italian towns were kept busy just making marble columns and statues for the hotel; the plumbing fixtures are so numerous they could be used to build a rest room every quarter mile between Las Vegas and Los Angeles; and each of the hotel's 600 chandeliers involves at least two tons of crystal!

Bally's is one of the two largest luxury resort hotels in the world. It ranks as a tourist attraction in its own right—like Boulder Dam or Versailles—and people detour just to see it. Others spend their entire vacation here, never going anywhere else.

If I start describing the hotel's entrance floor and branch out, you'll be lost before I get halfway through the casino. It's bigger than a football field with both end zones. Within its chandeliered precincts enclosed by a genuine imported Italian marble balustrade, you'll find about 1,000 slot machines, 10 craps layouts, 90 blackjack tables, 9 roulette wheels, 3 baccarat tables, 16 poker set-ups, a sports and race book, and a 100-seat keno lounge with closed-circuit TV to other areas. That's just for openers. So I'll skip to rooms and rates first. Then I'll return to the nearest thing to open Marlboro Country I've seen—indoors.

There are 2,900 basic, grand, and deluxe bedrooms, player's suites, and town-house suites, reachable via 24 high-speed elevators. Some sumptuous royal suites run $1,000 a day (double occupancy), but if the entire budget for your Las Vegas vacation is well below $1,000, there's hope.

MOVIES FOR TWO: Film buffs can take in such oldies as *Anastasia, Little Women, The Adventures of Huckleberry Finn,* and *The Mark of Zorro* (with Tyrone Power) at Bally's movie house. They're the originals, uncut, and they're nostalgic fun. Displacing the usual seating setup are love seats—for two. It's like a private screening room. Admission is $3.50 for adults, $2.75 for children aged 11 and under; senior citizens pay $2. There are showings nightly at 5:30, 8, and 10:30 p.m., and matinees on Saturday and Sunday at 12:30 and 3 p.m. The double couches are cozy.

Guest rooms for one or two with king-size beds or two double beds (often called double-doubles) are pegged at $85 to $120. Each has separate living-room space, color TV, a direct-dial phone with message light, an AM/FM clock radio, individually controlled air conditioning, and nightly turndown service. They're decorated with flair.

Some rooms have round beds with mirrored ceilings, for $120 a night.

Suites with one bedroom and a living room are priced from $190 to $225, ascending to a lofty $268 to $530 for a two-bedroom suite.

In a Technicolor aside, columnist Rex Reed referred to a suite he occupied as having lime draperies, pink furniture, a Popsicle-orange bedspread, a butterscotch and tomato-red bar, and a passion-purple bath. Said he: "I trudged off to my 14-color banana-split bedroom."

Each individual room or suite has a brass star on the door, signifying that "every guest at Bally's is a star." There's also a peephole through the star so guests can see who's knocking before they open the door. Hallways are hung with black-and-white photos, picturing such MGM luminaries as Clark Gable, Katharine Hepburn, Greta Garbo, Gene Kelly, Rosalind Russell, Wallace Beery, and others.

Be sure to ask about the Bally package plan for three days and two nights, which includes a deluxe guest room and either the *Jubilee* show in the Ziegfeld Room or a superstar, such as Tom Jones or Frank Sinatra, in the Celebrity Room, including cocktails.

Now, back to the hotel's public areas. Facing the Strip, but set back about a block from the boulevard, is the marqueed drive-up entrance—your first stop. It juts out over the double-lane roadway, and it's fronted by a bronze statuary grouping. From there, the check-in and registration counters are to your left, the casino to your right. Separating casino and lobby segments are colonnaded pillars and white marble statuary.

Behind the hotel are the swimming pools. The smaller one is a therapy pool seating 50 people, where water flows through jets at 800 gallons a minute. The bigger pool has a 320,000-gallon capacity.

On the floor below the lobby is a 40-store shopping arcade that offers an old-fashioned candy store with decor as tempting as the candied delights, a barbershop, a beauty salon, a florist, a jewelry emporium, furs, women's froufrou, etc.

And, of course, an important facility for those traveling with kids is the Youth Center, offering video arcade games and an ice-cream parlor.

Restaurants

No fewer than six restaurants offer dining to suit your mood. Most are located along Restaurant Court, a movie re-creation of an old-world street. The food is international, running the gamut from pâté de foie gras to hot pastrami, with plentiful selections in between. More gee-whiz statistics: the hotel keeps shrimp on hand by the boxcar load, 10,000 pounds to be exact; and the seven sparkling kitchens use about 12,000 eggs each day. Bally's 350 cooks turn out about 18,000 meals a day.

The **Café Gigi** is the hotel's poshest haute-cuisine eatery, with decor designed to reflect the Palace of Versailles no less. Intimate dining alcoves are framed by luxurious draperies. Walls and ceilings are a soft green, highlighted with gold leaf. The room is further enhanced by crystal chandeliers as well as gold-detailed mural wall panels and mirrors from the movie *Marie Antoinette*. The booths themselves are beautifully upholstered in rose velvet.

Your meal at Gigi might begin with smoked Scottish salmon served with dark bread, coquilles St-Jacques—creamy scallops in wine—or marrow on toast with truffle sauce. Since this is the kind of place for leisurely European-style multicourse feasting, you might proceed to a soup course—it could be anything from lobster bisque with cognac to French onion au gratin, perhaps followed by a wilted-spinach or Caesar salad. There's a considerable choice of entrees in the $27 to $40 range, among them steak Diane, braised fresh salmon in champagne and grapes, filet mignon with sauce béarnaise, roast duckling in orange or cherry sauce, and baby rack of lamb with fresh vegetables. Side orders of ratatouille niçoise or asparagus in hollandaise sauce are available, and, of course, there's a fine list of wines to complement your meal. As for desserts, they range from flambé specialties such as crêpes Suzette to a platter of fresh fruits and imported cheeses. Though you may not want to order such a complete meal as the above, this is not a place for skimping; as with a yacht, if you have to worry about the price, you can't afford Gigi. Save it for a night when you've made a killing at the casinos.

Café Gigi is open Wednesday through Sunday from 6 to 11 p.m.

Tracy's is named after Spencer Tracy (don't tell me you didn't guess it), who was nominated 11 times for an Academy Award. He insisted that he was an "unromantic type" despite the fact that he appeared with nearly every top female star in Hollywood. The escalator ride to the restaurant takes you through a wonderland of beveled glass, with reflections of a spectacular crystal chandelier glittering everywhere. A large montage from the old MGM studios—with movie poster blow-ups of Tracy and his costars from *Thirty Seconds Over Tokyo, Woman of the Year, Pat and Mike,* and *Boys Town*—assures you that you're in the right place.

The interior is done in soft shades of coral, with large gold pillars and two-story-high windows dominating the room. Each round table is lit by a small white-shaded lamp and has comfortable chairs.

Dinner can begin with imported prosciutto and melon, creamy marinated herring, a cup of double chicken consommé with noodles or chilled borscht, or perhaps Tracy's salad bowl with Belgian endive, artichokes, fresh mushrooms, and watercress. Entrees include mignonette of prime beef sauté with goose liver and truffle sauce, and broiled double-rib spring lamb chops with mint jelly, among other choices. All dinners are served with soup or salad, potatoes, and vegetables; entrees are $14 to $25. A large selection of desserts (such as fresh strawberry shortcake and French pastries) is available, and there's a good wine list.

If all this is not enough, there is a special Chinese menu as well. Appetizers include paper-wrapped chicken, rumaki with water chestnuts, and a combination plate with barbecued spareribs, eggroll, paper-wrapped chicken, fried prawns, and fried wonton. Soups range from egg flower to chicken broth with noodles and pork. There's a spicy Szechuan chicken with sautéed Chinese vegetables as well as Mongolian beef and fresh shrimps with sautéed vegetables. Other selections include lemon chicken and lobster Cantonese. All entrees are served with steamed rice, Chinese tea, and fortune cookies. Desserts include fresh pineapple, Chinese kumquats and lichee nuts, and homemade almond cookies. Entrees range in price from $13 to $20.

LAS VEGAS STRIP

KEY TO NUMBERED REFERENCES ON OUR MAP OF THE LAS VEGAS STRIP: 1—Vegas World; 2—Sahara; 3—Algiers; 4—Main Post Office; 5—Circus Circus; 6—Riviera; 7—Westward Ho; 8—La Concha; 9—El Morocco; 10—Stardust; 11—Villa Roma; 12—Landmark; 13—Las Vegas Hilton; 14—Convention Center; 15—Fashion Show Mall; 16—Convention Center Lodge; 17—Frontier; 18—Desert Inn; 19—Brooks Rent-a-Car; 20—Golden Nugget on the Strip; 21—Imperial 400; 22—Tam O'Shanter; 23—Sands; 24—Holiday Inn Center Strip; 25—Imperial Palace; 26—Caesars Palace; 27—Flamingo Hilton; 28—Barbary Coast; 29—Maxim; 30—Dunes; 31—Bally's–Las Vegas; 32—Mini-Price (Koval Lane); 33—Ambassador Inn; 34—Holiday Inn South; 35—Aladdin; 36—Hacienda; 37—Tropicana; 38—Motel 6.

Dinner at Tracy's is served Friday through Tuesday from 5 to 11 p.m.

Venice is the theme of **Caruso's,** Bally's elegant Italian restaurant. Hand-painted murals of Venetian scenes frame the entrance of this unique rust-toned room with its marble entry; cobblestone-motif carpeted floors, antique iron ovens, brilliant chandeliers, and classical statuary complete the decor. The menu offers a wide variety of choices. A good beginning to your meal is an antipasto platter or an appetizer of shrimp cocktail. All entrees are served with garlic bread toasted with sharp cheeses, and pasta or potato. There are several fish and seafood items—lobster tails sauté oreganata, mountain brook trout sauté amandine, Caruso shellfish stew, as well as Italian specialties like veal (scaloppine or parmigiana), homemade Italian sausages with roasted green peppers, and eggplant parmigiana. Of course you can also order a pasta dish—such as fettuccine in cream and butter with grated parmesan, spaghetti with meatballs or sausages, or lasagne—as an entree or side order. Among the à la carte desserts are rum cake and the excellent strawberry cheesecake. Entrees at Caruso's range from $15 to $25.

Caruso's is open from Friday through Tuesday from 6 to 11 p.m.

Barrymore's honors America's most famous theatrical family—John, Ethel, and Lionel (not to mention Drew)—who during their careers earned, collectively, over $10 million and managed to die penniless. The planked ceiling of hand-rubbed hardwoods is complemented by carpeting of planked design, combining with carved oak bas-relief panels and copper accents to create a warm and comfortable ambience.

The cuisine is gourmet quality, featuring steak and seafood for the most part. You can begin with such appetizers as escargots bourguignonne and bluepoint oysters or cherrystone clams on the halfshell. Specialties from the open hearth include French-cut lamb chops, roast prime rib of beef au jus, and filet mignon with sautéed mushrooms. Seafood entrees offer an excellent selection, ranging from blackened red fish New Orleans Style, to sautéed orange roughy, to a 2½-pound lobster. All entrees are served with potato and vegetable du jour; they range in price from $18 to $50. For dessert you might select one of the assorted French pastries, a plate of assorted homemade ice creams and sherberts, or chocolate twist torte.

Barrymore's is open nightly from 6 to 11 p.m.

The **Deli** is a New York-style eatery, its walls lined with caricatures of MGM stars. Its immense menu offers an astounding number of choices. Combination sandwiches include salami, Swiss cheese, turkey breast, coleslaw, and Russian dressing. And among the traditional favorites are cream cheese and Nova Scotia salmon on a bagel; pastrami on rye; a Reuben with corned beef, Swiss cheese, and sauerkraut, grilled on rye; matzoh ball soup; brisket on rye; all for $5 to $12. For dessert try the deep-dish fruit pies with vanilla ice cream.

The Deli is open daily from 8 a.m. to 1 a.m.

The **Orleans Coffee House** is open around the clock and features a French Quarter decor. Most of the above-mentioned Deli fare is available here too, but you can also get hot entrees such as fried prawns with a choice of soup or salad, fresh vegetable, potato du jour, and rolls and butter.

Finally, there's a snackbar by the pool, and a **Swensen's** ice-cream parlor in the shopping arcade.

CAESARS PALACE: 3570 Las Vegas Blvd. South, Las Vegas, NV 89109 (tel. 702/731-7110, or toll free 800/634-6001, 800/634-6661 for reservations).

From the day it opened on August 6, 1966, Caesars Palace has purveyed Lucullan luxuries under the name of the Caesars. The big hotel can no longer claim to be the biggest, but the invitation to lounge while being fed grapes by an adoring and nubile slavery is the image the Palace has continued to maintain.

At night, Caesars Palace bathes itself in a blue-green light, which glows from behind the grillwork that sheathes the hotel.

Out front, the towering row of fountains puts on a magnificent display and takes up a couple of city blocks of valuable land. When the wind blusters across the desert, however, the fountains are liable to douse anything within a hundred feet. That's given rise to the quip that the Palace is "the biggest Italian car wash in town."

Alongside the beautiful fountains are 50-foot-high cypresses in double rows, slim and green. Reproductions of classic statuary —*The Rape of the Sabines, Winged Victory of Samothrace, Venus de Milo*—complement the sweeping scene, and inside and out the hotel has enough marble in balustrades, columns, statues, and gewgaws to have depleted Italy's Carrara marble quarries.

A few years ago a dramatic innovation to the Caesars Palace façade was constructed—the People Mover, an arcaded automatic sidewalk facilitating entry into the hotel from the street, 240 feet away. It originates at a colonnaded Temple of Diana, its centerpiece an exact Carrara marble replica of that goddess of the hunt. A more recent addition is the Olympic Tower People Mover that connects the Strip with the Omnimax Theatre, a thrilling entertainment (about which more in Chapter VI). Its geodesic-dome entrance mirrors the shape of the theater, and the Omnimax exterior light show is visible from the Strip. Within the hotel is an awesome 18-foot-high replica of Michelangelo's *David* in the center of the Appian Way, an elite arcade with such prestigious shops as Gucci and Ted Lapidus.

In June 1988 Caesars Palace broke ground for what will become **The Forum at Caesars**—an enclosed, air-conditioned 150-store shopping complex and a 1½-acre open-air Roman village bazaar. If you don't part with your whole bankroll at the gambling tables, the Forum is intended to help you dispense with the rest of it. Ultimately, the grand design will encompass 875,000 square feet, with parking facilities for 3,000 cars; the first phase (expansion to 575,000 square feet) is scheduled for completion in 1990.

Caesars Palace has 1,600 rooms and suites. On its fourth anniversary the hotel opened a 14-story addition topped by a pair of two-story duplex suites with four bedrooms each. In 1974 another tower was added—this time with 375 rooms and suites with eight bedrooms. And in November 1979 the 24-story, 600-room Olympic Tower came into being. Its luxurious rooms have velvet-covered walls and sunken Roman tubs; its suites contain a seven-foot-diameter pool and Jacuzzi overlooking the Strip. The Olympic Tower also houses the above-mentioned Omnimax Theatre, a circular bar offering nightly entertainment, and a race and sports book lounge that bears a striking resemblance to a commodities exchange.

Seven restaurants, several cocktail lounges, and a wide variety of entertainment options are some of the facilities piled into the complex. But that's not quite the whole show. There are an Olympic-size swimming pool, and one shaped like a Roman shield and situated in the "Garden of the Gods," its landscaping copied from the Pompeii Baths of Rome; eight outdoor tennis courts (two of which are night-lit); and complete health-club facilities for men and women. Golf can be arranged nearby. As for the casino, it is lit by two majestic crystal-and-brass chandeliers—the largest in existence—and the domed ceiling above the craps and blackjack areas is supported by 20 Italian black marble columns trimmed with white marble and gold leaf. And then there's a cocktail lounge that floats in its own lagoon. It's called **Cleopatra's Barge,** and I'll get to it later. First, the rooms:

Single and double rates run from $110 to $160 for standard accommodations. One-bedroom suites are $230 to $560, and two-bedroom suites are in the $375 to $900 range. The most expensive of these are the Olympic Tower and Villa suites. Two-bedroom Villa duplex suites begin at $690. Add $15 for a third person in a standard room.

These prices are reasonable for what you get. Every room is an invitation to wallow in luxury, with sink-in carpets, entire walls of mirrors, chaises, some beds on raised platforms with steps and mirrored ceiling—separated from the living area (cum sofas) by arched dividers. Even the drinking glasses in the baths are wrapped in gold metal foil rather than in the usual waxed paper. The decor is colorful (fuchsia, purple, red), the entire effect airy, plush-grand, and comfortable. Hallways in the towers are lined with niches exhibiting more statuary. The decorators certainly went wild, but their efforts succeeded. The rooms at Caesars Palace achieve luxury with a fun angle.

Restaurants

Most typical of Caesars Palace is the **Bacchanal.** A quotation from the menu says it all: "I, Caesar, welcome you to the most resplendent arena of gustatory delights . . . the BACCHANAL!

"My staff has in every way attempted to anticipate and satisfy your slightest wish . . . both in the magnificence of your surroundings and in the abundance and superlative quality of the cuisine. Here, you shall embark upon an adventure in gourmet dining unparalleled outside my empire . . . created and composed by my Master Chefs. Each component part of my dinner has been selected to complement each other item within that dinner. Three selected wines appropriate to the entrees are included in the price of the dinner." (Currently, dinner at the Bacchanal is about $60 per person.)

Inside the menu are ostensible words of wisdom of the Roman emperors—Caligula's "Apud mensam plenam homini rostrum deliges" ("Tie the man by the beak to a well-filled table," or possibly more accurately, "Choose a well-stocked table as a rostrum for a man").

The setting is, of course, fittingly sumptuous. The entrance to the room is guarded by two golden lions, and the interior highlighted by a marble-walled lighted pool with a statue at its center; displayed around the pool are huge bowls of fruit, pastries, and ice-sculpture swans. Walls are white latticework or fluted columns interspersed with deep-purple swagged velvet curtains, the beamed blue ceiling suggests an open sky, and a grape arbor loops from beam to beam. Diners are comfortably ensconced in posh red-leather booths. Service is equally lavish; beautiful wine girls in sexy harem outfits (known as the "Wine Goddesses") pour wine from shoulder height into ornate chalices. Only in Vegas! As for the meal itself, it's a veritable orgy of seven courses, lacking only a minion to feed you grapes: tidbits served with an aperitif; an hors d'oeuvres tray; tureens of soup; a "Roman piscatorian delight" (fish course); a "parade of gastronomical surprises fit for all of the twelve Caesars" (main course); vegetables; flambé desserts and pastries, cheeses, fruits, and coffee—and lots of wine to wash it all down. The menu is preselected with seasonal entrees. The cost is $60 including wine.

The Bacchanal is open for dinner Tuesday through Sunday. There are two seatings, 6 to 6:30 p.m. and 9 to 9:30 p.m. Reservations recommended.

Just as lavish, but with a Venetian palazzo theme, the circular **Palace Court** is filled with art treasures. Reached via a crystal-and-bronze elevator, it is framed by a bronze-balustraded spiral staircase and illuminated by a Venini crystal chandelier; its white-latticed windows overlook the pool. The walls are hung with heroic paintings attributed to the School of Peter Paul Rubens and portraits of the 12 Caesars by a 17th-century painter, Camillo Procaccini (these used to hang in New York's posh Four Seasons restaurant). Tables are covered with Czechoslovakian lace cloths, set with gold-and-white Lenox china, vermeil flatware, and hand-blown crystal, and lit by silver candelabras. The centerpiece of the room is a domed stained-glass skylight (an orange-and-yellow sunburst), under which is a weeping fig tree shading a buffet display of fruits, cheeses, desserts, and ice sculpture. Around the tree are six terra-cotta pots of smaller trees and chrysanthemums, a lamppost with an exquisite glass glove in front of each. Statuary, faïence, and polished steel furnishings with velvet upholstery complete the picture. Adjoining is a piano bar with its own minicasino under a huge crystal chandelier. Gentlemen are required to wear jackets at the Palace Court.

Luncheon at the Palace Court might begin with an appetizer of pâté du chef with port wine in pastry crust, or imported Westphalian ham with white asparagus. Salmon mousse with sorrel sauce, sliced cold capon and papaya in light curry sauce, and poached egg in baked potato with cream and hollandaise sauce are just a few of the delicious entrees, which range in price from $9 to $17. For dessert the chocolate mousse with marinated strawberries is superb.

Dinner offers a wider and, of course, pricier selection. Hors d'oeuvres range from pâté of goose liver Strasbourg to pike mousse, and soups from lobster bisque flamed with Armagnac to chilled cream of cucumber topped with caviar. Among the entrees (which cost $25 to $55) are Maine lobster in tarragon butter with saffron rice, rock Cornish game hen in truffle sauce, steak Diane with wine sauce and mushrooms prepared tableside, and twin baby lamb chops with mint sauce. The sommelier will be happy to assist you in selecting the right wine to go with your entree. For dessert, perhaps a flamed liqueur coffee with petit fours.

The Palace Court is open for lunch Thursday to Sunday from 11:30 a.m. to 2:30 p.m. And for dinner, nightly, there are two seatings, 6 to 6:30 p.m. and 9 to 9:30 p.m.

Primavera, overlooking the Garden of the Gods swimming pool and spa, offers gourmet Italian cuisine with specialties from the North and South of Italy. For a first course, the antipasti cart presents an outstanding array of cold appetizers. Or you might defer to a house speciality such as the fried mozzarella or the elegant consommé garnished with egg flakes, spinach, and grated cheese.

The entree list begins with pasta, all homemade, including the chef's specialty of ravioli lightly filled with spinach and essence of veal, served with your choice of bolognese, marinara, or butter sauce. Several of the pasta entrees are also available as side dishes.

The many veal entrees range from the veal marsala to a simple veal with prosciutto and fresh sage. One of the unusual poultry choices features thin slices of sautéed breast of chicken with kiwi fruit and lemon butter, finished with rich sherry wine. Prime sirloin steak is served sautéed and topped with a tomato sauce, or panfried with a touch of garlic. Maine Lobster is served in a spicy marinara sauce. And look for the chef's specialty each evening.

Primavera offers a pastry cart of Italian specialties, as well as cheese with fresh fruit in season. Ice-cream desserts are meals in themselves—say, the Cassata Caligula with layers of pistachio, zabaglione, and chocolate ice cream.

Meat or seafood entrees cost $24 to $45, pasta dishes are $10 to $15, and appetizers $7 to $17. To help sustain your appetite, Primavera offers a good selection of still and sparkling Italian wines.

Primavera is open daily for breakfast at 7:30 to 11 a.m., for luncheon at 11:30 a.m. to 2:30 p.m., and for dinner at 6 to 11:30 p.m.

A few steps from the Roman Forum Casino is **Ah' So,** is Caesars' Oriental restaurant, a Disney-esque creation of plastic trees, thousands of artificial flowers, arched bridges over pools and grottoes, bamboo paneling, Japanese paper lanterns, and grass-like carpeting. A waterfall cascading over lava-like rock embedded with colorful foliage takes up one entire wall, and there are even electric fireflies amid the delicate blossoms of Nipponese fruit trees.

The six-course $44.50 prix-fixe teppan yaki meal is served by waitresses appropriately attired in kimonos and obis. All cooking is done tableside. Dinner includes an appetizer; miso or clear soup; tempura seafood and vegetables; a salad of marinated cucumber and shredded crabmeat; an entree of boneless chicken breast, steak, or lobster tail; an assortment of Japanese vegetables; steamed rice; green tea; plenty of sake; fresh fruit; and dessert.

Apart from the teppan yaki prix-fixe dinner, the Ah' So also offers tuna sashimi, as well as sushi prepared with salmon, tuna, sea vegetable roll, and shrimp.

Ah' So is open nightly from 6 to 11:30 p.m.

The **Spanish Steps** offers à la carte Spanish specialties, seafood, and steak. The restaurant is named for the 18th-century Piazza di Spagna in Rome. Designed in the style of Granada's Alhambra Palace, it has an imposing Moorish-design brass-and-copper entranceway, the geometric pattern repeated in layered copper walls and ceiling, marquetry tables, and terra-cotta tile floors. Variations of copper and brass are the main colors; tables are set with copper plates and candle lamps; and the open kitchen is agleam with copperware. Waiters and waitresses are dressed in dramatic gaucho costumes.

A good way to begin your dinner (à la carte) is with the house special margarita, which you can sip while perusing the menu. Among the recommended appetizers are the ceviche, and scampi prepared tableside with red and green salsa flambé. An excellent soup course is the clear clam broth with a crown of sherry whipped cream. Among the Spanish entrees are paella Valenciana and zarzuela de mariscos—a mixture of lobster, shrimp, clams, and squid in a rich red sauce. Choices from the grill include a T-bone steak and double-thick broiled lamb chops. The price range for entrees at the Spanish Steps is $17 to $45. Desserts run the gamut from a traditional flan to assorted French pastries, and a pitcher of sangría is a good accompaniment to your meal.

The Spanish Steps is open nightly from 6 to 11:30 p.m.

The **Palatium** is dedicated to serving lavish buffets for breakfast ($6.95), lunch ($7.95), and dinner ($10.95), with a fixed price for each. The restaurant is all etched glass, gold trim, and now and then Caesars statuary. Breakfast is served from 7:30 to 10:30 a.m. weekdays, and from 8:30 a.m. to 2:30 p.m. Saturday and Sunday; lunch from 11 to 2:30 p.m. daily; dinner from 4:30 to 10 p.m. Sunday through Thursday, till 11 p.m. Friday and Saturday.

And last, but by no means the least, there's an award-winning champagne brunch ($14.50; $9.50 for children under 12) every Sunday from 9:30 a.m. to 2 p.m. in the **Circus Maximus** showroom, presented in the grand tradition of Roman feasts, with the added flair of the bubbly.

Food orgies are all well and good, but should you want lighter fare and more casual surroundings, there is the immense **Café Roma**, a 24-hour coffeeshop. Done in warm colors—golds, oranges, reds, and yellows—the Café Roma has its share of fancy decor: classic columns and arches, etchings of ancient Roman scenes, and striped awnings over a colonnade; however, you can dine here comfortably in your jeans.

The fare ranges in price from $7 to $25 for a hot pastrami sandwich, lox and bagel, or filet mignon served with soup or salad, potatoes, and roll and butter, not to mention borscht with sour cream, crab Louie, and veal parmigiana. After 5 p.m., Café Roma also has an extensive Chinese menu, ranging from $6 to $9 for appetizers, from $12 to $30 for entrees.

There's one more option for daily sustenance—the **Post Time Deli.** The Deli is more for the convenience of the race and sports book fans who don't want to leave the area and will settle for a hamburger, hot dog, or a delicious sandwich. Wine, beer, and soft drinks are also available. It's open seven days from 9 a.m. to midnight.

THE LAS VEGAS HILTON: 3000 Paradise Rd. (adjacent to

the Las Vegas Convention Center), Las Vegas, NV 89109 (tel. 702/732-5111, or toll free 800/732-7117).

Set on 63 acres, the Hilton is the largest resort hotel in the world, with 3,174 rooms, a reception desk that measures 100 feet, a core of international restaurants, an appropriately plush casino, shops, and much, much more. Its 375-foot tower dominates the desert horizon.

You'll need time to explore the Hilton, including the land-scaped ten-acre outdoor recreation deck on the third-floor roof with six tennis courts, an 18-hole putting green, shuffleboard, and a swimming pool that's the biggest in Nevada. (In addition to the deck facilities, guests can use the 18-hole course next door at the Las Vegas Country Club; greens fee is $50.)

The Hilton is too sumptuous to be called rococo, too heady with the grandeur of Louis XIV, XV, XVI, and other unnumbered potentates to be reduced to ordinary narrative. I lost count of the chandeliers in the casino when I became absorbed with the Grecian-style frieze of bas-reliefs bordering the ceilings and the neon rainbows over slot machines.

Your passport to stay at the Hilton is $70 to $130 a day, single or double; suites cost $325 to $950. At that rate for one or two (an extra person is $15; no charge for children sharing a room with their parents), you'll get a very large room facing outside. Each floor of rooms is decorated in the motif of a different country—Spanish, French, Oriental, etc. All have remote-control color TV with a special gaming-instruction channel. A dresser with nine deep drawers is placed beneath an embellished wood-framed mirror. Upholstered easy chairs, of course, deep closets, a marble-topped dressing table with sink, and a completely separate tub-shower bath round out the layout. Colors are chosen with an eye for the elegant. Hallways are curved, and some of the room doors are recessed for a foyer effect. There are lanai suites on the third level near the pool at $275 a night.

Furthermore, in a town that has very few facilities for children, the Hilton has gone all out for family business. It has a completely self-contained $2-million **Youth Hotel** within the premises, a separate place with dormitories for girls and boys age 3 through 18. (Sleeping quarters are monitored by closed-circuit TV.) The Youth Hotel is supervised 24 hours a day by qualified educators and recreation specialists, meals and snacks are served, and rates and amounts for milkshakes and goodies are settled by parents in advance and added to their bill. It's like a summer camp. Fencing, boxing, tumbling, arts and crafts, table tennis, arcade games, teenage dances, an outdoor playground, basketball, volleyball, magic shows, desert field trips, and a stage where the children produce and mount their own skits and plays are among the many recreational outlets. Rates: $4.50 an hour for each child. Overnight stays are $25 per child. (This rate covers the hours of midnight to 8 a.m.) The Youth Hotel is open from 8 a.m. to 10 p.m. daily year round; kids can stay overnight seven days a week from mid-June until Labor Day, and weekends and holidays during the rest of the year.

Adults will appreciate the health spa for men and women, with exercise rooms, sauna and steam rooms, and a whirlpool bath. The spa also offers all kinds of refreshing relief from those late hours of cigarettes and alcohol over the blackjack tables: massage, specially invigorating baths, hot packs, cosmetic beauty baths, even oxygen pep-ups and a treatment in a wonder body machine called Panthermal, which is claimed to remove every form of weariness, increase muscular working capacity, clean your skin, stimulate body functions, diminish weight, and eliminate cellulite!

The ultimate bargain at the Las Vegas Hilton is a three-day/two-night "Winners Holiday" package. A Sunday-through-Thursday arrival is $42.50, Friday or Saturday is $54.50, per person, double occupancy; you get accommodations, admission to the show in the main showroom with two cocktails, or dinner for two in any designated restaurant.

Restaurants

Just about every dining mood can be accommodated at the Hilton. There are offerings from the delicate delights of Japan, the light pastas and veal dishes of Italy, the subtle and elegant cuisine of France, as well as the finest beef fare selected for Hilton steaks and prime ribs.

Le Montrachet, the pride of the Las Vegas Hilton, features continental cuisine and a wine cellar with over 400 wines from around the world.

Le Montrachet was created to achieve the utmost in elegant dining. The dark walls, plush banquettes, and flattering light create a rich, relaxed atmosphere, conducive to appreciation of the chef's superb creations.

Dinner at Le Montrachet was one of the finest I have had at any restaurant from New York to California. Ordering from the six-course, prix-fixe menu I began my meal with chilled foie gras of duck on a checkerboard of miniature green beans. Then came poached oysters on the halfshell, topped with orange butter glaze, followed by a delicate sweet basil sorbet. Choice of entrees was between roast rack of lamb marinated with sweet basil, fresh dill, mint, shallots, and tarragon; or medallions of veal and morel mushrooms with Noilly cream sauce. (Are your salivary glands coming to life?) A salad of lamb lettuce, endive, and watercress—tossed with walnuts, Dijon mustard, and lemon juice—was next, and all of the above was capped by a hot apple tart topped with caramel ice cream. The prix-fixe dinner is $60—about $25 less than if each course is ordered individually.

Should you decide to order à la carte, I suggest that you try something a bit different—and then wait for a very pleasant surprise. You might choose the raviolis of fresh crabmeat and morel mushrooms, or the mousse of lobster wrapped in a flaky strudel. A first or second course might be the chilled avocado soup topped with fresh beluga caviar.

Entrees include seafood choices from Maine lobster to Dover sole either grilled or boned and filled with mousse of lobster and served with truffle slices. And consider the medallions of venison or the sautéed breast of pheasant stuffed with duck liver. The broiled veal chop stuffed with wild mushrooms and served with Madeira sauce and truffles is excellent too, as is the broiled filet mignon served with a puff pastry shell of wild mushrooms and a pinot noir and Sandeman port wine sauce.

Then by all means review the pastry cart. If by some quirk nothing catches your eye, scan the dessert list and consider the Swiss chocolate soufflé, crème anglaise with Cointreau, or the Painter's Palette with sorbets and fresh fruits of the season.

Hors d'oeuvres range from $10 to $23, soup or salad from $7 to $9. Entrees are about $23 to $38, desserts $7 to $11.

Most dramatic of the restaurants is **Benihana Village,** a complex of three dining areas and four cocktail lounges set in a Japanese village with lush foliage, a three-story palace, and running streams. There are a hibachi dining room, a robata (Japanese barbecue) room, and a tempura room. Seating is under pagoda roofs and a giant umbrella, and special effects include thunder and lightning followed by pouring rain (not on diners, however), dancing waters bathed in colored lights, and electronic fireworks. An arched wooden bridge over a stream connects dining areas. There are also several cocktail areas, including one in which you can enjoy cocktails in your own private rickshaw.

In the hibachi rooms, all cooking is done tableside by chefs who wield their carving knives with the expertise of samurai warriors. Full dinners include a hibachi shrimp appetizer, soup, salad, rice, vegetable, green tea, and ice cream or sherbet; they're priced at $15 to $40. Hibachi chicken, sukiyaki steak, hibachi steak, and filet mignon are all on the menu. You can also order a carafe of sake with your meal. In the tempura room full dinners include Japanese-style onion soup, salad, green tea, rice, and dessert (try the green tea or ginger ice cream). Entrees, ranging from $13 to $35, include shrimp tempura, lobster tempura, and a combination of beef tempura and lobster tail. The meal in the robata rooms contains pretty much the same accompaniments except for the vegetables—a choice of corn on the cob, skewer of mushrooms, or onions and green peppers instead of tempura vegetables. Entrees of barbecued chicken, New York-cut sirloin, filet mignon, and steak-and-chicken or steak-and-shrimp combination are available for $13 to $35. You can order à la carte from any of the menus, all of which also offer half-price dinners for children under 12.

Benihana is open nightly for cocktails from 5 p.m. to midnight, for dining from 6 to 11 p.m.

For light Italian fare, the new, lovely **Andiamo** features an open kitchen where guests can watch the chefs busily turning out delicious meals.

The à la carte lunch and dinner menus both offer a remarkable selection. Lunch at Andiamo might begin with hot or cold antipasti, including such delectables as fresh asparagus with sweet pepper sauce, and crisply fried squid with fresh tomato sauce. Pizzas are decidedly not those found at your local parlor—the Porcini e Salsiccia, for example, is composed of porcini mushrooms, Italian sausage, and tomato sauce with mozzarella, fontina, and provolone. Pasta? Try the Ravioli Neri all' Aragosta with lobster, tarragon, and lobster sauce. An impressive list of entrees includes selections such as salmon, swordfish, a sirloin minute steak, and osso buco Andiamo. Your tab for lunch, without antipasti, wine, dessert, or coffee, will be about $9 to $16.

Andiamo's dinner menu is expansive, and the antipasti include one of my favorites, Carpaccio di Manzo—wafer-thin slices of tenderloin of beef blessed with parmesan, olive oil, and lemon juice. Among the pasta entrees, you might choose the Fettuccine Verdi al Pomodoro e Melanzane—spinach egg noodles with eggplant, tomatoes, and sweet basil. Other entrees are exceptional too—a whole baby salmon sautéed in butter, a veal chop with morel mushrooms and marsala sauce, or a charcoal-broiled filet mignon with Barolo Riserva red wine sauce. Pasta entrees run $10 to $16; seafood and meat courses will set you back $14 to $17.

Should you still have space for dessert, and the patience to wait 30 minutes, the soufflés at $5.50 are heavenly—there's a choice of Amaretto, Galliano, or lemon. Or you might consider the Venetian Dream of white espresso ice cream in a chocolate gondola.

Andiamo is open daily for lunch from 11:30 a.m. to 2:30 p.m. and for dinner from 6 to 11 p.m. Reservations are suggested.

Within the rustic western **Hilton Steak House,** there's an open charcoal kitchen, meat is displayed in a glass-doored refrigerator case, and rough-hewn barnwood or stucco walls are hung with farm implements and antlers. Railroad lamps and saddles are suspended from the log-beamed ceiling overhead.

You can order a filet mignon, New York steak, or a 20-ounce T-bone or combination steak and lobster. Alternatives to steak are broiled whitefish and barbecued pork ribs. Entrees cost $17 to $30, and are served with salad, corn on the cob or baked potato, and cheese-topped sourdough bread. Side orders of baked potato, acorn squash, or fresh mushrooms are also available. Desserts are traditional: chocolate mousse cake, apple pie à la mode, and a less than traditional pecan-apple cheesecake.

The Hilton Steak House is open nightly from 6 to 11:30 p.m.

Also western in decor is **Mamchen's Deli,** complete with swinging saloon doors, leaded-glass windows, mahogany paneling and beams, oak floors, and branding tools hanging over the old-fashioned marble bar. It's not totally western, though—Mamchen's is lettered in Hebrew-style characters, and the menu features the likes of smoked salmon, onions and cream cheese on a bagel, pastrami on homemade rye, chicken soup with kreplach, and chopped liver sandwiches, all in the $7 to $10 range. And of course there's strudel for dessert.

Mamchen's is open daily from 11:30 a.m. to 10 p.m.

Other dining options include the following:

The **Barronshire Prime Rib Room** offers prime-rib dinners, with Yorkshire pudding, mousseline potatoes, and creamed horseradish, at $19.75 to $25, depending on the cut. It has a hushed library ambience, complete with book-lined walls and a desk with an antique typewriter and open dictionary. The Barronshire Prime Rib Room is open nightly from 6 p.m. to 11 p.m.

The **Café Eclair,** an authentic Viennese café stube, offers such light fare as sandwiches, ice cream, pastries, and Viennese *torten* (cakes), to eat or take out. It's open daily from 7 a.m. to 9 p.m.

Market Plaza, the Hilton's spacious coffeeshop, is open round the clock and is conveniently located just off the main lobby next to the casino. You can get a quick continental breakfast or a variety of three-egg omelets here, depending upon the size of your appetite. The Plaza also offers fitness specialties such as cholesterol-free eggs. Full breakfasts cost $6.50 to $9.25. Lunch and dinner menus offer a good array of salads, sandwiches, and burgers, as well as more substantive choices such as chicken piccata, fried prawns, and sirloin steak, in the range of $9.50 to $13.50. Lunch and late-night favorites also include thick Sicilian pizza.

And finally, there's the **Paddock Snack Bar,** located in the SuperBook. The Paddock offers sandwiches, light bites, pizza, and soft drinks. Inside information has it that the corned beef sandwich served here is "the best" and will last through an entire football game. The snackbar is open from 7 a.m. to 10 p.m. Sunday through Thursday, to midnight Friday and Saturday.

DESERT INN COUNTRY CLUB AND SPA: 3145 Las Vegas Blvd. South (directly opposite the Frontier Hotel), Las Vegas, NV 89109 (tel. 702/733-4444, or toll free 800/634-6906).

A Strip fixture since 1950, the Desert Inn opened with 310 rooms built on 275 acres at a cost of $5 million. Two years later an 18-hole, par-72, championship golf course was created—a course that has played host to some of the nation's most famous golf tournaments. The golf course is part of a prestigious country club, which boasts its own two-story building complete with pro shop, locker rooms, and a distinguished restaurant and bar. The fee for 18 holes is $65 for guests, $110 for nonguests. You can buy sports apparel there, and rent golf and tennis equipment. Ten tournament-class tennis courts (all night-lit) are for the use of guests only (no extra charge). Lessons may be arranged. Other facilities include an Olympic-size swimming pool, about a dozen Jacuzzi baths scattered throughout the property, 14,000 square feet of shops, six restaurants, and, of course, a fine casino.

This abundance of existent facilities notwithstanding, in 1975 the Desert Inn undertook a $55-million expansion program. In this project, the Desert Inn was transformed into one of the most desirable hotels in town. It certainly has the most class of any hotel on the Strip, the usual ostentatious opulence replaced here by an understated (for Vegas) elegance. It has been redesigned and rebuilt, inside and out, from the foundation up. It now has the most attractive façade in town—a modular effect combining sand-colored stone and bronze reflective glass. A hexagonal module concept also unifies the accommodations buildings. Most notable is the previously unheard-of-in-Vegas, really good, refined taste throughout. The Desert Inn's buildings are situated on 200 acres of beautifully landscaped grounds, containing a lake, a waterfall, the pool, and sundecks. Considerable use of bronze glass is pleasantly dazzling, reflecting the brightly colored canvas patio awnings and expanses of water, grass, and palms.

To complete the total resort experience, the Desert Inn spent $3 million constructing a luxury health spa. It is second to none as a relaxation and fitness facility, including a gym, spas, saunas, massage, skin care, and a nutrition program that flies in the face of all that you've probably been eating and drinking in Las Vegas.

Golf- and tennis-themed buildings contain 818 beautiful rooms and suites. The least expensive rooms are in the Augusta Tower, and even these offer a tasteful beige, plum, and sienna decor and handsome beds (double-doubles or king-size) with brass headboards. They also have large dressing rooms, one full wall of window overlooking the Strip or the property, backgammon tables, cable TVs with movie channel, AM/FM radios, onyx baths, and every other modern amenity. The only thing lacking in Augusta that you'll find in all other units here—Pebble Beach, Forest Hills, Wimbledon, and Saint Andrews—is a bathroom phone. Particularly spectacular are the suites, decorated to reflect exotic regions—Guadalajara, Kashmir, Cannes, Isfahan, Kuala Lumpur, etc. Some of the suites even have their own private swimming pools, but all abound in luxury. Rooms at the Desert Inn are priced from $90 to $175, single or double; the higher rate is for a minisuite complete with wet bar, sunken marble tub, and other such luxuries. One-bedroom suites are $200 to $560; one- to four-bedroom private-pool suites, $500 to $1,500; with ultra luxurious accommodations ascending to $2,000.

Last but not least of many changes is the casino, sporting a plush decor dominated by 30 impressive circular brass chandeliers. And as you might expect, headliners play the showroom.

The Desert Inn is one of the most recommendable hotels on the Strip.

Restaurants

No shortage here. I'll begin with the **Monte Carlo Room,** its walls a vivid red and hung with many mirrors and French paintings. From the burgundy velvet-upholstered booths and Louis XVI–style chairs to the crystal chandeliers and wall lamps, from the stained-glass doors to the elaborate flower arrangements, the Monte Carlo Room is the last word in plush.

You can get off to a fittingly *haute* start by ordering hors d'oeuvres from marinated herring to beluga caviar. Entrees, including Monte Carlo specialties such as steak au poivre flambé Armagnac, Nevada Bob White quails Véronique, and broiled lobster tail in butter, range from $22 to $40. A bit pricey, but what the heck—how often do you get a chance to eat quail? For dessert, a selection from the pastry cart will add $4 to your bill. One comforting thought: even if you linger over after-dinner drinks, your meal will probably be less expensive than an evening spent at the tables.

The Monte Carlo Room is open nightly from 6:30 p.m. to midnight.

The **Portofino,** situated on the balcony, overlooks the casino action below, which tends to lend an air of excitement. It's quite luxurious, with Carrara marble and oak floors, black velvet booths, potted palm fronds, and an adjoining piano bar furnished with plush sienna chairs. The restaurant's centerpiece is a huge hexagonal structure filled with plants.

The Portofino, which specializes in northern Italian cuisine, features tableside cooking. The menu offers so many tempting northern Italian and continental specialties that you may find the choosing hard. If one could only have them all. For openers, the smoked salmon and the melon with prosciutto are great, but so are the crab legs, the fresh poached salmon served with cucumber salad and mustard sauce, and the shrimp, lobster, tuna, and crab mixed with artichoke heart, anchovies, romaine, and dressing. That's just the appetizer dilemma, and I won't even go into the soups and salads. As for the entrees, there are veal scaloppine rolled around a mixture of seasoned meat and cheese, simmered in wine; whole trout stuffed with crabmeat and served with drawn butter and lemon; seared beef tenderloin with mushrooms, shallots, red wine sauce, and sour cream; and whole New England lobster with tomalley (a sauce of lobster livers); and of course, osso buco. Entrees are priced from $19.50 to $30. Side orders of cannelloni, gnocchi, and fettuccine Alfredo are also available. And if after all that you're still up for a rich dessert, there's zabaglione with fruit, or mousse pie.

The Portofino is open Tuesday through Saturday from 6 p.m. to midnight. Jackets and reservations are necessary.

The Desert Inn has the touch of Far Eastern elegance with **HoWan,** located on the mezzanine above the casino. A blend of plush modern and antique Oriental, the room is decorated with two Chinese silk panels that are more than 100 years old. Bold brass columns with Chinese etching, an authentic gold bas-relief, distinctive woven carpeting, and subtle shades of burgundy, salmon, and gray complete the intimate decor of the room.

HoWan means "good fortune"—certainly for those who dine here. The menu offers a variety of soups and appetizers to start you off, including minced squab HoWan, crabmeat puff, shark's fin soup, and Eight Precious Soup with diced chicken, ham, prawns, lean pork, mushrooms, bean curd, and water chestnuts in a rich chicken broth. For your main course there's a complete selection of northern and southern Chinese dishes, including such specialties as Peking duck, beef with oyster sauce, lobster HoWan, and almond pressed duck. HoWan entrees range in price from $12 to $40. Chinese standards, such as egg foo yung, chow mein, and fried rice in a variety of flavors, all in the $5 to $12 range, can also be ordered.

HoWan is open Tuesday through Sunday from 6 to 11 p.m.

The distinguished country-club restaurant is the **Grill Room,** serving breakfast, lunch, and drinks. Its decor is sportive, with tartan plaids, forest-green leather-and-corduroy booths, and brown chairs. A wall of windows overlooks the golf course, and there are golf trophies on display. Stone walls add a rustic note.

Breakfast fare ranges from $5 to $9.50, encompassing everything from the conventional breakfast choices to scrambled eggs with lox and chives. At lunch there's a wide choice of reasonably priced hot and cold sandwiches, salads, and burgers (most under $9).

The Grill Room hours are 6:30 a.m. to 3:30 p.m. daily.

La Promenade, on the casino floor, is the Desert Inn's 24-hour coffeeshop, considerably more elegant than the usual of this genre with its beige velvet booths and magenta upholstered chrome chairs under immense tasseled gold umbrellas. The umbrellas are supported by massive copper-and-gold columns, each with six very delicate chandelier lamps attached and flowers and plants at its base. A tinted window offers a view of the pool.

A complete dinner is offered for $17, including soup, salad, entree (perhaps a broiled half spring chicken or fried filet of sole with white wine and mushrooms), potato or vegetable, dessert, and beverage. That's in addition to a wide choice of à la carte items available at all times. Breakfast options range from fresh-baked blueberry muffins to kippered herring.

FLAMINGO HILTON: 3555 Las Vegas Blvd. South, Las Vegas, NV 89109 (tel. 702/733-3111, or toll free 800/732-2111).

Inside and out, the Flamingo Hilton is one of my favorite

Vegas hotels. I love the electronic masterpiece that beckons visitors at the entrance with neon pink-and-orange flamingos grazing among graceful reeds. The use of pink plate mirror in the background creates the famous prismatic Hilton rainbow effect; it's also an energy-conscious way to keep wattage low.

The Flamingo has come a long way since it opened in 1946. Now it's the second-largest resort hotel in the world; then it was a 98-room oasis, so luxurious for its time that even the janitors wore tuxedos. Jimmy Durante was the opening headliner, and the wealthy and famous flocked to the beautifully landscaped resort festooned with lush palms and tropical plants.

Today the grounds are still lush. The original palms and sycamores are now complemented by Russian and Chinese elms and olive trees, cobblestoned pathways, fountains, and flower gardens. In the midst of it all are an Olympic-size swimming pool, sundeck, and the Little Vienna outdoor restaurant of the Crown Room Buffet.

Remodeling expanded the size of the casino; it has 7 craps layouts, 60 blackjack tables, 6 roulette tables, a Big Six wheel, a 90-seat keno lounge, and an 1,150-machine slot arcade where a Pot-O-Gold Jackpot and progressive slots offer potential winnings up to $1 million. Though the Flamingo offers almost every imaginable amenity, guests are welcome to use the facilities of the nearby Las Vegas Hilton, including the above-mentioned Youth Hotel for children aged 3 to 18.

Both old and new rooms (the former completely refurbished) are extremely attractive. The new 800-room tower accommodations have coordinated drapes and wallpaper in one of five color schemes: rust, blue, green, beige/yellow, or peach. They're large and handsomely furnished, and they offer views of the Strip or garden. A gaming-instruction channel on your color TV is one of many extras. Rooms in the old building are storybook homey, with old-fashioned lamps and cotton quilts, and pretty paintings on the walls. The tower has a health club, indoor/outdoor pool, tennis courts for day and night play, and a new gourmet restaurant, the Flamingo Room. Room rates are $70 to $118 a night, single or double, depending on location. There are a total of 2,920 rooms and suites.

Restaurants

The Flamingo Hilton has introduced a different restaurant concept to Las Vegas with its **Food Fantasy,** a 24-hour weekend "buffeteria" that allows you to select the items you wish from large, attractive displays. On weekdays it's open for breakfast, lunch, and dinner from 6 a.m. to 9 p.m. If you want dinner at 8 a.m., it's there. Modeled after the restaurant of the same name at the Hilton Hawaiian Village in Honolulu, it has a light and airy garden decor with brick floor, an abundance of plants, and a garden/pool view. A large salad bar is part of the offerings.

Breakfast fare ranges from $4 to $8 for cheese blintzes (three) with blueberries and sour cream to eggs Benedict. On weekends, early-morning breakfasters (midnight to 7 a.m.) can feast on two eggs with toast, hash browns, and bacon or sausage. There is a large selection of sandwiches—such as sliced breast of turkey or a hoagie (a French roll filled with ham, cheese, turkey, pickles, salad, etc.) or a French-dip roast beef sandwich with fries. Also available are salads—perhaps avocado or tomato stuffed with seafood or chicken salad—and hot entrees like broiled lamb chops with mint jelly, southern fried chicken with biscuits and honey, and New York–cut sirloin steak with onion rings. And many luscious desserts are on glorious, tempting display.

Also on the premises is a **Beef Barron,** an institution throughout the Hilton Chain. The elegant decor reflects the Old West, with fine western art displayed on the walls. A warm ambience is effected by a gold, rust, and brown color scheme; soft lighting emanates from steer-horn chandeliers, and western artifacts—guns, saddles, etc.—are on display.

It's a Beef Barron tradition to begin your dinner with the house specialty—black-bean soup with sherry. A full dinner— priced at $46 for two—includes soup, salad, sirloin steak carved tableside, corn on the cob, baked potato, a fresh vegetable, a decanter of house wine, and a selection from the pastry cart. À la carte you might consider half a barbecued chicken on the spit, prime rib au jus with creamy horseradish, or the steak-and-lobster combination. All cost $13 to $27.50, and are served with salad, fresh vegetables, and home-baked ranch rye bread.

The Beef Barron is open nightly from 5 to 11:30 p.m.

Just outside the Beef Barron is the hotel's **Promenade Bar,** a piano bar where you can sit, relax, and listen to some delightfully gentle music.

A red rickshaw sits outside the **Peking Market,** the interior of which is designed to suggest an open marketplace in a bustling Chinese city. Merchandise—foodstuffs, kites, tea, dishes, fans, etc.—is displayed in cases lining the walls. An open wood-burning brick oven adds a cozy note, overhead are bamboo and rattan fans, and Chinese music is played in the background.

A full dinner for two, priced at $15 per person, includes eggrolls, barbecued pork, fried wonton, egg flower soup, tender sautéed beef with green pepper, sweet-and-sour pork, fried rice with shrimp and pork, cashew chicken, fortune or almond cookies, ice cream, and tea. À la carte entrees cost $9 to $16. You might order crisp chicken with lemon sauce, boned duckling with toasted almonds served with sweet-and-sour sauce, or prawns and sautéed fresh tomatoes.

The Peking Market is open nightly from 5:30 to 11:30 p.m.

Adjoining the restaurant is **The Spirits of Dr. Wu,** an exotic Oriental bar furnished with peacock chairs. A photomural of a real Chinese market adorns one wall. Dr. Wu specializes in potent drinks like the Mongolian Kick, a blend of coconut cream, pineapple juice, light rum, vodka, and cream.

Then there's **Lindy's,** patterned after the New York deli and featuring the cheesecake that made it famous. Its marble tables, bentwood chairs, white tile floors, ceiling fans, and canopy awnings evoke a turn-of-the-century marketplace.

Its menu offers breakfast, lunch, and dinner, all in the $5 to $12 range. Waffles with whipped butter and maple-flavored syrup or two eggs with hash browns, juice, toast, and a beverage are offered for breakfast lovers. Sandwiches run the gamut from braunschweiger liverwurst to kosher-style salami to smoked beef tongue. Those with bigger appetites might enjoy the broiled New York minute steak. The deli platters provide some great alternatives like smoked salmon with Bermuda onion, sliced tomatoes, a bagel, and cream cheese. Burgers come smothered with onions and other goodies. There are also entrees of filet of sole, grilled beef liver with onions, and barbecued meaty beef rib bones. The fountain offers only superlatives, from "mammouth malts" to "gigantic banana splits." There are also beer and wine. Lindy's offers the classic New York deli beverage—Dr. Brown's soda, in several flavors, including black cherry.

Lindy's is open 24 hours a day.

The newest restaurant is the **Flamingo Room.** It's a pleasant place to relax over breakfast, lunch, or dinner. The room is done in pastels, light woods, with soft recessed lighting and a large expanse of windows overlooking the pool. The salad bar for lunch has an appetizing array (one of the largest in town) of beautifully fresh choices, including large shrimp. Dinner entrees offer a good selection of fresh fish, steaks, and rack of lamb for $15 to $26, though an average is about $18. Among the specialties of the house are a delicious mixed grill and the Flamingo barbecue.

The Flamingo Room is open daily from 7 a.m. to 11 a.m. for breakfast, 11:30 a.m. to 2 p.m. for lunch, and 5 to 11 p.m. for dinner.

Finally, there's the **Crown Room Buffet,** a bright area buffet dining room located next to the Little Venice pool terrace. The Crown Room features a breakfast buffet at $5 from 7 to 11:30 a.m., and a dinner buffet at $6.50 from 4:30 to 9:30 p.m.

THE TROPICANA RAMADA RESORT & CASINO:
3801 Las Vegas Blvd. South, Las Vegas, NV 89109 (tel. 702/739-2222, or toll free 800/634-4000, 24 hours).
A new era of luxury has begun at the Tropicana. When this resort hotel opened in 1957, it was one of the most lavish in the state and was known as "the Tiffany of the Strip." Two years later it added more rooms, and brought in the *Folies Bergère* direct from Paris (it's still running). By 1961 the hotel had added an 18-hole golf course and a country club.

In 1979 Ramada Inns, Inc., acquired the property, marking that company's first venture into the luxury hotel field as well as its first gaming hotel. They set out to renew the image of the Tropicana. The first major change was the addition of a 22-story tower to increase the room count to 1,150. The casino was doubled in size and redecorated in a grand and very plush European style.

A second reconstruction began in 1984. By 1986 the Tropicana had completed a $70-million expansion to give the resort hotel a totally new image and to expand its casino. Another 22-story tower was added with 806 guest rooms, increasing the total number to 1,913. Four of the six elevators in the new Island Tower are glass-enclosed and run up the face of the building.

The focal point of the expansion is a spectacular five-acre water park and "island" within the resort hotel grounds. For all those who enjoy swimming, the Tropicana now has the largest indoor/outdoor swimming pool in the world, plus a water slide and three Jacuzzis. One end of the pool can be heated during winter months and (can you believe it?) has swim-up blackjack tables! Where you might choose to keep your money is something else again, but suffice it to say that the hotel has a money-drier should the bills get soaked. If you just want to watch, there are lagoons with penguins, swans, Koi fish in an array of colors, and flamingos. The "island" also features variety acts during the day.

With expansion of the casino, a good deal of redesign has taken place. The Baccarat Room is now a thing of beauty to behold—

remodeled with mirrors, wall sconces, and crystal chandeliers befitting the game's historically elegant image.

Rooms in the new Island Tower are light, airy, and spacious. Furnishings are bamboo trim, and the drapes, bedspreads, and carpeting are in pastel hues that carry through the tropical feeling. As with the other tower and lanai rooms in the wings, all offer every modern amenity.

One of the most talked-about features of the Tropicana is its tennis layout. For 24-hour play, the Tropicana Racquet Club has four outdoor tennis courts. They're beautiful to look at, and if you're a watcher, you can observe from the cozy, plush, and paneled Paradise Cove lounge on a mezzanine balcony overlooking the courts. No greater comfort has ever been installed for kibitzers.

Room rates are $70 to $110, single or double; suites are priced at either $260 or $525.

Restaurants

Seven restaurants offer sumptuous repasts.

The Tropicana's requisite 24-hour eatery is the **Java Java Coffee Room,** decorated in a cheerful, predominantly green-and-yellow tropical color scheme. In addition to a full range of breakfast items served at any hour, there's a menu of salads, soups, etc. You can order anything from a kosher frank with chili or sauerkraut to a full meal of fried chicken with soup or salad, vegetable, potato, and rolls and butter—all for $6 to $12.

El Gaucho is a steak-lover's delight. It's done in an Argentinian motif—beamed ceilings, hides on the walls, bits, branding irons, halters, cinches, stirrups, woven shawls. Beef is the specialty of the house: steaks, ribs, and combination plates. Entrees range from $15 to $27.50; the top end of the range is a steak-and-seafood platter. El Gaucho has a select list of imported and domestic wines.

El Gaucho is open only for dinner, from 6 to 11 p.m.

The **Rhapsody** offers an excellent selection of entrees for all tastes. Whether you're moved toward Long Island duckling, veal piccata, filet mignon, rack of spring lamb, scampi, rainbow trout, Columbia River salmon, cioppino (San Francisco), or broiled Australian lobster tails, the Rhapsody will delight your appetite. And the desserts are not to be ignored: there's peach Melba, baked Alaska, French pastries, chocolate mousse—many of those wonderful things you never seem to have enough room for.

Most entrees cost $16.50 to $27.50 per person, but some of the dishes are priced for two—for example, the Châteaubriand for

$39.50. The menu is à la carte. The Rhapsody is open Tuesday through Saturday from 6 to 10:30 p.m.

The Tropics is just that—a Polynesian aura with beaded curtains, colorful banners, tiki figures, lighting glowing from large shells, and its own waterfall running through the center of the restaurant. The view to the outside is lovely. The restaurant has three tiers, glassed in, which overlook the "island" and all the activities and shows. The Tropics serves breakfast, lunch, and dinner from 7 a.m. to 10 p.m. Polynesian delights are the specialty of the house. Breakfast will cost $5 to $7.50; lunch, $7 to $13; and dinner, $12 to $19. The Tropics is closed Wednesday and Thursday.

An additional dining option is the **Island Buffet,** a decadent display of irresistible delights laid out in a dramatic setting, the old multitiered pink-and-blue Tiffany Theatre. Buffet breakfasts, served from 7 to 11 a.m., cost $4; lunches, served from 11:30 a.m. to 4 p.m., cost $5; and dinners, served from 4 to 10 p.m., cost $6.

Rounding out the dining choices at the Tropicana are the Japanese **Mizuno's Teppan Dining** and **Antonio's Pizzeria** (for pasta, pizza, salads, and Italian sandwiches).

THE RIVIERA HOTEL: 2901 Las Vegas Blvd. South, Las Vegas, NV 89109 (tel. 702/734-5110, or toll free 800/634-6753).

Labeled one of the most refined hotels along the posh central Strip, the Riviera is in a class almost by itself. The front building is T-shaped, of 9 to 18 stories, wrapped partially around an Olympic-size swimming pool and gardens. Other rooms are located in the lanai wing. Everything runs smoothly here, and that's what the hotel is known for.

Liberace, candelabra and all, was on hand for the gala opening of the Riviera on April 18, 1955.

You enter the lobby without having to weave your way through a maze of slot machines and casino crushes. (Games are discreetly off to one side.) An arcade of boutiques lines the hotel's promenade.

The addition of the Lanai Tower brought the Riviera's room capacity to 1,250. A third tower, under construction, will raise the room count to 3,975. Completion is scheduled for the end of 1989, at which time there will also be a total of nine showrooms.

The Lanai Tower is tastefully furnished, with bedroom and bath separated by a walk-through closet. Rooms cost $55 to $94 a night for double or single occupancy; suites run $120 to $575. All rooms have double or king-size beds.

And for an indefinite period, the Riviera offers its "Gambler's

Spree," with fantastic comps that include special room rates, show tickets, meals at the gourmet buffet, and cash rebates for qualified $5 bettors who certify that they have completed eight hours of gambling during their stay at the Riviera. When you call for information, ask for details about the "Gambler's Spree;" reservations are on a space-available basis.

The area surrounding the Riviera's pool is spacious, with manicured lawns, piped-in music, a sundeck, and a snackbar. Facilities also include ten championship tennis courts (free to guests), and babysitting services are available.

Although the casino at the Riviera is big and grand, it has an intimate quality that makes it one of the most popular along the Strip. Headliners perform in the Versailles Room.

The Riviera completed another expansion in July 1984. It offers hotel guests and visitors a new casino arcade, complete with a Burger King restaurant and a "Walk of Fame," styled after Mann's Chinese Theatre in Hollywood, featuring the hand- and footprints of celebrities. Already "immortalized" in the concrete are Mel Tillis, the Smothers Brothers, Rich Little, and Ginger Rogers.

Among the hotel's guest amenities is Le Bistro Bar, a lounge with continuous entertainment from afternoon to the wee morning hours. And the Riviera features annual events like gaming competitions, and even the "Armadillo Alympics" for enthusiasts of a different sort.

Restaurants

Among the posh Riviera dining facilities is the very romantic **Ristorante Italiano,** where a talented chef carefully supervises the preparation of delectable pastas, veal dishes, and seafood. Kenny Rogers, Steve Martin, Steve Lawrence and Eydie Gorme, Paul Anka, and Barry Manilow are among the stars who have turned out to sample linguine under the stars. For the ceiling here is atwinkle with stars, and the decor evokes Venice, with windows looking out on murals of St. Mark's Square, the Rialto, the Bridge of Sighs, and the canals. The Italiano is, in fact, a recreation of an actual open-air rooftop restaurant in Venice that overlooks those sights. Exposed brick walls are hung with copies of famous paintings, and furnishings are bright red; candlelight and Italian music complete the ambience.

A meal at the Italiano might get off to a hearty start with a soup of macaroni and beans, although the baked clams casino seems a more apt choice. Among the entrees, priced from $16 to $32, there's a choice of about ten veal preparations ranging from saltimbocca (sautéed slices of veal with prosciutto and mozzarella) to osso buco (veal shank sautéed in olive oil with tomatoes, onions, celery, green peppers, and Italian herbs). Other options include broiled steak with fresh mushrooms, chicken parmigiana, and a platter of shrimp, scallops, and clams cooked in a light sauce with wine, butter, mushrooms, green peppers, and onions. All entrees are served with spaghetti, except for pasta dishes like linguine with red or white clam sauce and lasagne. Desserts range from light fare like Italian ices or melon to such caloric delights as cannoli and Italian rum sponge cake.

Ristorante Italiano is open nightly from 6 p.m. to 11 p.m.

Recalling the charm of its namesake once in the Wall Street district of New York, the newly reopened and redecorated **Delmonico** offers a refined atmosphere in which the components are rich pearl-gray walls adorned with framed prints and paintings; tables set with exquisite china, gleaming silver, and sparkling crystal; soft lighting from magnificent cut-crystal chandeliers overhead; and dark wood chairs with gray cushioning.

Open your handsome leather-bound menu and you'll find an original continental listing. There's a large choice of hot and cold appetizers from escargots in mushrooms with a red wine, garlic sauce to fresh pâtés created daily; or you might begin with a Caesar salad or a fresh spinach salad with bacon dressing. For the main course, priced at $17 to $35, some interesting options are roast boneless breast of chicken in champagne cream sauce with pink peppercorns, and sautéed medallions of veal with fresh melon and port wine. A distinguished wine list is available. Leave room for a selection from the gleaming cart of pastries.

Delmonico is open nightly from 6 p.m. to 11 p.m.

The **Rik'Shaw,** the Riviera's new Chinese restaurant—all done in bamboo and Chinese red, with temple paintings, dragons, and rickshaws—is a pleasant, warm place for reasonably priced dining.

Entrees cover the range of beef, pork, seafood, and poultry favorites such as roast pork with bok choy, lobster Cantonese, and sweet and sour chicken. Chef's specialties include lemon chicken (delicious) and pineapple duck, among others. Prices range from $8.95 to $13.95. Combination dinners, which include appetizer, soup, and entree, cost $11.95 to $14.95. One very pleasant note: I found the service at Rik'Shaw to be superior to that of many other restaurants where entrees were twice the price. Open nightly from 5 to 11 p.m.

Kady's Brasserie is the Riviera's 24-hour poolside

coffeeshop. Its offerings range in price from $6.50 to $22.50, and include everything from deli fare such as corned beef with potato salad to a full meal of double-rib lamb chops with french fries, not to mention salads, sandwiches, eggs and omelets, etc.

Don't mention it to a soul, but for the best snack bargain in town, go to the Riviera's **Mardi Gras Plaza** snackbar (near the Burger King)—they've got a super-delicious seafood cocktail for 99¢. The place is hard to find, but it's worth the effort.

ALADDIN HOTEL & CASINO: 3667 Las Vegas Blvd. South, Las Vegas, NV 89109 (tel. 702/736-0111, or toll free 800/634-3424).

The Japanese seem convinced of Las Vegas's success in the high-stakes contest for top billing as the gambling, entertainment, and convention center of the country. After all, Las Vegas is just a short jump from the La Costa Resort in Carlsbad—purchased by the Japanese in 1987 for $250 million. And La Costa—or any one of several Japanese-owned hotels in San Francisco—is little more than a five-hour hop from Japanese holdings in Hawaii.

In January 1986, Ginji Yasuda, a Korean-born resident of Japan, bought the Aladdin Hotel & Casino (then in bankruptcy) for over $54 million. Mr. Yasuda became the first non-U.S. citizen to own a casino on the Strip, and the first to be licensed to operate a casino in the U.S.

The Aladdin has 1,100 modern, spacious rooms, totally redecorated and refurnished. Furnishings are beige and gold and convey a luxury theme whether you choose to stay in one of the remodeled rooms or in a newly created duplex suite. Room rates are $70 to $100 per night, single or double occupancy. One- and two-bedroom suites are $400 to $700, and the duplex, super-suite extravaganza is $2,500.

To keep you fit, comfortable, and relaxed, the Aladdin sports a rooftop recreation center with a pool, lighted tennis courts for night play, and a snackbar for the lounge lizards.

The Aladdin has three entertainment venues: the 700-seat Bagdad Showroom, the 100-seat Sinbad Lounge, and topping all the hotels in Las Vegas, the 7,000-seat Aladdin Theatre for the Performing Arts—the largest theater in Las Vegas (apart from that at the University) and undoubtedly the one with the best acoustics. The theater has featured a remarkable range of performers from Rudolf Nureyev to Anita Baker, Fleetwood Mac, Tina Turner, and, in a historic charity reunion, the Doobie Brothers.

And what would a Las Vegas hotel be without its own version

of a perpetual-motion machine—the nonstop, 24-hour casino. Among the usual games, the Aladdin also features a new poker room and a high-limit race and sports book.

Restaurants

The Aladdin has three excellent restaurants, a deli, and the usual 24-hour coffeeshop so necessary to survival in Las Vegas. Most prestigious of the eateries is **The Florentine,** which offers French, Italian, and continental cuisine prepared tableside. This elegant restaurant, as its name suggests, is graced with Florentine frosted-glass panels, as well as floral murals and crystal chandeliers. House specialties are veal marsala and sumptuous braised sweetbreads. Entrees on the à la carte menu are priced from $22 to $48. Wines from cellars all over the world are available here. Open Wednesday through Sunday from 6 to 12 p.m.; reservations are suggested.

Another handsomely designed restaurant is **Wellington's,** an American version of an English pub—very masculine, with dark woods, brick floors, wrought-iron chandeliers, hunting prints, and, in the center of it all, a brass rotisserie. This beef house features certified black Angus aged beef, as well as first-rate steaks and barbecued selections. Wellington's prepares excellent salads tableside and offers an extensive wine list. Entrees range from $18 to $25. Open Friday through Tuesday from 6 to 12 p.m.; reservations suggested.

Fisherman's Port has been a hit with diners from the day it opened. The restaurant features fresh seafood flown in from the East Coast. Despite the Cajun character of much of its cuisine, Fisherman's Port looks more New England than New Orleans, with its board floors, stanchions, captain's chairs, netting, and seascapes. The menu features soups, bisques, and bouillabaisse, and entrees range from orange roughy to Alaskan king crab, crawfish étouffé, and blackened red fish, all accompanied by hush puppies and black-eyed peas; the popular Cajun dishes are served spicy or mild, to suit your taste. Entree prices range from $15 to $23. There is a special wine list to complement the unique cuisine. The Fisherman's Port is open Wednesday through Sunday from 6 to 12 p.m.

The Delicatessen looks like an oldtime deli—dark wood chairs with red cushions, red-and-black carpeting, and a counter that looks like an old-fashioned bar. You can watch the specialties of the house being prepared in an open kitchen—everything from scrambled eggs with lox and onions to cheese blintzes with sour cream or blueberries. Combination sandwiches, in an incredible variety, are served on three slices of thin corn rye and accompanied by potato salad, relish bowl, and garnish. For dinner, you can order the likes of boiled chicken in the pot, pot roast, or linguine and clams or shrimp. Should you feel you have room for dessert, everything from cheesecake (five varieties) to a banana split can be enjoyed while watching the keno board. Prices for luncheon or dinner range from $4 to $10, for breakfast from $2 to $5. The Delicatessen is open daily from 10 a.m. to midnight.

And **The Oasis,** the Aladdin's 24-hour coffeeshop, is ready whenever you are with sandwiches, salads, main dishes, desserts, and fountain selections. Prices go up to $10.

THE DUNES HOTEL AND COUNTRY CLUB: 3650 Las Vegas Blvd. South, Las Vegas, NV 89109 (tel. 702/737-4110, or toll free 800/634-6971).

Opened in 1955 as a modest 194-room hotel, the Dunes today consists of a 24-story high-rise tower (actually 21 stories—there are no floors numbered 11, 12, or 13), the connecting Sea Horse and Olympic Wings, and a newer 17-story, 400-room tower. Part of a $75-million expansion program, the tower wing brought the Dunes' room count to 1,285. The newest addition is a shiny black-glass building called the Oasis. A striking sidewalk of colored mosaic tile leads you to it.

The Dunes is one of the many Las Vegas hotels recently acquired by Japanese investors. It was purchased in August 1987 for the tidy sum of $157.7 million, and it has been announced that the owners intend to spend $300 million more to double the hotel's capacity.

When it comes to facilities, the Dunes has always been well equipped. It has two immense swimming pools (both Olympic-size), an 18-hole golf course (greens fee is $30) and a country club, a large and opulent casino doubled in size, a complete health club for men and women, and shops proffering everything from toys for children to fine furs.

As for the rooms, they're luxurious to a fault. Spacious and attractively color coordinated, they're furnished with king-size, twin, or double-double beds. Running ice water on tap and a makeup area with theatrical lighting are just a few of the extras, and, of course, all the modern amenities are as you'd expect. Rates are $60 to $90 per night, single or double occupancy. Suites, at $140 to $1,800, are particularly sumptuous.

The Dunes also has a year-round "Drive-In" package for three days/two nights. Weekdays the total package price is $110, double or single occupancy; weekends the cost is $140. The package includes accommodations, one buffet breakfast, the Oasis Lounge show with two drinks, the main show (Comedy Store) with two drinks, a free keno ticket, a $100-value fun book, and all taxes and gratuities.

Restaurants

There are four restaurants at the Dunes. Most prestigious is the **Sultan's Table,** serving gourmet continental cuisine. A year after it opened it was awarded the title of "America's finest and most beautiful new restaurant" by Diners Club. Now, some two decades later, it is still winning laurels, with its Kismet pleasure-palace theme. This exotic eatery has a tented entrance, an interior done in royal purple, plum, and rich blues, beveled bronze mirrors, dripping crystal chandeliers galore, and stained-glass windows from Germany designed after an illustration from an antique book of the original *Kismet.* The windows are flanked by 300 yards of hand-loomed draperies. Colored lights play on a waterfall, and a cocktail lounge off the entrance is adorned with imported marble tables and jewel-toned banquettes.

You can begin your haute-cuisine feast with such classy hors d'oeuvres as foie gras with truffles, escargots de Bourgogne, or Scottish smoked salmon. Among the entrees, priced at $20 to $27.50 (or for some, $50 for two), are breast of capon Kiev with wild rice, frogs' legs provençal, tournedos sauce périgourdine, and Châteaubriand with vegetables in sauce béarnaise. Vegetables—such as broccoli hollandaise or hearts of palm amandine—are à la carte, and desserts range from simple sherbets to sumptuous choices like baked Alaska flambé and strawberries Romanoff. The wine list offers an excellent selection of imported and domestic vintages, reasonably priced.

The Sultan's Table is open nightly from 6 to 11 p.m. Jackets are required for men.

Another spectacularly designed restaurant is the **Dome of the Sea,** where you dine in a large seashell-shaped affair while a steady movement of flying fish is projected slowly around the walls. Varicolored lights pour through a domed ceiling, the tablecloths are blue and green, and a mermaid in a gondola even plays the harp. You'll feel as if you're dining in a magical undersea kingdom.

Hot and cold seafood appetizers include chilled melon with prosciutto, imported smoked Scottish salmon, and scampi sauté

Dijonese. There's a wide choice of entrees: seafood nouvelle cuisine with sautéed crabmeat, lobster, and shrimp; Maine lobster thermidor; a traditional bouillabaisse; and imported Dover sole, sautéed in lemon butter or lemon and capers. Non–seafood fanciers can get a New York–cut steak or filet mignon. All entrees are served with a vegetable and potato du jour, and range in price from $25 to $35. Desserts once again feature flambé specialties like cherries jubilee, although you can also select a French pastry.

The Dome of the Sea is open nightly from 6 to midnight. Jackets are required for men.

The newest Dunes eatery is the **Chinese Kitchen,** located in the Savoy, which offers typical Chinese fare such as chow mein, sweet-and-sour shrimp, and pork or beef with mixed Chinese vegetables for $5 to $15. It's open nightly for dinner from 6 p.m. to midnight.

The **Savoy** is the Dunes' 24-hour coffeeshop. It offers the usual kind of menu for the genre: salads, sandwiches, and burgers for $6 to $12, and hot entrees for $12 to $19.

THE SANDS HOTEL & CASINO: 3355 Las Vegas Blvd. South, Las Vegas, NV 89109 (tel. 702/733-5000, or toll free 800/634-6901).

Located in the center of the Strip, the Sands is a modern, 18-story circular skyscraper with half-moon balconies winging out around the upper floors. Not obvious is a collection of smaller units named after famous racetracks—the Del Mar, Triple Crown, Hollywood Park, and Aqueduct, for instance—which are grouped over a manicured expanse of palmed gardens and a putting green. There are two very large swimming pools and six tennis courts, all of them lit for night play.

Rates for single or double occupancy run from $65 to $95 ($15 for a third person in a room), with the higher prices charged for poolside and tower rooms. (Except in the high tower and the Aqueduct building, second-floor rooms in the other units are walk-ups.) There are 730 rooms in the entire complex, including 50 luxurious suites that begin at $180 a night, single or double occupancy, for a parlor/bedroom combination. A one-bedroom suite with parlor is $225 to $325; a two-bedroom, $300 to $650.

Rooms at the Sands are proportioned for spacious appeal and decorated in understated color blends, with easy chairs, sit-down tables, wall-to-wall carpeting. Closets are wide, and the baths have tub/showers with glass doors. Some rooms have small private patios and Jaccuzis.

Although a pleasant walk through the gardens to outlying

buildings will take only a moment or two, a bell car will take you if you wish.

In addition to its plush casino, the Sands has wining and dining rooms aplenty. And the multiple services of a resort are available: barbershop, beauty salon, gift shop, boutiques, massage rooms, saunas, health club (for men and women), round-the-clock room service, and car-rental desk. Tennis pros are available for lessons to the public on the courts, and equipment may either be rented or purchased in the fully stocked pro shop.

The Sands offers a three-day/two-night "Sands Select Package." Priced at $80 per night per person, double occupancy, it includes accommodations, breakfast in the Garden Terrace, tips, taxes, and bellman's gratuities. Another package is the "Sands Select Gambling Package" for $100 per person per night, double occupancy, which features the above plus $50 in nonnegotiable gaming chips.

Restaurants

The Sands boasts a major gourmet restaurant, the **Regency Room.** Exquisite carved-wood paneling throughout is interspersed with tapestries and built-in cabinets filled with objets d'art. Seating is in comfortable armchairs and large black tufted-leather booths; tables are handsomely clothed in beige and brown and set with the Regency's own china. The decor is further enhanced by copies of Greek classical sculpture and opulent crystal chandeliers overhead.

The menu lists à la carte French/continental gourmet specialties, beginning with hors d'oeuvres like crêpes Mornay and a terrine of pâté de foie gras. For an entree you might select roast prime rib of beef au jus with Yorkshire pudding, stone crab with mustard and butter sauce, or roast duckling with peach. Entrees are $19 to $45. Other menu choices include salad, potato, fresh fruits and petit fours, and tea or coffee. Flaming desserts like baked Alaska and cherries jubilee are a specialty, although you could opt for cheese or mousse au chocolat.

The Regency Room is open nightly from 6 to 11 p.m.

The **Garden Terrace** offers 24-hour dining—you guessed it —on the terrace, with a wide range of breakfast, lunch, and dinner choices.

Breakfast, served around the clock, offers a variety of omelets, scrambled eggs with nova and onions, eggs "your way," blintzes, griddle cakes, danish, and the usual assortment of beverages, juices, and fruit. For midday hunger pangs there is a good selection of sandwiches, including "create your own" hamburgers and a few good waist-watchers such as lemon baked chicken and a delicious vegetable plate. Dinner entrees range from tenderloin of pork or prime rib to stuffed red snapper. For the incurable steak-lover, the Garden Terrace has sirloin or filet mignon.

In addition to all of the above, the Garden Terrace has a Chinese menu during dinner hours. The Chinese Kitchen lists everything you expect, and a lot you do not, from shredded pork in brown sauce (the most famous Peking-style dish) to Peking duck (on 24-hour advance notice).

The Occidental menu ranges from $6 to $19. The Chinese Kitchen entrees are $11 to $27.50, the average being about $14; top of the line is the Peking duck.

The Garden Terrace is open daily and serves breakfast around the clock, lunch from 11 a.m. to 3 p.m., and dinner from 5 to 11 p.m. The Chinese Kitchen serves from 5 p.m. to 2 a.m.

What would a Las Vegas hotel be without a restaurant serving Italian specialties? The **Mediterranean** offers an enticing selection of antipasti, hot and cold, from the shrimp sautéed in garlic with cream and basil sauce, to the antipasto Freddi with marinated vegetables, calamari salad, roasted peppers, and mushrooms. Entrees include chicken breast prepared several ways, any one of which is bound to please you—chicken Angelo is simmered with artichoke hearts, mushrooms, and grapes in a white wine sauce; Romano is sautéed and finished with a cream sauce and strips of red and green peppers; and Sicilian is sautéed with zucchini, summer squash, and eggplant, touched with a hint of garlic and flamed with white wine. The Mediterranean also prepares delectable standards such as veal marsala and veal milanese. Seafood focuses on shrimp or scampi prepared fra diavolo or on pescattore with garlic, basil, and white wine.

The à la carte dinner entrees are $9.50 to $14. The Mediterranean is open daily from 5 p.m. to 1 a.m.

FRONTIER HOTEL: 3120 Las Vegas Blvd. South, Las Vegas, NV 89109 (tel. 702/734-0110, or toll free 800/634-6966).

Opened in July 1967, the Frontier contains 600 rooms in a ring-shaped, seven-story building and one three-story lanai wing. It is horseshoed around beautiful garden acres of manicured grass and towering palms, an Olympic-size swimming pool, fountains, and little rustic bridges over reflecting pools. In the very heartland of the Strip, it's one of the most attractive and successful of the properties operated by the Summa Corporation, the company once run by Howard Hughes.

You can't miss the Frontier. Its huge sign out near the street fairly blasts out its name in electric lights. A couple of hundred feet high, it is reputed to have cost more than a million dollars.

Two tennis courts at the Frontier are busy day and night (both are lit for night play); they're for hotel guests only. Guests at the Frontier may play golf at the Desert Inn. And rounding out the facilities are convention space, a putting green, a fine casino, car-rental desk, babysitting service, three restaurants, three cocktail lounges, a first-rate showroom, and 8,000 square feet of shops.

Rooms are all stunningly decorated in bright mauves, teals, and blues; all have color-coordinated cultured-marble bathrooms, color TVs with free-ESPN sports and a closed-circuit gaming-instruction station, and direct-dial phones with message lights. They're priced at $60 to $110, single or double, depending on view and location; poolside rooms are more expensive. One-bedroom suites cost from $210; two-bedroom suites, from $300.

Restaurants

The **Branding Iron Steak House** captures the romance of a stately ranch-house dining room where hearty, well-prepared meals are the rule. Specialties here include steaks of every description, Florida stone crab on ice, and seafood cooked over mesquite. Entrees range in price from $14 to $29.50.

The Branding Iron is open for dinner nightly from 5 to 11 p.m., closed Wednesday and Thursday.

At **Diamond Jim's** you'll find a down-home mix of Gay Nineties and Southern atmosphere. In contrast to the ambience, the menu is decidedly upscale. Appetizers include oysters Rockefeller, clams casino, and snails Escoffier. For a simpler approach, there are Blue Point oysters or cherrystone clams on the halfshell. The Florida stone crab featured in the Branding Iron restaurant is also on the appetizer list here.

Diamond Jim's list of specialties has something for everyone —roast prime rib served with Yorkshire pudding, Long Island duckling à l'orange roasted and basted in Grand Marnier, or, for seafood-lovers, bouillabaisse with garlic bread, a whole Dover sole, or shrimp "inferno"—spicy hot jumbo shrimp said to have been created for Diamond Jim himself. All veal dishes, from veal Oscar to veal française, are served with linguine tossed in oil and butter, or with fettuccini Alfredo.

Entrees are $19 to $26 à la carte. A daily "special" full-course dinner is always available; the price varies with the entree.

Diamond Jim's tempting dessert list includes your turn-of-the-century peach Melba and, if you're going all out, an impressive list of flambé specialties for two, including baked Alaska flambéed at your table, cherries jubilee, and crêpes Suzette.

Diamond Jim's is open Wednesday through Sunday from 6 p.m. to midnight.

The requisite 24-hour coffeeshop is called the **Longhorn Café.** In addition to the usual Vegas coffeeshop fare, it dishes up southern fried chicken with hot biscuits, honey, and corn fritters, and jumbo fried shrimp with red sauce and french fries. And it may be the only place on the Strip where you can get grits. Two of the most popular items are a prime rib dinner for $6.95 and a barbe-cued ribs special for $5.95.

HOLIDAY INN HOTEL AND CASINO AT CENTER STRIP: 3473 Las Vegas Blvd. South, Las Vegas, NV 89109 (tel. 702/369-5000, or toll free 800/634-6765).

This is another Las Vegas superlative, the largest Holiday Inn in this country, with 1,000 rooms. Except for the traditional Holi-day Inn sign, the first thing you'll notice is not the size of the prop-erty but the fanciful façade of the casino facing the Strip. It's a reproduction of a sidewheel Mississippi River gambling boat, complete with mannequin passengers and even Tom Sawyer and Huck Finn on a raft.

Inside, the Holiday Theater above the casino offers the long-running show, Rocky Senne's *The Roaring '20s Revue,* Monday through Saturday. The casino interior maintains the riverboat theme with red-flocked wall coverings, pink globe chandeliers, and a general feeling of old New Orleans.

The hotel has been completely remodeled, and the new rooms are beautifully appointed. They're larger than before and have either double-double, queen-size, or king-size beds. All have free Showtime movies on color TVs, AM/FM clock radios, direct-dial phones, custom soaps in the baths and tub/shower combinations with showerhead massage. The rooms are furnished in soft hues, with dramatic wall graphics of abstract designs taking the place of the more usual painting over the bed. Singles and dou-bles run $55 to $85; an extra person is $10. In addition to the reg-ular rooms, there are petite suites for $110. These are exceptionally spacious, and include a living area as well as a bed-room. Some are equipped with wet bars as well as conference ta-bles.

Since this is a family hotel, the casino is actually separated from the lobby, and great care has been taken to ensure that children do not have to venture anywhere near the casino. Even the shopping and game arcade, swimming pool, and health spa are separated from the action. Also of interest to families is the complete laundry facility available for guests.

The lobby area has also been completely redecorated with plants, skylights, and plenty of places to sit and enjoy the passing parade. The casino now features all your favorite slot machines, a keno lounge, Bingo parlor, poker room, and a 24-hour race and sports book. And read on for your options when pangs of hunger strike.

Restaurants

The Holiday Inn Hotel and Casino's gourmet dining facility, **Claudine's Steakhouse,** is a candlelit room that seats only 80 and offers steaks and seafood. Dinner might begin with smoked salmon with horseradish-mustard sauce or fettuccine du chef. Entrees, ranging in price from $15 to $28, include a variety of steaks— T-bone, filet mignon, roast prime rib—and such seafood as lobster tails, salmon steak, shrimp, and scallops. Each entree is served with potato or rice and Claudine's specialty bread. Dessert selections, including pastries and ice cream, change daily.

Claudine's is open nightly from 5:30 to 11 p.m.

The hotel's coffeeshop, the **Veranda,** features sandwiches, full dinners, and breakfast. There's a daily breakfast special for $4.25, and luncheon with soup or salad and sandwich for $5.50. Dinner specials range from $9 to $13. The Veranda is open daily from 7 a.m. to 10:30 p.m.

New Orleans meets Las Vegas in the newest of the Holiday Inn restaurants, **Joe's Bayou.** A great selection of "starters," as well as high-quality gumbos, stews, salads, blackened fare, jambalaya, and bayou specialties, is available. Each of the starters is a meal in itself, but one of the most interesting is the "bayou sampler"— an array of tidbits, including a pork rib, prawn, chicken, frog's leg, and catfish, with Cajun dressing. Or you might order stew (red or white) with scallops, oysters, or clams, or a combination of all three served with plantation greens (otherwise known as salad) and a choice of baked yams, potatoes, rice, okra, or hush puppies.

Considering salad as your main course? Joe's Bayou serves a shrimp, barbecued-chicken, or crab salad in a crisp pastry shell, accompanied by corn bread or baguette.

Blackened fare includes not only the usual red fish but also an interesting choice of scallops, shrimp, or catfish. Bayou specialties range from shrimp and ham jambalaya to fried catfish. If you're not in the mood for a big meal, some great sandwiches, like deep-fried oysters or barbecued chicken breast on toasted French bread, are an option.

If you make it through to dessert, there's southern pecan pie or banana fritters, among other thoroughly fattening choices.

Entree prices are $11 to $18. Joe's Bayou is open daily from 4:30 to 11 p.m.

And there's the **Galley Buffet.** Here you can partake of a 24-hour breakfast buffet for $2.99, a lunch buffet for $3.50 from 11 a.m. to 5 p.m., and a dinner buffet for $4 from 5 to 11 p.m.

GOLDEN NUGGET HOTEL AND CASINO: 129 E. Fremont St. (at the corner of Casino Center Boulevard), Las Vegas, NV 89101 (tel. 702/385-7111, or toll free 800/634-3454).

When you consider accommodations in Las Vegas, among the best and most luxurious are at the all-new Golden Nugget Hotel and Casino. Gone is the fantasy of the Wild West that once characterized the hotel. Today this extraordinary downtown establishment commands top rating among all hotel-casinos. A hint of its interior elegance is presented by a new façade of pure-white Grecian marble, cut, hand-carved, and polished by old-world artisans; by the white canopies, Tivoli lights, and beveled mirrors; and by a white-on-white motif subtly accented with brass. Hundreds of palm trees in planter beds surround the entire property.

As you enter the driveway, you arrive under a gleaming white portico. Oval etched-glass panels flank the doors, which lead directly to the hotel registration and lobby areas. (Happily, you do not have to work your way through a casino to arrive at the front desk.) Inside, the decor is opulent, from the verdi marble-inlaid floors inset with custom-woven wool carpet to the antique furnishings and stained-glass panels.

Oversize guest rooms have been decorated in soothing pastels, soft creams, and desert shades. All rooms are equipped with every modern amenity—direct-dial phones, AM/FM radios, color TVs, tub/shower baths, oversize terry towels, toilette articles, and more. Of course, the hotel affords the services of a concierge, 24-hour room service in addition to that of the coffeeshop, same-day laundry and dry-cleaning service, car-rental desk, valet parking, and other comfortable touches. The Golden Nugget prides itself on attention to detail, whether in the hotel's elegant appointments or in the extra effort extended by the staff to make a guest's stay enjoyable.

Set among beds of flowers and palm trees is an outdoor pool

(open May through October) with a whirlpool spa, a snackbar, and a poolside lounge area. If relaxing in the desert sun is too much of a good thing, there's always the spa—a health emporium geared for body building, exercise, and aerobics. There are separate men's and women's facilities for massages, steam rooms, sauna, and whirlpool spas. A full-service beauty salon provides services for men and women.

The 30,000-square-foot casino is handsomely styled and designed, and well equipped for the total comfort of its customers. There are 42 blackjack tables, 8 craps layouts, 3 roulette wheels, 13 poker tables, a Big Six wheel, 3 baccarat tables, and a luxurious keno lounge. A full assortment of more than 700 video and traditional slot machines, all brass-clad, add the finishing touch to the casino area.

In addition to fine restaurants, the Nugget offers two notably beautiful drinking establishments. The Canopy Bar, just off the casino, features a gleaming brass bar-top and richly colored stained glass depicting 19th-century saloon scenes; and the exquisite Victoria Bar contains overstuffed furnishings, marble-topped tables, a magnificent wood-and-mirrored bar, a 24-carat-gold-plated espresso/cappuccino machine, and a bar rail made of onyx.

Rates for the hotel's rooms are $65 to $95, single or double; suites start at $230 and go up to $800. Children under 12 stay free in a room with their parents; extra adults pay $10 a night.

Restaurants

Top of the line at the Golden Nugget is **Elaine's,** on the second level of the Spa Suite Tower. As you approach the ebony-black entry, you won't expect the classic French decor inside. The dining room is elegant, and the effect is rich. Your eye is caught by a superb Venetian crystal chandelier and the impressionist-style paintings. There's a feeling of privacy you rarely find in a dining room, undoubtedly effected by the curtained booths and well-spaced tables.

The menu is à la carte. Among Elaine's excellent specialties are rack of lamb, chicken with wild mushrooms, bouillabaisse, and a fabulous quail with a mousse of veal. Entrees range from $25 to $35. The wine list is of the same fine quality as the food. Jackets are required for men and reservations are suggested.

Elaine's is open nightly from 6 to 11 p.m.

Stefano's is the northern Italian restaurant in the Golden Nugget. As you enter, the feeling is that you're in an Italian garden. Stefano's has a varied menu with a wide range of choices among some dozen fresh pasta dishes, including an exceptional fettuccine with prosciutto, parmesan, and a silky cream sauce, as well as veal and fresh fish. A perennial search for the perfect veal piccata ended at Stefano's—delicate white veal, exquisitely tender, lightly touched with lemon, and served piping hot. It's the seemingly simple dishes that display the genius of the chef (this one is from Rome). If you've ever wanted to indulge a childlike urge to lick the plate, Stefano's will bring it on. Be sure to order the salad. It's light and so fresh there's sure to be a garden by the kitchen. And it's touched with just the right amount of delicate dressing.

All this beauty and superb food isn't cheap, but it's worth the price. And the service is attentive. The menu is à la carte and dinner entrees range from $17 to $35.

Stefano's is open daily for dinner from 5:30 to 11 p.m. Reservations are suggested.

Reflecting the decor of the hotel, **Lillie Langtry's,** named for the famed British actress who stole the heart of the infamous Judge Roy Bean, is a masterpiece of Victoriana. The walls are richly paneled in oak and mahogany, chairs plushly upholstered in a lovely floral velvet, tables handsomely set with wheat-colored linen. At the entrance is a stained-glass domed skylight, overhead globe chandeliers with dangling crystal; potted palms, brass railings, swagged velvet and lace café curtains, flickering gaslamps, fine murals of the Old West, and pressed-tin ceilings are among the many other elements that help create this gorgeous setting. Like every other part of this fine hotel, it is done in perfect taste.

The dinner menu at Lillie's place is Cantonese. You might begin your meal with an order of golden-fried shrimp or crispy rumaki—broiled chicken liver and water chestnut wrapped in bacon. Suggested entrees: lemon chicken, shrimp Cantonese (jumbo shrimp with minced pork, onion, garlic, bean sauce, and other spices); chicken sautéed with cashew nuts, water chestnuts, bamboo shoots, and peas; and ginger beef cooked in oyster sauce and onion. Entrees, which range from $12 to $20, are served with oolong tea, rice, and fortune cookies. Two American entrees are listed—prime rib with baked potato, salad, and vegetable; and barbecued spareribs with corn on the cob and onion rings. Exotic drinks are also featured at Lillie's: the Rangoon Ruby (vodka and cranberry juice), the Oriental Devil (banana and rum), the Great Wall of China (coconut, rum, and vodka), etc. What I most appreciate, however, is the presence of Western desserts on a Chinese menu. Here, Lillie comes through with class, offering not only fresh-baked cakes but Häagen-Dazs ice cream.

Lillie Langtry's is open nightly from 5 to 11 p.m.

MODERATELY PRICED HOTELS

SAHARA HOTEL AND CASINO: Las Vegas Boulevard South and Sahara Avenue, Las Vegas, NV 89101 (tel. 702/737-2111, or toll free 800/634-6666 or 800/323-3466).

With its 24-story tower, the Sahara is the tallest structure at the north end of the Strip, farthest from the airport. It's dominated by a huge lighted "S," and beneath that flash temperature and time signals. The 222-foot sign, spelling out S-A-H-A-R-A in letters 18 feet high and 10 feet wide, is the tallest free-standing sign in the world. Ten other buildings, including a second tower of 14 stories, tote up to a hotel plant of considerable proportions. The Sahara's come a long way since it opened in 1952 with just 200 rooms.

With a reputed 100% occupancy in its 932 rooms every weekend of the year, it holds its own as one of the most successful hotels in the U.S.

Now under the management and ownership of Sahara Resorts, Inc., the Sahara has undergone extensive renovations.

Rates for rooms are $60 to $110, single or double occupancy; suites are $180 to $550. All rooms have wall-to-wall carpeting, neat and simple modern decor and furnishings, good drawer space, a separate dressing unit with a big, big mirror, and all modern amenities, including clock radios.

Facilities include two pools (one Olympic-size), a showroom, a huge convention hall called the Space Center, shops, and services. A parking lot with space for 2,200 cars is connected to the hotel by an air-conditioned, carpeted walkway. Guests can use the golf facilities at the Sahara Country Club.

Restaurants

For openers, the Sahara offers very reasonable all-you-can-eat buffets in the **Garden Room.** Breakfast ($4) and lunch ($4.75) are served Monday through Friday from 7:30 to 10:30 a.m. and 11 a.m. to 2:30 p.m., respectively; dinner ($5.75) from 4 to 10 p.m. Weekend brunch ($5.95), which includes unlimited champagne, is served from 8 a.m. to 3 p.m. Every night the cuisine of a different country is featured: Monday is continental, Tuesday German, Wednesday Italian, Thursday mixed international, Friday Cape

Cod, Saturday western barbecue, and Sunday Polynesian. In addition to the foreign fare, you can also get conventional buffet items like roast beef on any given night.

The **House of Windsor** is one of the premier gourmet restaurants in Las Vegas. Mostly steak and seafood à la carte specialties are offered here in an intimate English setting—an ambience composed of heavy wood beams, rich wood paneling, stained glass, pewter, and such.

The menu features old favorites as well as new, specially developed dishes. Char-broiled entrees include New York–cut sirloin or filet mignon béarnaise, and brochette of beef tenderloin bordelaise. In addition to steak and seafood there are also selections like breast of capon with wild rice, rack of lamb, and roast prime rib au jus, plus a gourmet's delight consisting of medallions of veal, beef, and lamb. Entrees cost $18 to $35 on the average. All entrees are served with baked potato, salad, fresh fruit, petit fours, and beverage. Flambéed desserts like crêpes Suzette, cherries jubilee, peach flambé, and baked Alaska are available.

The House of Windsor is open six nights a week from 6 p.m. to midnight. Closed Wednesday. Jackets are required for men.

Don the Beachcomber, part of the well-known chain, offers lush bamboo/rattan/palm-frond Polynesian island ambience and exotic South Seas fare. Before you begin to study the menu, order up one of those intoxicating concoctions with names like Cobra's Fang and Shark's Tooth—they help set the proper mood.

Full Polynesian dinners range from $14 to $26, the latter including assorted appetizers (fried shrimp, eggroll, crab puffs, and ribs). Your entree might be boned Mandarin duck with wild plum sauce and ground almonds; lobster in rice wine sauce with spring onions; sliced chicken with vegetables, imported mushrooms, and bamboo shoots—plus fried rice and tea. For the traditional eaters in your party, there are full American dinners available, these priced at $15 to $30 and featuring steak and/or lobster. You can also order à la carte items like lobster Hong Kong—pieces of lobster rolled in egg batter and sautéed with pineapple and green pepper. For dessert try the macadamia-nut ice cream.

Don the Beachcomber is open nightly, except Tuesday, from 5 to 11 p.m.

And, of course, there's a 24-hour coffeeshop, called the **Caravan Room.** In addition to all the usual fare, it offers specials for under $12 from 11 a.m. to 11 p.m., like beef stew with whipped potatoes, vegetable du jour, assorted rolls and butter, and coffee or tea for $7.95.

A full breakfast—anything from pancakes to eggs Benedict

—can be had for $4 to $10. Light fare, such as sandwiches, soups, and salads, costs $4 to $9. And hot entrees, like filet mignon or filet of sole, run $12 to $22.

HACIENDA HOTEL: 3950 Las Vegas Blvd. South, Las Vegas, NV 89119 (tel. 702/739-8911, or toll free 800/634-6713).

The Hacienda Hotel is the southernmost on Las Vegas Boulevard. She and her sister hotel, the Sahara, are getting to be known as "The Strip's Bookends."

The Hacienda has always maintained a reputation as a friendly place, with a downtown Vegas approach to hospitality. It was part of the masterly touch of a couple named Bayley. When Mr. Bayley died in 1964, his wife, Judy, took over and ran the place with a Midas touch until 1972, when she died. These days it's owned and operated by Sahara Resorts, Inc.

Rates are $41 to $81, single or double, for the hotel's 810 rooms, plus $10 extra for each additional occupant. Suites are $135 to $375, accommodating up to four persons. Children under 12 can stay free in a room with their parents.

All rooms are nicely color coordinated with contemporary flair. They aren't the lavish, sometimes excessively decorated accommodations you can find in other hotels, but they're meticulously kept. All have been redecorated in desert/earth tones. Baths are tiled and have glass-doored tub/showers. Furnishings throughout are simply stated pieces, and attractive.

A two-night/three-day package plan, called "Champagne Fiesta," is priced at $54.87 per person, based on double occupancy. It includes a buffet breakfast, a gourmet buffet dinner, a special show with two cocktails, free tennis, two cocktails at the Island Bar, champagne parties, bellman gratuities, and more. Champagne, a traditional extra at the Hacienda, still flows freely. The hotel, it's claimed, serves more champagne than any other place in Las Vegas.

The Hacienda has six tennis courts for day and night play: their use is free to hotel guests.

An interesting innovation at the hotel is the **Hacienda Camperland.** A trailer-camper park covering 27 landscaped acres adjacent to the hotel, it has spaces for 451 recreational vehicles. In addition to complete hookups, it has a country store, snackbar, laundromats, its own swimming pool and recreational hall, kiddie playground, picnic tables, barbecue pits, showers, and 24-hour security. This installation follows the successful pioneering efforts with similar parks at the Stardust and the Circus Circus, proving that there's a big market for such facilities. Camperland rates begin at $12 per vehicle per night, plus $1 per person and per pet.

Restaurants

The Hacienda's gourmet dining room is a steakhouse called the **Charcoal Room.** It's romantically candlelit, seating is in black-leather booths and chairs, and the walls are adorned with smoked mirrors and Spanish-motif oil paintings. It also features an exhibition kitchen.

The Charcoal Room offers fine seafood and steaks broiled over charcoal and mesquite. The menu is simple, including: the queen's and king's cut filet mignon, New York sirloin steak, broiled spring chicken, porterhouse steak, roast prime rib of beef au jus, Australian lobster tail with drawn butter, and sirloin-and-lobster combination. All of the entrees are in the $21 to $35 range, and are served with iced relishes, whipped cottage cheese and cheddar cheese spread, mixed greens and tomato wedges, Lyonnaise potatoes, a tureen of black-bean soup, sorbet with champagne, and freshly baked black-raisin bread topped with whipped butter. For dessert there are petit fours.

The Charcoal Room is open nightly from 6 to 11 p.m.

The **Garden Room Buffet,** a large buffet area overlooking the pool, offers reasonably priced brunch and dinner buffets with 12 hot entrees. Breakfast is $4.99, brunch and dinner $5.99, $6.99 on holidays.

In addition, there is **La Cocina Dining Room,** a 24-hour restaurant that offers a full breakfast and lunch, and features specialties such as chicken Kiev, steak au poivre, and cheese tortellini, as well as a complete Mexican menu. All dinner entrees are in the $8 to $18 price range.

THE BARBARY COAST: 3595 Las Vegas Blvd. South (at the corner of Flamingo Road), Las Vegas, NV 89109 (tel. 702/737-7111, or toll free 800/634-6755).

Evoking the romantic image of turn-of-the-century San Francisco—in the days when Chinatown opium dens, saloons, and gambling parlors flourished—the Barbary Coast is an exciting new addition to this rather sedate Strip corner. Opened in March 1979, it is a Gaughan enterprise (owned by Jackie Gaughan's son, Michael), and the Gaughans are noted for giving a great deal for the money.

Here, they've created 200 beautiful period rooms, all with oversize canopied brass beds, floral-design carpeting, black-and-white-striped wallpaper with matching bedspreads, barn-red ceilings, and crocheted white lace curtains on the windows. A parlor area is separated from the bedroom by gold-fringed scarlet curtains. It all combines to create an authentic Old West feeling. Facilities, however, are strictly up-to-date: tub/shower bath, direct-dial phone with message light, individually controlled heating and air-conditioning, and color TV with in-room movies. There are plans to add four floors to the building with 188 additional rooms.

The plush and lively casino is decorated in the same motif, with dangling crystal-globe chandeliers overhead. It has a big keno lounge which adjoins the entertainment lounge. This is one of my favorite places in town to enjoy the show while playing keno and imbibing drinks on the house. Other casino offerings include 700 slot machines, 28 blackjack tables, 5 craps layouts, minibaccarat, a poker room, and a race and sports book lounge.

There's lots of free indoor parking at the Barbary Coast, all of it convenient to the rooms and casino.

Rates for one or two people are $55 Sunday to Thursday night, $65 on Friday and Saturday night. Children 12 or under can stay free in a room with their parents; extra adults pay $8.

Restaurants

The 24-hour coffeeshop, the **Victorian Room,** has multipaned beveled mirrors lining the walls, giving the room a windowed effect. It serves all the requisite Vegas fare from a bagel with cream cheese and lox to a steak-and-lobster dinner with soup or salad, potato, and rolls and butter. It specializes in Chinese cuisine, from eggroll to Szechuan, served from noon to 5 a.m.

Breakfast and lighter fare here generally run $4 to $9; hot entrees are priced in the $10 to $24 range. Chinese entrees like almond chicken and sweet-and-sour pork are available, in the $6 to $10 range.

The newest addition to the Barbary Coast's dining facilities is the gourmet restaurant, **Michael's.** Located just across the casino from the front desk, it's entered via a frosted- and etched-glass door. Featuring a turn-of-the-century decor, Michael's has been designed for intimate dining; it seats just 70 people. The beautiful white-marble floor and brass accents are a cool contrast to the deep-burgundy walls lined with banquettes and booths. Elegant settings of hand-blown crystal and gold-rimmed white china are enhanced by single roses in silver bud vases on each burgundy- and white-lace-clothed table. Over the center of the room is a large stained-glass dome with 40 small lights adding to its glittery, gem-like effect.

The dinner menu includes a variety of appetizers such as marinated herring in sour cream and seafood cocktails of either Maryland lump crab or shrimp imported from Spain. In addition there are hot appetizers and soups, as well as a selection of salads like hearts of palm vinaigrette, beefsteak tomatoes with anchovies and pimentos, and Caesar salad for two. Entree selections include double-rib spring lamb chops with mint jelly, filet mignon, and Châteaubriand for two—all prepared over charcoal. Other choices: imported Dover sole and veal sautéed in butter and lemon. Entrees at Michael's are priced from $23 to $45. A distinguished wine list and desserts of cherries jubilee, strawberries Romanoff, and pastries round out the meals.

THE LANDMARK: 364 Convention Center Dr., Las Vegas, NV 89109 (tel. 702/733-1110, or toll free 800/634-6777, 800/458-2946 in California).

At 31 stories and 346 feet in height, the Landmark is topped for height by only one other building in the state of Nevada. (The Las Vegas Hilton is reputed to be 365 feet.) Opened in 1969, it was one of the many properties of the late Howard Hughes.

The main thrust of the Landmark is its hexagonal tower, which you can see from practically everywhere in town. It's capped by three glassed-in double floors in a round disk that cantilevers out over the main structure. These upper floors contain cocktail lounges, restaurants, and a place to dance. Topside may be reached by a glass-sided elevator for vertical rides with a view. From a distance the hotel appears similar to the space needles and towers that have been magnets of interest for millions at the Seattle World's Fair, at HemisFair in San Antonio, and at the Olympics in Munich.

Since late 1983 the Landmark has been under new management, and many positive changes have been made. Accommodations in the tower have been completely remodeled; all rooms there are now minisuites, with new decor in soft colors, lounging area, wet bar, and a king-size bed or two double beds. The 350 garden rooms have also been redecorated. In every respect, details of the rooms have been chosen with comfort in mind, but with a pleasant, contemporary simplicity.

During the high season, rates for single or double occupancy are $59 to $67. Suites range from $90 to $180. Rates are lower in summer and during the month of December.

The Landmark's current three-day/two-night package is called "The Landmark Showdown." For $55 per person, double occupancy, you get two buffet breakfasts, a cocktail in the Love

Song lounge, and a casino funbook; bellman's tips and taxes are included.

The award-winning pool at the Landmark is whale-shaped, 240 feet long by 52 feet wide, with a tropical island and sundeck in the center. Bridges connect the island with the pool deck, and a waterfall cascades over black lava rocks at one end. Other facilities include an arcade of shops (including an ice-cream parlor), and service desks, a showroom, and a casino.

Restaurants

Looking out across the pool to the waterfall is the **Cascade Terrace,** a 24-hour coffeeshop. It has an attractive wine, gray, and white decor.

The menu lists the usual breakfast fare (pancakes, omelets, cereal, danish, etc.). At lunch you might order an avocado stuffed with tuna salad with lettuce and a hard-boiled egg, a French dip roast beef sandwich on a roll with french fries, or a Reuben sandwich, all in the $5 to $8 price range. There is also a breakfast buffet for under $4, and a lunch buffet for under $6. Dinner entrees are heartier, ranging from Kentucky honey-fried ham with candied yams and a vegetable to prime rib with a baked potato and vegetable. They range in price from $7 to $12. For dessert, why not a hot fudge sundae or a piece of hot apple pie with cheese? Pastries are all baked fresh on the premises.

Up on the 27th floor is the candlelit **Sunset Room,** where an entire wall of windows provides a magnificent view of glittering Las Vegas at night. The interior, done in gold and turquoise for the most part, has a 1950s feel. Tablecloths and tufted-leather booths are gold, carpeting and lighting fixtures are turquoise, and there's a tile-and-copper bas-relief design on the walls.

The menu is continental, with an emphasis on steak and seafood; entrees range in price from $12 to $24. All entrees include a choice of soup or salad-bar offerings, hot rolls and butter, vegetable, and rice or potato with sour cream and chives. Possibilities include jumbo king crab legs, red snapper in brown butter sauce, prime rib au jus, salmon stuffed with crabmeat, and boneless double breast of chicken in red wine.

HOLIDAY INN: 3745 Las Vegas Blvd. South, Las Vegas, NV 89109 (tel. 702/369-5000, or toll free 800/238-8000).

Located near the Aladdin Hotel, this Holiday Inn is in the quieter southern section of the Strip. It has 203 rooms spread out in two buildings—one of six stories, one of four stories.

The rooms here are spacious (with two double beds or one king-size bed), neat, well arranged, and appointed for comfort. Each has color television, direct-dial phone with message light, and tub-shower bath. Prices are $64 to $89 for a single, $71 to $89 for a double. An extra person in the room is $10. There's no extra charge for kids 18 and under in the same room as their parents.

There's a restaurant on the premises called Pipers that serves breakfast and lunch from 6:30 a.m. to 2 p.m., and dinner from 5 to 10 p.m.

This charming Holiday Inn has no casino, but it's within a short walk of several, and it does have two big pools constantly in use.

STARDUST HOTEL: 3000 Las Vegas Blvd. South, Las Vegas, NV 89109 (tel. 702/732-6111, or toll free 800/634-6757).

Until the International (now the Hilton) was opened, the Stardust was the biggest hotel in Las Vegas, its 1,400 rooms located in six buildings and a tower. It has an Olympic-size swimming pool and four restaurants; it's also the home of the ultra-extravagant *Lido de Paris* spectacular—a not-to-be-missed Vegas production. The 183-foot-high, multiprogrammed sign out front, and the glittering neon tower with a whimsical star (among several different lighting combinations, that illuminate the full length of the hotel's façade), are a longtime Vegas fixture. The location of the Stardust is excellent too, at the most central point on the Strip, for easy access to other areas in all directions.

The big hotel opened in 1958, and has gone through a multi-million-dollar remodeling. Facilities include two-story château suites, with one or two bedrooms and a living room with wet bar. At poolside locations, they have sliding glass doors leading to small terraces. An internal circular staircase leads to the upstairs sleeping quarters, and furnishings are brightly contemporary, colorful, and handsome. They're priced from $140 a night. One-bedroom tower suites or poolside minisuites begin at $140 a night. Regular poolside rooms are $89 to $112 a night, single or double.

The Stardust offers package plans to suit a wide variety of vacation needs; ask the hotel for details.

The Stardust has pioneered another accommodations approach: campsites on the Strip. The setup, called **Camperland,** has 350 spaces on grounds behind the hotel. Camperland has two swimming pools, laundry and shower rooms, a dog run, and a small convenience store. Spaces begin at $10, which includes hookup. Use of Camperland is on a first-come, first-served basis. Camperland is open year round to campers, travel trailers, motor homes, and tent trailers.

The Stardust casino is one of the largest—and busiest—on the Strip. It includes a huge race and sports book lounge. All the other popular games of chance are represented here as well. There is lounge entertainment nightly, except Monday.

Restaurants

There's a **Tony Roma's** restaurant at the Stardust, one of the famous nationwide chain featuring barbecued ribs. It is open nightly from 5 to 11 p.m. Tony Roma's has another Las Vegas location, about which more in Chapter III.

Ralph's Diner is the Stardust's contribution to memories of places where some of us ate in the '50's and early '60's. There are a black-and-white checkerboard tile floor, stainless-steel everything, an old juke box, tiered booths, and a snackbar/soda fountain. About the only items missing are pictures of James Dean, Marilyn, and Elvis.

Can you guess what, besides nostalgia, is served in Ralph's Diner? Hamburgers, fries, steaks, and those fountain drinks that somehow don't taste quite the same now. Meals cost $3.75 to $10.95. The diner is open daily from 6:30 a.m. to 2 a.m.

William B's is a toned-down version of a Texas steakhouse—dark, masculine, and woody. The prime attraction here is steak and more steak, with seafood running a strong second. Steaks range from the usual New York steak, filet, and rib eye to prime rib, all of which are offered at $12.95 to $25.

William B's is open from 5 to 11 p.m. Sunday through Thursday, till midnight Friday and Saturday.

It looks like St. Patrick's Day the year round at the 24-hour **Temporary Coffeeshop,** with green palm-frond carpeting and wallpaper, green chairs and booths. However, the Irish look is purely unintentional, and the menu is typical of the genre, ranging from the special prime rib dinner at $6.95 to hot pastrami sandwiches. Cakes and pies—try the German chocolate cake ($1.75)—are baked on the premises.

Also included in the hotel's dining facilities is the **Buffet Room,** a multimirrored affair with marquee lights and a predominantly red decor. An all-you-can-eat brunch, served from 7 a.m. to 2 p.m. daily, is $4.50; and a roast beef dinner, served from 4 p.m. to midnight, is $6.95. All nonalcoholic beverages are included.

Next to the race and sports book in the Stardust is the **Shortstop Snack Bar,** where you can get a super sandwich from $3.50

to $6, beer or soft drinks, and watch the games, fights, races, or whatever, without interruption.

MAXIM: 160 E. Flamingo Rd., Las Vegas, NV 89109 (tel. 702/731-4300, or toll free 800/634-6987).

A relative newcomer to the part of the Strip known as the "Golden Corner" (locale of Bally's—Las Vegas, Caesars Palace, and other prestigious hostelries), the Maxim opened its doors in July 1977. Though somewhat more modest than its neighbors, it offers all the big-hotel features: a swimming pool and sundeck, a large attractive casino with entertainment lounge, showroom, convention facilities, shops, three restaurants, and two cocktail lounges; tennis and golf can be arranged.

Its 800 rooms are housed in 17-story twin towers. They are attractively modernistic, done in a rust, brown, and blue color scheme. All have one wall covered in silver foil, upholstered chrome furnishings, and bed units that encompass a framed rug with a super-graphic design; all are equipped with every amenity, including a closed-circuit gaming station on your color TV. They're priced at $60 a night, single or double on weekends, $42 on weekdays.

Restaurants

The **Tree House,** off the casino, is the requisite 24-hour eatery. It has smoked-mirror walls and columns, oak butcher-block tables, and cane-backed chrome chairs, as well as lots of hanging plants. The menu gets you through the day, from pancakes or eggs Benedict with Canadian bacon in the $5 to $9 range, to salads and hot or cold sandwiches for $6 to $11, to rainbow trout or a New York steak with all the trimmings for $9 to $17. And there are terrific specials available, like roast chicken for $4.95, fish fillet for $5.95, and prime rib for $6.95.

Maxim's gourmet restaurant, **Da Vinci,** has likenesses of the great man in etched glass at the entrance but is otherwise similar in decor to the rest of the hotel. It has modernistic lighting, rust-and-brown suede-upholstered chairs and booths, and chrome designs on the walls.

The menu is continental, and it starts things off with delicious appetizers such as giant prawns scampi, escargots bourguignonne, and crab legs dipped in cheese batter and sautéed in butter, lemon, and sherry. All are served with garlic bread. The French onion soup au gratin, served in an earthenware tureen, is also a recommendable beginning. However, a plate of fresh vegetables with dip is served gratis to all, so you might even skip over the appetizers. Among the entrees are roast prime rib with creamy horseradish sauce and Yorkshire pudding, chicken in a butter and mushroom sauce, and veal Oscar—with crabmeat and asparagus topped with a mushroom cap and béarnaise sauce. There's a fine variety of wines available to complement your meal. Entrees range in price from $15 to $28. Flambé desserts are featured, and pastries are also available.

The Da Vinci is open nightly from 6 p.m. to midnight.

IMPERIAL PALACE: 3535 Las Vegas Blvd. South, Las Vegas, NV 89109 (tel. 702/731-3311, or toll free 800/634-6441).

A blue pagoda-topped 19-story white stucco structure, the Imperial Palace is an only-in-Vegas, East-meets-West proposition. For instance, only in Vegas could the traditional Japanese sunken tub emerge as a marble Luv Tub with mirrored walls and ceilings. Cocktail waitresses are attired in shortened kimonos, and the Oriental theme is carried out throughout the hotel in many other ways as well. Actually, all this Eastern splendor works quite well in the middle of the Strip opposite Caesars Palace.

The hotel added another tower in 1986, bringing the total number of rooms to 2,100. Accommodations are all equipped with color TVs, direct-dial phones, and air conditioning. The decor features bamboo furnishings, Oriental-motif wallpaper and drapes, and Oriental art prints.

And 100 rooms feature the above-mentioned love tubs; these rooms also have canopied beds on platforms with mirrored ceilings. Should the urge for a wedding come over you, there is always a minister on call.

Rates for the standard tower and East Building rooms are $50 to $105 a night, single or double, $10 for an extra person in the room; the Luv Tub rooms are in the higher range. Suites are $160 to $500.

Facilities include 30,000 square feet of convention space. The 50,000-square-foot casino has blue neon-lit pagoda-topped slot carousels and Oriental-design overhead beams decorated with dragons. And since this is, after all, a desert, there are no fewer than six cocktail lounges, including a bar by the pool. The Sake Bar, Ginza Bar, Geisha Bar, and Mai Tai Lounge are all convenient to the casino. All the bars offer a selection of Polynesian drinks in exotic settings. Dozens of specialty shops can be found on a main-floor arcade. Also on the premises are a large swimming pool and

Jacuzzi, with a rock-walled waterfall and sundeck. The Imperial Theater showroom, which seats 869, features dance extravaganzas as well as headliner entertainment.

The hotel offers two unique attractions in addition to the above: the management found that visitors were often reluctant to approach the tables for fear of being embarrassed by lack of knowledge. So they opened a **school of gaming** on the fourth floor, providing complimentary gaming classes to all Las Vegas visitors, not just hotel guests. The classes are held four times a day and cover the basics of the games found on the casino floor.

The **Imperial Palace Auto Collection** is one of the largest in the country and was voted one of the ten best collections in the world by *Car and Driver* magazine. An elevator off the lobby whisks you up to the fifth floor of the display facility, and years back in time. The cars, valued in the millions, include those owned by Adolf Hitler, Howard Hughes, Mrs. Henry Ford, and the King of Siam. Hitler's 1939 Mercedes Benz is complete with armor plating and a self-destruct mechanism which causes the gas tank to blow up. Howard Hughes's 1954 Chrysler was altered to include a specially engineered $15,000 air-purification system. For car buffs who appreciate rare examples of early models, over 200 antique, classic, and special-interest autos are on display daily from 9:30 a.m. to 11:30 p.m. in a plush, gallery-like setting.

Restaurants

The **Kobe Steak House** is located on the fourth floor above the casino. The Kobe offers a wide range of steak and seafood dinners in the $12 to $35 range. The various appetizers include clams casino, oysters Imperial, and escargots à la Vineberg. For an entree you might choose a top sirloin, steak-and-lobster combination, or Alaskan king crab legs. Impossible-to-resist French and Bavarian pastries are brought to your table for a dessert selection.

The Kobe is open nightly from 5 p.m. to midnight. Reservations are suggested.

The **Fourth Floor Rib Room** serves—you guessed it— barbecued beef and pork ribs, as well as barbecued chicken. These meaty entrees range from $9 to $15. In addition, the Rib Room features specialty side dishes like fried mozzarella and fried potato skins.

The Fourth Floor Rib Room is open nightly from 5 p.m. to midnight.

The **Teahouse** is a 24-hour coffeeshop, with overhanging eaves, Oriental-design chairs, and straw baskets of cloth flowers. The fare is mostly Western, running the gamut from a chef's salad to a hot turkey sandwich. Concessions to the East are teriyaki tidbits—pieces of beef tenderloin sautéed in teriyaki sauce and served in a casserole—and Polynesian chicken. There is also a nightly prime rib special at $8.95. For those who like to indulge in the morning, there's a lavish weekday brunch buffet from 8 a.m. to 3 p.m. for $6.95, and a weekend champagne brunch for $7.50.

The **Ming Terrace** is Oriental not only in name and decor but also in cuisine. Red and gold, the traditional Chinese colors, predominate. There are sprigs of cherry blossom here and there, walls are covered in grasspaper, furnishings are bamboo, and Chinese-design dividers separate the booths. Mongolian beef, lemon chicken, abalone with black mushrooms, and hot bean curd sautéed in spicy meat sauce are among the offerings, which range in price from $9 to $27.

The Ming Terrace is open daily from 11 a.m. to midnight.

The adjoining **Mai Tai Bar** serves exotic drinks in a Polynesian setting.

On the third floor of the hotel's convention center is the **Emperor's Buffet,** where all-you-can-eat spreads are offered from 7 a.m. to 11 p.m. Breakfast and lunch cost $3.50, plus beverage; dinner is $5, plus beverage.

MINT HOTEL AND CASINO: 100 E. Fremont St. (at the corner of First Street), Las Vegas, NV 89101 (tel. 702/387-6468, or toll free 800/622-MINT).

Also in the heart of the downtown area, the Mint's 26 stories dominate the scene with enough flashing lights to illuminate a good-size town. A glass-enclosed elevator zips nonstop up 26 stories on the outside of the hotel and allows a panoramic view of the spectacular desert, the Strip, the mountains, and the closer downtown area. The Sky Deck swimming pool is located on the roof.

The lobby of this 300-room hotel is off First Street. Enter the hotel from Fremont or any other direction and you'll be in the midst of slot machines by the acre, craps and blackjack tables, roulette—the whole gamut of fun and games in one of Nevada's largest, most opulent casinos, complete with a stage for live entertainment. And there's a pinball arcade to keep the kids happy while you gamble.

The Mint is Las Vegas in virtual stereotype. It bulges with capacity bookings on weekends all year long. Rooms are priced from $44 to $68, single or double, and the secret to the lower rates is to request a room on a lower floor. Rooms on the three top floors have balconies. Since all rooms are similar, you miss only the wider view. All rooms have been refurbished, and they're nicely proportioned and coordinated with attractive colors. Some have plush velvet-upholstered headboards. There are color TVs, direct-dial phones, and selected radio channels in every air-conditioned room.

The hotel is famous for its annual Mint 400 Desert Race, in which about 450 worldwide entrants race cars through 400 miles of rough desert terrain. They also sponsor two big trap-shooting tournaments each year.

But these activities notwithstanding, the Mint's excellent facilities and low rates make it one of the better bargains in Vegas.

Restaurants

For openers, take the glass-walled elevator to the **Skye Room,** where you'll find a bar and cocktail lounge for drinks and dancing, and a gourmet restaurant for dining. The Skye Room is well known for deft service, fine food, and a superb overview of the whole city and the surrounding desert and mountains. It's particularly stunning at sunset, when the mountains turn color and the Strip begins to light up. The decor is elegant, with mauve and black drapes and curtains, room-high mirrors, and soft indirect lighting. The lounge has a starlight ceiling at night, and a pianist and singer entertain from 7 p.m. to midnight.

The menu is actually quite simple. You might order an appetizer of shrimp scampi or escargots bourguignonne. Dinners, which range from $17 to $38, include spinach salad or tossed green salad, and baked or steakhouse potatoes. There's a choice of four cuts of steak as well as prime rib, broiled chicken, broiled halibut, shrimp sautéed or broiled with wine and garlic butter, and broiled Australian lobster tails. This is one of those restaurants that offers a few items very well prepared. A small but good wine list is inside the menu, and for dessert, rum cake is the specialty.

The Skye Room is open nightly from 5 to 11 p.m.; closed Monday and Tuesday.

Spaghetti Red's is (you guessed it) Italian all the way, from the extensive list of pasta specialties to the veal and chicken dishes the house features. And it's all served at a reasonable price in a cozy, warm, enthusiastically Italian atmosphere, complete with singing waiters.

Beginning, as you should, with the antipasti, there's fried mozzarella served with spicy tomato sauce, or sautéed shrimp in a tomato, basil, and wine sauce.

There's a lot to choose from in the pasta column—your basic spaghetti entrees (with a variety of sauces), linguine, lasagna, or manicotti, through to an exceptionally good house cannelloni stuffed with a combination of ground veal, spinach, and ricotta, and baked with cheese and tomato sauce. The price range for pasta is $5.95 to $9.50.

Spaghetti Red's is family-oriented, which is a help when it comes to cost and portion size. You can order a child's portion of pasta (for children 12 and under) for $3.50. For the family, you can choose any four pasta items served on a large platter, together with a dish of meatballs and Italian sausages, for $9 per person. Side dishes of meatballs, Italian sausages, meat or cheese ravioli, or spiral noodles (fusilli) with meat sauce and Romano cheese are offered for $2.25 to $2.50.

Veal and chicken dishes, shrimp, baked salmon, and New York steak Sicilian style (with mushrooms, sliced olives, green peppers, garlic) top off the menu and range from $9 to $14. All entrees are served with Italiano salad (greens with garbanzo beans, green peppers, and olives) and garlic cheese bread; meat or fish entrees also come with a choice of spaghetti, linguine, or fettuccine. Buon appetito.

Dessert, from cannoli to cassata Siciliano, if you can handle it after any of the above, will add $2.25 to $3.

Spaghetti Red's is open for dinner from 5 to 10:30 p.m. Sunday through Tuesday, till 11 p.m. Friday and Saturday; it's closed Wednesday and Thursday.

The Mint's 24-hour coffeeshop is called the **Second-Story Café**. Its round-the-clock offerings range from a hot turkey sandwich with mashed potatoes and cranberry sauce to deep-fried Eastern scallops with coleslaw, french fries, and a roll and butter. Breakfast entrees here average $4 to $9; lunch and dinner run $7 to $15.

UNION PLAZA HOTEL: 1 Main St. (at Fremont Street), Las Vegas, NV 89101 (tel. 702/386-2110, or toll free 800/634-6575, 800/634-6821 in California).

Opened on August 1, 1971, the Union Plaza celebrated its first birthday with the "World's Biggest Birthday Cake." At the top of the brilliant Fremont Street light show on the site where the old Union Pacific Depot used to be, its double-towered, three-block-long frontage has permanently altered the Las Vegas downtown skyline.

The 1,037-room, $100-million Union Plaza is one of the largest hotels in downtown Las Vegas.

Immaculate rooms with cable TV, direct-dial phones with message light, tub/shower bath, and two queen-size beds are standard accommodations at the hotel. There also are some rooms with king-size beds and a separate love seat that converts to a small bed, rooms with round beds; and a number of suites. Decor throughout the hotel is contemporary, with liberal use of walnut veneer and draperies and bedspreads in big, splashy patterns. The rooms are pretty and homey.

The Union Plaza's 650-seat showroom opened with *Fiddler on the Roof*, a smash hit, and it continues to feature Broadway-style musical productions or comedies, most recently *Your House or Mine*, with Avery Schreiber. A 24-hour casino, entertainment lounge, several dining rooms and bars, a shopping arcade, a sports deck with four lighted tennis courts and a quarter-mile jogging track, a pool, parking for 1,400 cars (including a five-story covered ramp), a huge casino, and a race and sports book lounge seating 300 complete the layout.

Rates for standard rooms at the Union Plaza are $45 to $65 single, $50 to $70 double. Each additional person pays $8.

A few facts about the Union Plaza: Adjacent to the hotel's parking ramps is the main Greyhound Terminal. . . . The Amtrack Railroad Station is right in the hotel. . . . The Union Plaza is a joint venture of the Union Pacific Railroad and the Plaza Corporation of Las Vegas. So again a railroad has spurred new business in the West. . . . Shortly after the opening of the Union Plaza, Interstate 15 (linking Las Vegas with metropolitan Los Angeles, 289 miles to the southwest) was extended into the Casino Center, allowing drivers to go the entire distance from the Pacific Ocean to downtown Las Vegas without encountering a single traffic light.

Restaurants

The Union Plaza's gourmet restaurant is the **Center Stage.** It's located under a glass dome on the second floor of the hotel's north tower, with a spectacular nighttime view of the bright lights of downtown along Fremont Street. Adjacent to the Center Stage is a cocktail lounge, where piano entertainment is featured nightly. The restaurant's decor is soothing and attractive forest green and cream. You might begin dinner with an à la carte appetizer such as smoked salmon or coquilles St-Jacques, or you can proceed directly to a complete dinner that begins with Act One—black-bean soup served with chopped egg, onions, and sherry. Act Two is a salad, Act Three the entree, and Act Four a fresh fruit basket with assorted nuts, and tea or coffee. Entrees, which are priced at $19 to $35, include Rocky Mountain brook trout, grenadine of beef with either béarnaise or bordelaise sauce, and roast prime rib.

In addition to all the Acts listed above, meals include a baked potato, fresh vegetable, and French or garlic bread. There's also an à la carte selection, and a nice wine list.

The Center Stage is open daily for dinner from 5 to 11 p.m.

Another dining establishment at the Union Plaza is the **Kung Fu Plaza.** The foyer of this Chinese-Thai restaurant is Oriental indeed, with a Buddha, elephant statues, and dragon columns. Inside it more resembles a garden, with leaf-print wallpaper, white latticework, and plants everywhere. The Kung Fu Plaza offers traditional Chinese fare: moo goo gai pan, beef with snow peas, Chinese soy sauce duck (unlike Peking duck, the skin is soft), and the expected array of appetizers including barbecued spareribs, egg rolls, and wonton soup.

Recently the restaurant added a delicious selection of Thai entrees to its menu. Dishes may be ordered to whatever degree of spiciness you prefer. Specialties of the house include spicy, crispy catfish—a favorite of mine; chicken chili mint—cooked with garlic and ground chili and served with chopped mint for a marvelous flavor; barbecue pork satay—marinated with Thai curry and served with a peanut butter sauce for dipping, as well as a special house cucumber sauce. And if you enjoy noodle dishes as much as I do, Kung Fu Plaza is famous for its Pad Thai noodles prepared with Thai chili powder and panfried with bay shrimp, bean sprouts, and peanuts.

If you've never tried Thai food, King Fu Plaza is a great place to begin. Entrees range from $6 to $9.50. The restaurant is open daily from 11 a.m. to 11 p.m.

The Union Plaza's 24-hour coffeeshop is the **Plaza Diner,** located off the casino on the main floor. In addition to the usual fare, the Plaza Diner offers daily specials of soup or salad, vegetable, bread, entree, and beverage. Lunch specials, available from 11 a.m. to 5 p.m., include shrimp or pork chops, and run $5 to $8. Dinner might be a delicacy like New York steak, prime rib, or brook trout, for $6 to $14. The Plaza Diner also features a bargain breakfast around the clock.

FOUR QUEENS HOTEL: 202 E. Fremont St. (at Casino Center Boulevard), Las Vegas, NV 89101 (tel. 702/385-4011, or toll free 800/634-6045).

When the Four Queens first opened in 1965, it was a casino operation; the hotel followed later. These days it's a major downtown property with 720 rooms, occupying an entire block, and has been decorated in a turn-of-the-century New Orleans French

Quarter motif. The Four Queens offers 24-hour gaming and continuous entertainment featuring jazz and Dixieland artists, in addition to complete hotel services. There's also a Ripley's Believe It or Not Museum with over 1,000 exhibits.

With singles and doubles $52 Sunday through Thursday, $60 on Friday and Saturday, and $8 for each additional occupant in any room, this is an excellent choice. Rates decrease substantially during summer and winter. The 720 rooms are attractively decorated in a contemporary mode, with wall-to-wall carpeting, good-sized closets with double sliding doors, and prettily coordinated draperies and bedspreads. They're equipped with color TVs, direct-dial phones, and baths with glass-walled tubs and/or showers.

Restaurants
Magnolia's Veranda offers excellent food in a plush garden setting overlooking the casino. It's a pleasant alternative to the usual 24-hour coffeeshop. The food is nicely prepared, whether it's a full-course meal or a quick snack. The service is good too.

Hugo's Cellar features an abundant tableside salad cart and entrees like fresh fish, prime rib, lamb, and duckling. Full dinners cost $17.50 to $32 and come with salad-cart selections, fresh vegetables, baked lavosh and cheese, and sherbet in between courses to refresh your palate. The finishing touch is light- and dark-chocolate-dipped fruits served with fresh whipped cream.

In addition, guests can enjoy nightly entertainment (jazz is featured), not to mention shrimp cocktail, in the **French Quarter Lounge.** And for your sweet tooth, there's an old-fashioned **Ice Cream Shoppe,** which serves up delectable concoctions in a variety of flavors.

FITZGERALD'S HOTEL & CASINO: At Third and Fremont Streets, Las Vegas, NV 89101 (tel. 702/382-6111, or toll free 800/634-6519).
This hotel, which had its grand opening on July 2, 1980, as the Sundance Hotel, is housed in a 34-story tan and reflective-glass building. The casino dominates the ground floor. It's decorated in earth tones, and offers 50,000 square feet of gambling facilities, including 920 slot machines, 24 blackjack tables, a poker room, 4 craps tables, and keno. Public areas of the hotel are situated on two levels, with the casino, lobby, and entertainment lounge on the ground floor, restaurants and a lounge on the upper level.

The hotel's 650 rooms are modern and attractive, equipped with direct-dial phones, color TVs, etc. There's free indoor parking for guests. Rates are $30 to $48 on weekdays, $55 to $85 on weekends, single or double. An extra person in the room pays $8.

Restaurants

Cassidy's Steak House is a dim and intimate eatery with tufted booths and old cowboy photos on the walls. Beef dishes like filet mignon with mushrooms are a specialty, but there are also seafood dishes, such as a combination of shrimp, scallops, oysters, and clams, and other special items like veal piccata and duckling à l'orange. Entrees range in price from $12 to $24. For dessert, Cassidy's features flaming items like peaches or cherries flambé. Outside the restaurant there's a small lounge where you can enjoy a before-dinner cocktail or a postprandial liqueur.

Cassidy's is open for dinner nightly from 5 to 11 p.m.

Next to Cassidy's is **Chicago Joe's,** a small Italian restaurant with lace curtains, red carpeting, and small tables with upholstered chairs that match the wallpaper. The lunch menu features pasta dishes like lasagne, spaghetti, and rigatoni, and sandwiches filled with roast beef or Italian meatballs, all in the $6 to $12 range. At dinner, such Italian specialties as veal or shrimp parmesan and chicken cooked in garlic butter are offered for $11 to $17.

Chicago Joe's is open Tuesday through Saturday from 11:30 a.m. to 11 p.m., on Monday from 5 to 11 p.m.

The Sundance also has a 24-hour coffeeshop, and a buffet offering all-you-can-eat meals. The breakfast buffet is available from 8 to 11 a.m. for $3.99, lunch is from 11 a.m. to 3:30 p.m. for $4.50, and dinner is from 4 to 9 p.m. (to 10 p.m. on Friday and Saturday) for $6.50.

SHOWBOAT HOTEL: 2800 E. Fremont St. (between Eastern and Boulder Highway), Las Vegas, NV 89104 (tel. 702/385-9123, or toll free 800/634-3484).

A hike from the downtown section, in an area that's lined mostly with motels, the Showboat is popular with locals for bowling, Bingo, and an attractive Mississippi River–motif casino complete with flocked wallpaper and globe chandeliers. More than most hotels in Las Vegas, it's a family place, with plenty of diversions for both juniors and seniors.

The Showboat looks exactly like an oldtime showboat that's been stranded on flat land. Two stories of streetside façade have a big paddlewheel and porched decks with columns and banisters. They're topped by a "poop deck" and steering-wheel room. The riverboats were gambling saloons once upon a time, so the innovations are in keeping with the Vegas scene.

The 500 rooms are large and attractive, equipped with color TVs, direct-dial phones, and tub/shower baths. There are 350 housed in an 18-story tower, the rest in three low buildings situated around a big swimming pool. Singles and doubles are $48 a night; an extra person pays $8. Suites are $100 to $145 for one to two bedrooms.

The Showboat is a sportsman's delight. One of the biggest and busiest lures is its 106 bowling alleys, open 24 hours. (They're the site of the Pro Bowlers' Association events twice a year.) There's a snackbar facing the alleys for candy, and a playroom (with attendant) where you can leave kids aged 2 to 7 for up to three hours at no charge.

A recent addition is a 45,000-square-foot **Sports Pavilion** where professional wrestling and boxing matches are staged, and sometimes televised on the cable sports networks. WBC championships have been presented here, and the Russian and Yugoslav national boxing teams have appeared in exhibitions.

Another recent acquisition is the **Showboat Country Club,** complete with two lighted tennis courts, swimming pool, and a championship golf course. The club also has a clubhouse with restaurant, bar, and tennis and golf pro shop, as well as a driving range and putting green. A shuttle bus runs a regular route between the hotel and club.

There's a game arcade for kids. The hotel also has a barbershop and beauty salon, a gift shop, and shuttle bus to the airport.

The coffeeshop is open around the clock for meals ranging from a burger and fries to prime filet mignon with mushroom caps, plus all the requisite breakfast fare, deli items, sandwiches, and salads. Breakfast ranges from $4.50 to $8; lunch and dinner, from $7 to $22.

Large buffets are set out weekdays from 10 a.m. to 3:30 p.m. ($5.25), Sunday for brunch from 8:30 a.m. to 2:30 p.m. ($6.95), and at dinner nightly from 4:30 to 10 p.m. Kids' meals cost less.

There's a hometown attitude at the Showboat, which makes it most agreeable to regular repeat guests, who find all the amusement they want here without ranging out into the downtown area or to the Strip.

LOWER-PRICED HOTELS

THE CIRCUS CIRCUS HOTEL: 2880 Las Vegas Blvd. South, Las Vegas, NV 89109 (tel. 702/734-0410, or toll free 800/634-3450).

The Circus Circus is the only hotel in town that caters as unabashedly to children as it does to adults. From the clown-shaped marquee to the Circus Sky Shuttle to the tent-shaped Big Top, the Circus Circus is a delight for kids of all ages.

The hotel, which is located behind the immense casino-circus complex, is 15 stories high and has 800 rooms and suites. Another 805 rooms are located across the street in five three-story buildings known as Circus Circus Manor.

Rooms are priced from just $22 to $45 a night, single or double (prices are lower during the summer and December). An extra adult is $5. A typical room has two double beds or one king-size bed, a big mirror above the dressing table, color TV, direct-dial phone, wall-to-wall carpeting, and pleasant decor. The bath is separated from the dressing room by a big walk-through closet.

The focus of the hotel is, of course, the Big Top. On the main floor, casino action includes all the popular table games, a large keno lounge, lots of slots, and video gaming machines (blackjack, poker, etc.). Originally the circus acts were presented directly over the casino in full view of all, but the daring acrobats and tightrope walkers were a distraction for the gamblers, and that's a definite no-no in Las Vegas. Now a sound-cushion ceiling insulates the main body of the casino from the circus goings-on, although the action can still be seen from selected parts of the casino floor.

On the mezzanine, the circus proper is ringed by carnival games offering nice prizes, arcades of electronic games, snack stands for grabbing a quick bite. There's even a booth where kids (and lighthearted grownups) can be painted up like clowns. The one concession to the adults on this level is a revolving carousel bar; there's no gambling up here at all.

And of course there are the circus acts. Thirteen hours a day, from 11 a.m. to midnight, on the hour, you can see tumblers and trained animals, jugglers and magicians. Trapeze artists soar through space, and aerial ballerinas perform on swaying carousel ponies. The atmosphere is nothing short of electric, and of course the smiles are contagious.

Gift shops and boutiques, swimming pool, and other fun things are tucked into the Circus Circus cornucopia of goodies, a sensational (to use one of those superlatives that really are necessary in this case) hotel-casino-circus-spa that has to be seen to be believed. There's even a wedding chapel, if you'd like to get married under the Big Top.

Restaurants

Dining at the Circus Circus can mean anything from a hot dog to a full veal scaloppine dinner.

The **Steak House** is located on the main floor near the elevators. The decor is traditional with rich woods, gleaming brass, leather-upholstered chairs, and soft lighting.

There's an open-hearth charcoal grill in full view of the dining area, so you can watch your steak being cooked. All the steaks are from midwestern beef aged 21 days in a glassed-in area just to the side of the restaurant. Good choices for steak-lovers are the sirloin tip and the filet mignon, but there are also prime rib and lobster tail. Entrees costing $15 to $28 are served with a loaf of sourdough dark sweet bread and a choice of a one-pound baked potato or potato wedges with cheese. There is an extensive list of domestic and imported wines.

The room is open daily from 5 p.m. to midnight. A bar and lounge adjoin.

Another dining choice is the **Circus Pizzeria,** located on the mezzanine. It's decorated in cheery red, white, and green, with striped poles and red-and-white-checked tablecloths. The specialty here is—of course—pizza, either traditional or deep-dish. The dough is made fresh daily, as is the pasta, another dining choice. Pizzas range in price from $7 to $14, depending on size (small, medium, large) and number of toppings. Pasta, such as spaghetti, rigatoni, and linguine, runs $5 to $9. You can order sodas by the glass or pitcher, and beer and wine are available for those over 21. The pizzeria is open daily from 11 a.m. to 1 a.m.

A DELUXE MOTOR CAMP: A few years ago, Circus Circus opened the luxurious **Circusland RV Park** adjacent to the Circus Circus Hotel/Casino and just steps away from the Strip. The RV park has all the informality and economy that RVers look for, plus the resort luxury of Las Vegas. There are spaces for 421 vehicles, all with up to 50-amp full-utility hookups. Well lit and attractively landscaped, the Circusland offers swimming pools for adults and a wading pool for tots, a fenced playground, saunas, Jacuzzis, a community room, games arcade, fenced pet runs, laundromat, disposal station, and 24-hour convenience store. A free minibus provides transportation to and from the hotel. Rates are $8 to $12 per vehicle per night.

The **Circus Circus Buffet,** served in a room off the casino, is an all-you-can-eat affair with over 40 items of all kinds priced at $2.50 for breakfast (beverage extra), served from 6 to 11:30 a.m. Lunch, served from noon to 4 p.m. ($2.75), and dinner, served from 4:30 to 11 p.m. ($3.95), include beverage. Dinner includes carved-to-order roast beef and baked ham.

The **Snack Train,** on the mezzanine level, offers fast-food service, and the plushly pink **Pink Pony** (off the casino) is the requisite Vegas 24-hour coffeeshop.

On the second level of Circus Circus, the **Skyrise Dining Room** offers a way to fill the urge for a one-pound New York steak or prime rib dinner at a great price. It's not posh-decor dining, but then it's hard to beat $6.95 when the entree also comes with soup or salad, potato, vegetable, and bread. The Skyrise Dining Room is open nightly from 5 to 11 p.m. There's also the **Skyrise Snack Bar,** offering fast-food service on the second level.

LA MIRAGE HOTEL & CASINO: 377 E. Flamingo Rd. (at Paradise Road), Las Vegas, NV 89109 (tel. 702/733-7777, or toll free 800/634-6617).

La Mirage offers 320 modern rooms each with color TV, tub/shower bath, direct-dial phone, wet bar, refrigerator, and kitchenette. There's a large outdoor swimming pool, a Jacuzzi, laundry rooms, beauty and gift shops, a 24-hour coffeeshop, Oasis Café, a cocktail lounge with entertainment, and a medium-size casino.

Rooms are housed in six three-story buildings set in a lush landscape amid waterfalls, fish ponds, and babbling brooks. Sunday through Thursday, rates are $35, single or double occupancy. On Friday, Saturday, and holidays they rise to $42 a night. Children under 12 can stay free in their parents' room, and extra adults pay $8.

VILLA ROMA: 220 Convention Center Dr., Las Vegas, NV 89109 (tel. 702/735-4151, or toll free 800/634-6535).

Although the two-story Villa Roma was opened in 1964, a new and attractive creamy white paint job outside has improved its image. It has 100 rooms, walk-ups (no elevator) to the second floor.

The fairly big rooms are furnished with king-size beds or two doubles, sofas, and tables, with two chairs. Closets have sliding doors, and the baths have tub/showers with glass doors. There's color TV in every room, and local calls are free on your direct-dial phone. In-room coffee and refrigerators are convenient extras. Out back there's also a big swimming pool surrounded by Astroturf. And for those so inclined, there's a wedding chapel on the premises.

Rooms are in the bargain category, and especially notable for their excellent mid-Strip location. Single or double occupancy is $39. Shopping, several big hotels and showrooms, and Strip buses are within close walking distance. Limo service is available.

ALGIERS HOTEL: 2845 Las Vegas Blvd. South, Las Vegas, NV 89109 (tel. 702/735-3311).

This is one place that is surprisingly different . . . it has no casino. The hotel is much nicer than you might expect from the array of shops in front. The barrage of lights announcing "Cocktails," "Coffeeshop," "Souvenirs," "Gifts" dominates the façade to such a degree that you'll find the hotel sign barely noticeable. (It's across from Circus Circus.) But if you keep looking and take the underpass below the signs, you'll find yourself in a central court and pool area. And that's it. The two-story hotel is arranged in a U-shape around the pool; there are 105 rooms.

As you enter the court at the Algiers, the small and informal office is to your left. Off it is the cozy cocktail lounge with bar and leatherette seats in reds. The cocktail bar is open from 11 a.m. to 3 a.m. daily; the adjoining coffeeshop, from 7 a.m. to 11 p.m.

It's quite plush for a coffeeshp, with gold vinyl-upholstered chairs and horseshoe-shaped booths; red-and-gold-flocked wallpaper and smoked-glass mirrors on the walls; lighting emanating from candlelight, crystal chandeliers, and wall sconces; and a small waterfall in a copper-chimneyed fireplace. You can also dine on an enclosed patio café area overlooking the pool. Luncheon specials are an unbeatable bargain—like fried chicken or ocean perch, served with soup or salad, rolls and butter, and dessert, for under $7. Steaks are $9.50 to $11.95.

Rooms at the Algiers are priced at $39 single, $44 double, $51 triple, $56 for four persons. All rooms are the same, whether you wish twins or a double bed. Carpets and bedspreads are prettily colorful; walls are wood-paneled. Furniture is contemporary, painted white, with tables and chairs, double dressers, tiled baths with tub/showers, and big walk-in closets. The rooms are of adequate size and very pleasant, equipped with color TVs and direct-dial phones. All the rooms shine with good housekeeping too, which is especially impressive.

The Algiers Hotel is an informal place without the fanfare and the fuss and bother associated with most hotels along the Strip. It definitely does not attract the frenetic crowds that most casinos do. If you're simply looking for a pleasant hotel with a swimming pool, a place to eat, and a nice room, the Algiers is worth checking into. Its superior location along the Strip is an advantage too, for days and nights roaming the town.

MINI-PRICE MOTOR INN: 4155 Koval Lane, Las Vegas, NV 89109 (tel. 702/731-2111, or toll free 800/634-6541).

Well located, immaculate, cheerful, and fully equipped to meet your travel needs, these no-frills hostelries are among the best things to happen to budget travel since Arthur Frommer.

The Koval Lane establishment, directly behind Bally's—Las Vegas, couldn't be better placed. A stucco and shingled three-story building, it houses 360 well-proportioned rooms, quite pretty for the price with attractive matching spreads and drapes, gray carpeting, and peach-colored walls. Rooms are air-conditioned and equipped with shower baths, color TVs, and direct-dial phones. The rates during the week are $32, single or double. On weekends the rates increase by $8. An extra person is $5 per night.

Facilities include a swimming pool and sundeck, a Jacuzzi, a gift shop, and ample free parking. You pass through a small casino to register; a small restaurant and bar are off to one side. There are scores of restaurants in easy walking distance.

VEGAS WORLD HOTEL AND CASINO: 2000 Las Vegas Blvd. South (at St. Louis Boulevard), Las Vegas, NV 89104 (tel. 702/382-2000, or toll free 800/634-6277).

This hotel is different from the average Las Vegas hotel/casino complex. First, its position: it's neither on the Strip proper nor in downtown. It's somewhere in between, at the junction of Las Vegas Boulevard, Main Street, and St. Louis Boulevard. Second, the casino is always looking for new twists to the same old games. Vegas World claims that "Double Exposure 21" (the dealer's two first cards are both dealt face up) got its start here, as well as "crapless craps"—you can't lose on the first throw of the dice simply because 2, 3, or 12 (on the first throw) are points (See Chapter V for the rules of the game). Third, the hotel is not ablaze in neon. In fact, at night you have to look for it. Its exterior decor is positively Space Age: peeping through red-painted archways on the original structure is a building-size portrait of the moon; the tower depicts a blue-and-white planet Earth. A realistic depiction of the solar system on the 40-foot ceiling of the main lobby is done with fiber optics. It's replete with a replica of the Apollo Skylab and life-size astronaut models shown against a planetary background.

Vegas World has 600 rooms, divided between the main building and the 24-story tower. The rooms are moderate in size, each containing one king-size bed or two double beds. The decor is cheerful, and all the usual amenities are present—direct-dial phones, air conditioning, color TVs, modern bathrooms. (These last are quite small in the older building.) Room rates range from $47 to $62, single or double; $10 for each extra person.

Other facilities at Vegas World are a shopping arcade, two lounges, a video arcade, a beauty salon, the fully equipped casino, and a 1,200-seat showroom.

Restaurants

Vegas World's 24-hour coffeeshop is the **Copperhood Restaurant.** It's standard all the way, from the red leatherette booths lining the walls and the Formica tables to the menu. Breakfast (served around the clock) is everything from danish to steak and eggs, for $3 to $10. Light fare (also available 24 hours a day), in the $5 to $11 range, consists of sandwiches, burgers, and salads as well as Hobo Stew (beef chunks and vegetables in a tomato broth), Pop's Texas-style chili, and a daily chef's special. From 5 p.m. to 1 a.m. you can order hot entrees such as prime rib, batter-fried shrimp, or barbecued pork ribs, complete with soup or salad, vegetable, potato, rolls and butter, for $9 to $16.

Nearby is **Kelly and Cohen's Steakhouse.** It's a small, intimate place, decorated in ornate Victorian style with red tufted-velvet booths and an elaborate brass and red-globed chandelier. Overlooking the whole is a portrait of Kelly and Cohen, head to head. The steakhouse menu is presented on an easel; specialties include prime rib and broiled trout. Entrees range in price from $13 to $28.50.

Kelly and Cohen's is open for dinner nightly from 5 p.m. to midnight.

EL CORTEZ HOTEL: At Fremont and Sixth Streets, P.O. Box 680, Las Vegas, NV 89125 (tel. 702/385-5200, or toll free 800/634-6703).
This is one of Las Vegas's smaller hotels, and it's a gem.

Built around 1940, it was completely renovated a few years back. The result is what appears to be a pleasant five-story hotel, with a sparkling coffeeshop, lobby, dining room, an expanded keno lounge, and 308 guest rooms.

Slots at the El Cortez are "extra liberal," according to the hotel's promotional material, and they pay more than 7,000 jackpots every 24 hours. On the ground floor there's a lounge that never closes and is always crowded, and a round-the-clock coffeeshop, the **Emerald Room.** Needless to say, the casino is an all-day/all-night operation, 365 days a year.

Because the gambling action is so concentrated, some individuals almost never use their rooms. That's a shame, for not only are they nicely arranged and decorated, they're outstanding bargains at $22 to $30, single or double, and the rates are constant the year round. An extra person adds $3. Each room has individually controlled heat and air conditioning too, so you can keep temperatures at levels you prefer. They're also equipped with color TVs, direct-dial phones, and tub/shower baths.

Local Las Vegans always mention the El Cortez for top dining at reasonable prices. The food is excellent, served in **Roberta's Café,** a place popular with families. The room is so popular, in fact, that double lines during dinner hours extend through the entire casino. A 1¼-pound porterhouse steak with trimmings at $9.95 is the biggest draw, but whopping lobsters, really big enough for two at $12.95, and half-steak/half-lobster specials for $12.50 are other menu tantalizers. Dinner is served from 4 to 11 p.m.

The high-quality food at the El Cortez Hotel is famous in Las Vegas. But Jackie Gaughan, the hotel's dynamic owner, has adhered to old-line Las Vegas attitudes, really giving guests as much for their money as volume traffic will allow. He shaves prices to the bare minimum, resists the corporate trend to cut the extras that have attracted people to the city, and his approach has made him one of the most successful hotel-casino operators in Nevada.

OGDEN HOUSE: 651 E. Ogden (at Sixth Street), Las Vegas, NV 89101 (tel. 702/385-5200), or toll free 800/634-6703).

The Ogden House is a five-story hostelry located directly behind the El Cortez. The 102 rooms, all of which open off interior corridors, are simply but comfortably furnished, with one queen-size bed or two twin beds, air conditioning, phones, and color TVs. Room rates are a bargain at $21, single or double occupancy.

The hotel has no eating or gaming facilities of its own. In fact, it operates as a sort of an annex to the El Cortez, with which it shares its management and switchboard. And guests of the Ogden House have full access to all the amenities of the El Cortez.

GOLD SPIKE: 400 E. Ogden (at Fourth Street), Las Vegas, NV 89101 (tel. 702/384-8444, or toll free 800/634-6703).

The Gold Spike is located just a couple of blocks from the El Cortez and the Ogden House, and is also owned by Jackie

Gaughan. The hotel has 110 rooms and suites, the latter with balconies. All accommodations have phones, color TVs, and air conditioning. Prices are a very reasonable $19, single or double, and include free breakfast at the El Cortez; a suite is $31. An extra person adds on $3.

The Gold Spike has a small snackbar that features hot roast beef or ham dinners for under $4, as well as reasonably priced soup, sandwiches, and chili. And there are Marie Callender pies on sale for dessert. There's also a casino in the hotel, perfect for the "budget" gambler, with penny slot machines, 5¢ electronic keno machines, 40¢ live keno, 10¢ roulette, and 5¢ blackjack, as well as higher-stakes machines and games.

WESTERN HOTEL: 889 E. Fremont St. (at Ninth Street), Las Vegas, NV 89101 (tel. 702/384-4620, or toll free 800/634-6703).

The Western has the largest free-standing marquee (77 feet) in the downtown area, and its Bingo parlor is known as "the most comfortable, and the happiest in town." It certainly does attract a sizable crowd. So do the slots, live gaming, and keno lounge, the latter offering 40¢ keno with prizes up to $25,000.

The Western is three stories tall, with 115 rooms. It's about three short blocks from the most crowded casino area along Fremont Street, certainly within easy walking distance of all the downtown attractions.

Cozy and immaculate rooms of colorful contemporary design are located off central hallways, or off an open central porch on the top floor. They're priced at a mere $17 for a room with one queen-size bed or two twin beds, $21 for two doubles. And the hotel doesn't need a shill to tell anybody that it's one of the best price deals in Las Vegas. Rooms have mirrored dressing alcoves, and the baths have tubs or showers with glass doors. Closet space is abundant. Naturally, every room is air-conditioned and has direct-dial phone and color television.

"Western Fun Books," which guests may receive daily at the desk, are *really* fun books. They entitle you to some free meals, drinks, souvenirs, gifts, etc., at this and other Vegas establishments.

SAM BOYD'S FREMONT HOTEL & CASINO: 200 E. Fremont St. (at Casino Center Boulevard), Las Vegas, NV 89101 (tel. 702/385-3232, or toll free 800/634-6182).

Sam Boyd's Fremont Hotel & Casino, a downtown landmark since 1956, has recently undergone a $15-million renovation. The 450 rooms have been refurbished with comfortable double or king-size beds, color TVs, direct-dial phones, tub/shower baths, and wall-to-wall carpeting. For guests' protection and convenience, each room is equipped with a safe. Midweek rates are $33 for a single or double, and weekend rates are $46 for a single or double; $6 a day for an additional person.

The hotel is located smack in the center of downtown Las Vegas, where all-hour gaming spills through the hotel casinos, out into the streets, into the coffeeshops and restaurants, and keeps the nights day-bright. Time isn't measured by a.m. or p.m. in these precincts. Casino activities at the Fremont keep the action going with blackjack, craps, keno, race and sports book, Bingo, and, as you might suspect, lots of slots.

When the need for nourishment overwhelms you, there are three restaurants and a snackbar handy. The **Overland Stage Café** is open 24 hours and offers Chinese dishes in addition to a complete American menu. Dinner possibilities (for $9 to $17) range from lobster Cantonese to broiled Swiss steak.

The all-you-can-eat meals at the **Fremont Buffet** are among the best bargains in Vegas. Breakfast, served from 7 to 10:30 a.m., is $2.95; lunch, from 11 a.m. to 4 p.m., is $3.79; and dinner, from 4 to 10 p.m., goes for $4.95. The buffet features fresh vegetables and fruits at its salad bar, a variety of delicious hot entrees, pastries, and mixed berry sorbets. All meals include unlimited beverages, of the soft variety.

On the second floor of the Fremont is the **Hualapai,** a first-rate restaurant offering superb food in a warm, relaxed atmosphere. Specialties of the house are ribs, filet mignon, rib-eye steak, Australian lobster tail, and a great combination—"Shells and Bones," with crab legs or lobster plus a half-pound filet or half rack of ribs. And for dessert, if you've never had cheese cake with caramel sauce and spiced pecans, this is the place to go all out and order it.

Entrees average $12.50 to $19. The Hualapai is open from 5:30 to 11 p.m. Sunday through Thursday, till midnight Friday and Saturday. Reservations are suggested.

Roxy's Bar, in the main casino area, features live entertainment daily from noon to 6 a.m.

HORSESHOE HOTEL & CASINO: 128 Fremont St. (at Casino Center Boulevard), Las Vegas, NV 89101 (tel. 702/382-1600, or toll free 800/237-6537).

Located in the heart of downtown Las Vegas, the Horseshoe is often thought of simply as a casino, and most patrons never realize that it's a hotel. Not a big one, however. It has only 80 rooms on three floors. The hotel and casino are run by the Binion family, well known in gambling circles.

As you might guess, the casino is done up in the style of the Old West, with antique etched-glass chandeliers overhead; there are even antique slot machines.

The Horseshoe has some of the lowest-priced rooms in Las Vegas: $26 to $30 single, $28 to $33 double. Rooms in the main section are fairly plain. The annex rooms feature perky quilted spreads, matching wallpaper, brass or painted iron beds, closets with sliding doors, and tub/showers in the very nice tile baths. All rooms have small refrigerators. It isn't glamorous, nor should you expect to find boutiques and the sort of extras you pay for at some bigger establishments. But the location can't be beat in downtown Las Vegas.

One of the biggest draws at the Horseshoe Casino is a display of $1 million in cash, one hundred $10,000 bills. You can have your picture taken with the money free, and it's printed and ready in about two hours. Ted Binion, one of the family who works at the casino, told me that "the free picture deal costs the casino about $100 a day." He added: "It's so popular, it's worth it."

The Horseshoe is also the setting each spring for the World Series of Poker, in which all participants must begin with minimum stakes of $10,000.

Jack Binion occassionally strolls through the slot-machine areas handing out rolls of nickels, dimes, or quarters to those playing the slots. You also may be given $1 in nickels to play while you're waiting for your photo to be developed. There's not a set policy on these freebies, however. The casino also is unique for allowing craps table bets up to $5,000, reputed to be the highest sum allowed in Nevada in any casino for a single bet at craps. However, it's been said that if you've got a million to bet, the casino will take you on.

Restaurants

Although most Las Vegas bistros tend to turn into some decorator's idea of the bad and bawdy splendors of the rollicking Old West, the West that the Binions have created in their three restaurants is a civilized one indeed. In the back of the casino and down a flight of stairs, all the restaurants feature Victorian reproduction wallpapers and etched-glass panels.

The **coffeeshop** is less elegant than the Mexican Bar and Ranch House, but essentially the same decor prevails. Open 24 hours, it features such breakfast items as huevos rancheros and a large selection of omelets for $4 to $6. Lunch or dinner cost $6 to $17 for light fare like soups, sandwiches, salads and chili, as well as fried chicken plate served with country gravy, potato, biscuits, and apple cobbler.

The **Ranch House** features mesquite-broiled prime beef, like New York steak and a 20-ounce porterhouse steak, as well as lighter entrees like rainbow trout and chicken. Dinners, which cost $12 to $25, include salad and baked potato. It's open nightly from 5 to 11 p.m.

Next door is the **Mexican Bar,** where tacos, burritos, chili, enchiladas, chiles rellenos, and combination platters may be had for $5 to $10. The Mexican Bar is open daily from 11 a.m. to 10 p.m.

HOTEL NEVADA AND CASINO: 235 S. Main St. (at Bridger Avenue), Las Vegas, NV 89101 (tel. 702/385-7311).

Among the hotels in downtown Las Vegas, with 165 rooms behind a plain and unimposing façade, the Nevada was opened on July 1, 1974. The casino has been remodeled and the 155 rooms brightened up with new wallpaper, carpeting, wood paneling, and furnishings.

Standard rooms at the Nevada cost $22 a night, single or double, Sunday to Thursday; $28 on Friday and Saturday. An extra person in a room pays $3.

The Nevada has a fairly small casino with 200 slots, keno, and gaming tables, and a smallish restaurant open 24 hours. It's directly across the street from the bus terminal adjacent to the Union Plaza.

You won't find entertainment at the Nevada. It's meant to fulfill modest needs. Around the corner on Fremont Street, within a block, are the Golden Nugget, the Horseshoe, and other hotels where guests can find plentiful entertainment.

LAS VEGAS MOTELS

TAM O'SHANTER MOTEL: 3317 Las Vegas Blvd. South, Las Vegas, NV 89109 (tel. 702/735-7331, or toll free 800/835-7427, ext. 662).

Located in the very center of the Strip between the Sands and the Desert Inn, the Tam O'Shanter is a prime location for lively activities. It's within easy walking distance of most major hotels and the new Fashion Show Mall, a major shopping center with 130 stores including Saks Fifth Avenue, Bullock's, and Neiman Marcus.

The office is located to the left as you face the central court.

Bernard Zeldin, general manager, is a longtime resident of Las Vegas and bends over backward to welcome you to "his" motel and "his" city. He always keeps a good supply of fun books on hand for guests and free coffee in the lobby.

There's a total of 100 rooms housed in two sand-colored buildings. They cost $34 a night for a single, $38 for a double. On weekends, rooms are let at $43, single or double.

Rooms are attractively bracketed around a central court, where the swimming pool and parking spaces are located. A wall separates the pool from the street for privacy. Corridors leading to rooms are open-porch affairs along the outside of the buildings. The rooms have neatly paneled and papered walls, two easy chairs, direct-dial phones, large beds with massage units, and color TVs. The baths have glass-doored tile showers and/or tubs, and the dressing rooms have a handy table with a big mirror and a roomy closet without doors. Decor is simple and pleasant.

WESTWARD HO MOTEL & CASINO: 2900 Las Vegas Blvd. South, Las Vegas, NV 89109 (tel. 702/731-2900, or toll free 800/634-6803).

The largest motel in the world conveniently located, it has 1,000 air-conditioned rooms and, believe it or not, seven (!) swimming pools and whirlpools. In spite of its size, the staff are friendly and helpful; they treat their many guests as individuals.

Every room here has a color TV, phone, tub/shower bath, and dressing area. Special rooms for the handicapped are available. And the location, right in the heart of Strip activities, couldn't be better. Singles and doubles are $44 to $49 Sunday through Thursday, $50 to $55 on Friday and Saturday. Also available are two-bedroom apartments that can sleep up to six, and cost $64 to $74 Sunday through Thursday, $74 to $80 on Friday and Saturday, for four persons (there's a $2-per-night charge for each extra person up to six). They're ideal for families or larger groups traveling together.

The Westward Ho offers a special three-day/two-night package for $45 per person, based on double occupancy. Included in the package are accommodations, daily continental breakfast, lunch, and drinks, free slot tokens, casino party book, baggage handling, airport transportation, and tips. Children under 21 years get a special rate of $8 when they stay in their parents' room.

The Westward Ho has added an attractive Parisian-style promenade to its Strip Frontage, sheltered by brilliantly lighted umbrella-like structures. And the motel's casino has been expanded threefold and remodeled to the tune of $12 million. The casino lounge has free nightly entertainment. In addition to the usual automatic teller machines and other financial services offered in most casinos, the Westward Ho has a foreign-exchange desk where you can trade in your marks, francs, pounds, and yen for more negotiable currency.

Another feature is **La Café**, a 24-hour eatery decorated with latticed walls, a green lattice-patterned carpet, attractive tilework, ceiling fans, and lots of ferns. Breakfast is served around the clock for $4 to $8; lunch and dinner feature sandwiches and burgers, as well as hot food like barbecued ribs, fried chicken, and filet of sole, in the $7 to $15 range. A special New York steak or trout amandine dinner, with soup or salad, potato, rolls, and beverage, is available for $7. And if that's not enough of a bargain, there's a $5 luncheon buffet from 11:30 a.m. to 3:30 p.m., followed by a dinner buffet until 10 p.m. for only $6.

IMPERIAL MOTOR INN: 3265 Las Vegas Blvd. South, Las Vegas, NV 89109 (tel. 702/735-5102, or toll free 800/368-4400).

This motel is under the housekeeping care of a lady who takes pride in her work. It's neat! The three stories of rooms are wrapped on three sides of a square around the swimming pool, which is separated from the street by a cement-block barrier for privacy.

All rooms have been totally refurbished and attractively decorated in earth tones—rust, brown, gold, and beige. Singles pay $39 to $67 a night; doubles (with a queen-size bed or two double beds) are $45 to $67. Many of the rooms in this motel have private terraces, all have Formica-topped dressers with big mirrors, direct-dial phones, and color TVs with AM/FM radios. The clothes racks are built in, but there are no closets. The tiled baths with tub/showers have heat lights in the ceiling. There are ice machines on each floor, and there's adequate free parking. The front desk is helpful with show reservations and tours.

LA CONCHA MOTEL: 2955 Las Vegas Blvd. South, Las Vegas, NV 89109 (tel. 702/735-1255).

This is one place that can't easily be missed, for the reception room facing the street is housed in a contemporary architectural structure that demands notice—a shell-like, domed, and arched parabola. It's directly adjacent to the Riviera Hotel in one of the best locations along the Strip.

For lower-priced rooms, you should ask for a location on the side of the motel not facing the pool. The rates here are $37 to $45, single or double, either with two double beds or one king size bed. An extra person pays $3. There's also a suite with a living room, kitchen, and separate bedroom for $67.

Rooms at the La Concha are above average in quality. They have fully carpeted floors, and they're of excellent dimensions. All have color TVs, easy chairs, fancy flocked wallpaper, tables with chairs, radio, direct-dial phones, and good lighting. The baths are sleek, with tub/showers and marble sinks.

The motel has 100 rooms, and free parking is located adjacent to the room areas. The pool is large, and it has a pleasant sundeck. There is no dining facility at the La Concha, but there's room service from 7 a.m. to 10 p.m. from the coffeeshop at the El Morocco next door. Guests can use all the El Morocco's facilities —restaurant, casino, beauty salon, etc.

EL MOROCCO: 2975 Las Vegas Blvd. South, Las Vegas, NV 89109 (tel. 702/735-7145).

Contemporary in motif but somewhat Moorish in its reception room, the El Morocco shares facilities with the next-door La Concha. It boasts a restaurant, a bar, a small, friendly casino, a swimming pool, beauty salon, and gift shop.

The 252 rooms here are priced at $39 to $48, single or double; again, the secret to the lower price is to request a room not facing the pool. An extra person is charged $3.

Rooms are spacious, and have either double beds set up as twins or king-size beds. Furnishings are contemporary, and decor is Vegas plush, complete with a flocked red-and-gold mural behind your bed, marble-topped dressers, etc. Each room has a tub/shower bath, radio, color TV, clock, and direct-dial phone.

There's a good restaurant on the premises called the **Carving Cart.** Dimly lit (as are most restaurants in Las Vegas) and atmospheric, it has oversize plush pink tufted-leather booths and banquettes flanked by brass street lamps, and candlelit tables covered with red linen cloths. The menu features gourmet fare. Appetizers include escargots in garlic butter and fried zucchini. Entrees, which cost $14 to $25, run the gamut from shrimp curry with rice to a prime rib or steak and Alaskan king crab combination, both served with salad, baked potato with sour cream and chives, and Yorkshire puffs. For dessert: cherries jubilee.

The Carving Cart is open nightly from 5 to 11 p.m. An adjoining coffeeshop, the **Garden Room,** serves reasonably priced fare from 7 a.m. to 10 p.m.

Both El Morocco and La Concha are well run and friendly.

CONVENTION CENTER LODGE: 79 Convention Center Dr., Las Vegas, NV 89109 (tel. 702/735-1315, or toll free 800/634-6266).

Convention Center Lodge is right in the heart of the action, at "Stardust Corner." Its modern furnishings are comfortable and clean, all with private bath containing tub and/or shower, cable color TV, and direct-dial phone. Singles or doubles go for $28 to $38 on weeknights, $38 to $48 on weekends and holidays.

MOTEL 6: 195 E. Tropicana Ave. (at Koval Lane), Las Vegas, NV 89109 (tel. 702/798-0728).

Just two blocks off the Strip, this branch of the amazingly low-priced and well-located Motel 6 chain now has 877 units and is growing by the minute. It's the largest Motel 6 in the country. All rooms have air conditioning, free TV, phones in the rooms with free local calls, and a shower bath. There's even a swimming pool, plus a therapy pool. Room rates are $22.95 for one, $28.95 for two. Ask about the Family Plan if there are three or more of you. Be sure to reserve early and you'll not only enjoy very adequate accommodations, but save lots of money that will come in handy for shows and casinos.

ALLSTAR INN: 5085 S. Industrial Rd. (just south of Tropicana Avenue), Las Vegas, NV 89118 (tel. 702/739-6747).

This branch of Allstar Inns is one block west of the Strip. It's low priced, has handsome modern furnishings, and is very comfortable and meticulously clean. All rooms have a full tub and shower, and air conditioning. It's a very attractive bargain. And not only is there a swimming pool but, surprisingly enough, a putting green. TV is free, and so are local phone calls. Sunday through Thursday, room rates are $22.95 for one, $27.95 for two; on Friday and Saturday, $25.95 for one, $30.95 for two. From May through October prices are $3 higher.

There's another Allstar Inn at 4125 Boulder Hwy. (between

Desert Inn Road and Sahara Avenue), Las Vegas, NV 89121 (tel. 702/457-8051). Rates and accommodations are the same as above. There's a pool, but (alas) no putting green.

WINING AND DINING IN LAS VEGAS

□ □ □

"**S**uper-salad?" asked the waiter in the elegant restaurant, on the first evening of my visit to Las Vegas . . . sometime way back when.

Since everything in Las Vegas is promoted in a superlative way, I thought the waiter might be suggesting a concoction with a live, popout redhead, or something. I tried to keep my cool.

"Great!" I answered, smiling and hoping.

"Well, we have consommé, pea soup, French onion soup. And individual Caesar salad, or mixed greens with a choice of any dressing."

"Oh," I said, deflated, "soup or salad."

Anyhow, Las Vegas is a super food town, where you can find great American food in the most generous helpings available on the continent. The colossal buffet is a way of life. Along with noble efforts in American cooking, you'll also discover a wide selection of foreign and exotic cuisines.

The big hotels, glamour places to say the least, serve elaborate spreads, often at prices that make cooking at home almost unreasonable. So do gambling halls. While you're enjoying the casino games and slot machines, wandering hostesses in chorus-girl tights and miniskirts invite you to order any free drink you may wish—but don't forget the tip ("toke")—and many will even provide your favorite brand of cigarettes free. It's part of the game in Las Vegas—a "shill" at even the most renowned hotels and gaming places, to keep you from wandering from the tables.

The house wins, and so do you—they get the business and you get some of the easiest-to-take wining and dining in the U.S.A.

Topping the list of the Vegas food bargains are the buffets— amazingly low-priced all-you-can-eat breakfasts, lunches, brunches, and dinners. They're almost always in the $4 to $8 range, and at some the champagne flows freely, to boot. Among the hotels offering these sumptuous food orgies are the Aladdin, Bally's, Bourbon Street, Caesars Palace, Circus Circus, Dunes, Flamingo Hilton, Fremont, Golden Nugget, Hacienda, Holiday, Imperial Palace, Landmark, Maxim, Riviera, Sahara, Showboat, Silver Slipper, Stardust, Fitzgerald's, Tropicana, Union Plaza, and Westward Ho.

And signs all over town hawk 69¢ breakfasts, 99¢ shrimp cocktails, and the like.

In addition to the restaurant extravaganzas in the hotels, however, Vegas has plenty of good eating places. They have to offer a lot to compete with the hotel eateries and prices, and they also give you a chance to get away for a while from the razzle-dazzle, flashy neon ambience of the Strip and downtown. These are the places where the locals eat, and not only will you get an excellent meal at any of the upcoming listings, you'll also get to see another side of Vegas.

One last note: If you've never been to Las Vegas before, or have eaten only within the hotels, you may find the seafood to be adequate but not exceptional. It's certainly not up to the standards of the Oyster Bar in Grand Central Station in New York City, for example. All this may change with the advent of the Golden Nugget On The Strip. It's the intention of the hotel to have the finest seafood restaurant in the country, and what the Golden Nugget wants, the Golden Nugget usually gets. In the meanwhile, there are a number of good places to eat outside of the hotels.

WHERE TO DINE, INTERNATIONAL AND AMERICAN

THE GOLDEN STEER: 308 W. Sahara Ave., just west of the Strip (tel. 384-4470 or 387-9236).

(Note: directly after heading west on Sahara, turn into the lot after the Texaco sign on your right.)

The bar on your left as you enter the Golden Steer has an Old West look and feel—red leather, a forest-green ceiling, steer horns, antique guns, western paintings, framed silver dollars, and red velvet curtains. To one side there's a beautiful old glass-encased slot machine that's never had the opportunity to gobble up a single coin.

Among the excellent entrees offered, there are a number you would expect to find (and some you would not) in a restaurant called the Golden Steer. Choices range from one-half of a broiled spring chicken at $12 to the prime rib (called a Diamond Lil or Diamond Jim) at $19.50 or $24. But then you may prefer either the moist and delicious rack of lamb, or Châteaubriand for two at $24 per person.

You can also enjoy a somewhat more unusual and sumptuous meal of Bob White quail—a pair for $24 per person. A Beef and Bird entree offers some of the best of both worlds, with quail and a petit filet mignon accompanied by wild rice for $21.

There is nothing commonplace about the veal or chicken specialties, though you may have seen them listed on other restaurant menus. The quality is exceptional, whether you choose the veal française—dipped in egg batter and sautéed with mushrooms and lemon; or the Chicken of the Angels—a boneless breast sautéed with mushrooms and hearts of artichokes. Chicken and veal specialties, served with spaghetti or toasted ravioli, go for $16.50 to $17.50.

As for the seafood, the highlight of the menu is an extra-large imported Dover sole for $22, served à la carte with a baked potato. Other specialties from the sea include Australian lobster tail and Alaskan king crab legs priced according to market.

One of the pleasant surprises here: without a doubt, the Golden Steer has the best baked potato I've ever eaten in any restaurant at any time; it's indicative of the quality you may expect, whatever you order. I also hear from a good source that the restaurant has the best Caesar salad, bar none. I simply did not have room to try it.

The house offers a good selection of imported and domestic wines at reasonable prices. The Golden Steer menu identifies what it pours when you order your booze by its generic name—the quality, as you might expect, matches that of the food.

If you have room for dessert, there are several varieties of delicious cheese cake, or if you're a chocolate freak, the chocolate bomba ice cream may be just what it takes to hit the spot. Desserts range in price from $3 to $3.85.

You don't want to join the crowd at the Golden Steer if you plan to eat and run back to the baccarat table. Service here is appropriately paced for dining, not gulping. Open daily from 5 p.m. to midnight, closed on Thanksgiving and Christmas. Reservations are suggested.

THE ALPINE VILLAGE INN: 3003 Paradise Rd., across from the Hilton (tel. 734-6888).

Wiener schnitzel and sausages, sauerkraut and strudel— German delicacies galore are made on the premises in this outstanding restaurant, which opened in Las Vegas in 1950. It's privately owned, not a franchise in a restaurant chain with a similar name, and the attentiveness is impressive and personal.

Gemütlichkeit may be overworked to describe atmospheric qualities in German restaurants. In this case, it's appropriate. Fresh white table napery over red cloths makes an immediate cheerful impact. Roofing around the dining room's edges enhances the alpine ski-chalet/beer-garden texture. It's pretty, with little Christmas-card touches typical of the Tyrolean Alps. Service plates, bowls, ice-water mugs—all are pewter. Waiters and waitresses are in Tyrolean garb.

As a starter, a small pumpernickel loaf, cinnamon rolls, spicy gingerbreads, and salty Triscuits arrive at your table, warmed and folded in a napkin on a chopping block with a sharp knife. You'll also get a relish bowl with crackers and cottage cheese dip. Then the meal begins, a banquet really. First comes a pewter tureen of chicken suprême soup, followed by a tossed salad. Also included in the $14 to $22 price of your entree are alpine-seasoned green beans and sauerkraut, sweet-and-sour red cabbage, potato pancakes or a jumbo baked potato, dessert (ice cream or homemade apple strudel), and tea or coffee.

If you'd like to try a few dishes, order one of the combination entrees—like a platter of sauerbraten with fleischrouladen (beef roll) and kohlrouladen (cabbage roll). Also available are a beef roll stuffed with chestnut dressing, a tasty dish called hammelkeule— lean lamb baked with special seasonings and Wiener schnitzel topped with a poached egg, capers, and anchovies. Roast duckling stuffed with chopped meat, apples, prunes, celery, and onions, with lingonberry sauce, is a specialty. Ditto the fondue bourguignonne (filet beef cubes to cook at the table in a copper fondue pot). The beef cubes weigh 14 ounces, and they're lean. Steaks range from a ten-ounce filet mignon to an extra-large porterhouse. A bonus for families: children's portions are available for most entrees at less than half price.

Downstairs, the **Rathskeller** serves lighter fare—pizzas,

burgers, sandwiches, a salad bar—as well as meals of broiled chicken or catfish, complete with soup, salad bar, bread, and ice cream, all for $6 to $17.50. The Rathskeller adds songs, organ music, and, sometimes, a guitarist-folksinger; everybody sings along. If you're looking for informal fun, the Rathskeller is easy on the budget. Some people eat upstairs, then go down to the Rathskeller to round out the evening.

Both the restaurant and Rathskeller are open from 11:30 a.m. to 2:30 p.m. for lunch, and from 5 p.m. to midnight for dinner, and both offer reduced prices for children. Reservations are required upstairs at the restaurant.

The Alpine Village Inn attracts considerable business from local people, which speaks well for its quality.

At the restaurant's entrance, there's a gift shop. You'll find pewterware, crystal, dolls, German Black Forest clocks, cuckoo clocks, musical clocks, music boxes, etc. The shop will mail purchases.

PAMPLEMOUSSE: 400 E. Sahara Ave., one block east of the Strip (tel. 733-2066).

Step inside and you're no longer in Vegas but on the Côte d'Azur. Pamplemousse is an intimate and elegant restaurant decorated in subtle shades of pink and wine, with candles and flowers and ceiling fans. Classical music or light jazz plays softly in the background. There's a wood-burning fireplace that's used on cool evenings, and an outdoor garden area under a bit of tenting. For small private parties, there's a dining area secluded from the main dining room. It's all extremely charming and un-Vegasy.

The restaurant's name, by the way, which means grapefruit, was suggested by the late singer Bobby Darin; it just appealed to him for some reason. Darin was one of French owner Georges La Forge's numerous celebrity friends and patrons.

Pamplemousse has no fixed menu. The restaurant's talented chef prepares four entrees every evening from the freshest ingredients available. The house specialty is duck, served with one of four sauces—kiwi, orange, cherry, or banana rum. There are also fresh fish selections, and a beef or veal dish. But if there's something you're particularly craving, Pamplemousse will prepare a meal to order with 24 hours' notice. The price of your entree includes fresh breads, fresh boiled eggs, and a basket of fresh raw vegetables served with a dip. Entrees are $20 to $24. And to accompany your meal, you can select from perhaps the most extensive wine list in Las Vegas, chosen personally by Georges La Forge with great care.

Beer is also available; no hard liquor is served. And you can round out your meal with a delectable dessert—perhaps a tarte, a mousse, crème caramel, homemade ice cream, or a flambé.

Pamplemousse is open Tuesday through Sunday from 6 to 11 p.m. Reservations are essential. It has my highest recommendation.

KELLER AND FOX LTD.: 850 S. Rancho Dr., near Charleston (tel. 877-2711).

Keller and Fox Ltd. is as lacking in flamboyance as a Las Vegas restaurant can possibly be. A few minutes west of the Strip, the restaurant is well worth the detour for the food and the environment in which it's served. You'll find here the understated elegance of a beautiful English country home, a far cry from the decor of most Las Vegas eateries.

Luncheon specials at Keller and Fox change daily and generally include choices of pasta, crêpes, English pies, eggs, fish, fowl, or meat. Among the crêpes you might find one filled with beef Stroganoff, or one filled with chicken and duck curry. The savory English pies do not include the overworked standard of beef and kidney, but, rather, a more interesting choice of spinach, chicken, or vegetable. The roast game hen with fresh plum sauce tempted me, but I chose the salmon with lime and ginger, and it surpassed my best expectations.

Among the standard light-lunch selections are cold pasta primavera, salade niçoise, and a Windsor salad with poached breast of chicken in champagne sauce. Diehard beef-eaters are also accommodated here, though: the day of my lunch, a top sirloin au poivre was on the menu. Luncheon specials range from $4.75 to $8.50, standard entrees from $7.75 to $14.50.

Dinner is a delight. Keller and Fox serves surperb roast duckling—among the best I've ever had. The duckling is offered three ways: with garlic, herbs, duck stock, and cream; with raspberry sauce; or with fresh pineapple, sautéed bananas, and Jamaican rum. It isn't an easy choice. Nor does the rest of the menu make deciding any simpler. Lamb chops en croûte, individually wrapped in puff pastry with a veal and truffle filling, competed for my attention, as did the poached salmon with caviar mousseline, and the tournedos Valoise—two tenderloins of beef sautéed and garnished with artichoke hearts and mushrooms and served in a veal-stock and burgundy-hollandaise sauce. Entrees range from $16.50 to $22.50.

Desserts, or "confections" as they're dubbed here, are all made on the premises and vary daily; the price for each is $3.75.

The restaurant takes special care of its patrons and will prepare low-cholesterol and/or low-sodium menus on request in advance. Keller and Fox's quality is also reflected in the very attentive and helpful service of the immaculately attired waiters.

Open for lunch Monday through Friday from 11:30 a.m. to 2:30 p.m., for dinner Monday through Saturday from 6:30 to 10:30 p.m. Reservations advised.

OH NO TOKYO: 4455 W. Flamingo Rd., near Arville Street (tel. 876-4455).

As you pass through a simple granite courtyard, the small Japanese-style bridge on your left spans a pond that requires only a few koi (goldfish) to complete the tranquil introduction to Oh No Tokyo. The entry prepares you for the lovely California/Japanese interior, vertical black blinds, shoji screens, and hanging half-curtains that divide the serving areas from the main rooms. You can choose to dine at a table or in one of several tatami rooms (assuming that everyone in your party has socks of whole cloth—remember, shoes are removed before you enter).

The last time I had Japanese food of comparable quality and diversity to that served at Oh No Tokyo was in New York City. The à la carte sushi menu is quite broad; it includes seaweed rolls and specialty rolls, among which is a superb Emperor's roll with shrimp tempura, scallops, green onion, and masago (smelt eggs). Prices are $3 to $4 for a two-piece order; quail eggs are 50¢ each. Plates of assorted sushi range from $5.95 to $10.95 and are served with soup. Other Japanese dinners, priced from $6.95 to $10.95, include such standards as shrimp and vegetable tempura, beef and chicken teriyaki, sukiyaki, and grilled mackeral, salmon, or the catch-of-the-day. Special combination plates (teisuoku) offer a choice of one appetizer and two entrees, with soup, rice, tea, and ice cream, for the reasonable sum of $14.95. The lunch menu also offers a choice of delectable and light udon dishes (steaming noodle soup), with egg, chicken, or beef, at $4.25 to $5.95.

For more Occidental tastes, Oh No Tokyo adds charcoal-grilled dinners to the menu "in the tradition of Japanese boatmen." Entrees range from breast of chicken to steak and lobster, all served with soup, salad, vegetable kebab, and steamed rice. Prices begin at $7.95 and top at $19.95 for the steak and lobster.

Soft drinks are available, as are domestic and Japanese beers, Japanese draft beer, house wine by the glass or bottle, and plum wine by the glass.

Lunch is served weekdays from 11 a.m. to 2:30 p.m., dinner daily from 5 p.m. to 10:45 p.m., when the last order is taken.

FREDDIE G'S: 355 Convention Center Dr., near Paradise Road (tel. 735-3653).

Freddie G's, opened in January 1987, has a New England look, though it serves up food from many regions of the country. The characteristic brick, stone, vaulted ceilings, exposed beams, and seascapes are contrasted and complemented by warm rose-brown banquettes and tables. Soft-pink track lighting gives the room a feeling of intimacy. Delicate china, attractive stemware, Evian water served with a slim slice of lemon—all foretell a similar attention to detail in the food.

Hot sourdough bread (and it truly is hot) is served with your order. The presentation of the crab Louie that I ordered indicated a chef who took great pride in his work, and the tomatoes in the salad tasted wonderfully bush-ripened. Salads aren't your favorite for lunch? The broiled boneless breast of capon with sautéed mushrooms is thoroughly soul-satisfying. Or if you seek beef, there are huge San Francisco half-pound sourdough burgers, plain or with various combinations of American or mozzarella cheese, prosciutto, onions and peppers, bacon and green chilis, or avocado and bacon. Lunch will be about $5.50 to $8.75 for salads, $7.75 to $9.75 for entrees (the capon is $8), and $5.75 to $6.75 for the sourdough burgers.

But the exceptional dining experience at Freddie G's is the evening meal. A good selection of Cajun specialties (running from $16 to $22) includes chicken Dijon baked in bread crumbs with a distinctive mustard flavor, blackened redfish, and Freddie G's jambalaya, all served with salad, red beans and rice, and Cajun vegetables. Other entrees include "the ultimate Porterhouse," Piero's roast kosher chicken, Maine lobster, and Chicago-style calf's liver, at a range of $17 to $26 (the lobster priced according to market). Non-Cajun entrees are served with the house salad, baked potato, and a garden-fresh vegetable.

Desserts are excellent, and one of my favorites has always been the simple rice pudding, unadorned but certainly not pedestrian at Freddie G's. Fresh cinnamon, a raisin or two, cream, and the rice cooked to absolute perfection—it's scrumptious.

Freddie G's has a remarkable selection of wines, both domestic and imported.

And one of the fine touches to an enjoyable lunch or dinner: the service is very attentive and well informed without being intrusive.

Freddie G's is open for lunch weekdays from 11:30 a.m. to

2:30 p.m. Dinner is served nightly from 5 p.m. to midnight. Reservations are suggested for dinner.

CAFÉ SANTA FE: 1213 Las Vegas Blvd. South, near Charleston (tel. 384-4444).

Should you call the café, you will first reach the adjacent Thunderbird Hotel. As a matter of fact, you can dine, nap, get married, and drink in the café's all-night bar (though not necessarily in that order) within the same enclave, since the hotel has a wedding chapel.

The Café Santa Fe is just a bit away from the main action on the Strip, but it's well worth the visit. The Karamanos family has tried, by way of its southwestern menu and handsome restaurant design, to capture the feeling of the true Southwest. The pink stucco walls, wooden pillars, beamed ceiling, Native American rugs, straight-backed Spanish chairs, cacti, and tiled floors, all reflect the unique combination of Native American, Spanish, Mexican, and southwestern traditions found in the restaurant's cuisine.

If you arrive for breakfast, there are the usual gringo offerings as well as those with a southwestern flair. Among the "Omelettes Grandes" are the Santa Fe Joe, with ground beef, panfried onions, mushrooms, spinach, and Swiss cheese; and the South of the Border, with shredded beef chili, onions, and Monterey Jack cheese. The caballero with a hearty appetite might also order three fresh eggs served with medallions of beef tenderloin, chili relleno, and casera potatoes. All egg orders come with casera potatoes, buttermilk biscuits, and preserves. Breakfast ranges from $2.95 to $4.75; the eggs with beef tenderloin is $7.95.

Highlights of the luncheon menu are two freshly made beef patties with chili and cheese, the BBQ sliced pork in a zesty sauce, or the Santa Fe filet sandwich broiled and served open-faced with onion rings. The choices range from $4.75 to $5.75. Salads "from the pantry" include one with freshly cut greens topped with chili con carne, shredded cheese, diced tomato, sour cream, and guacamole; served with salsa and tostados. Salads, served with bread and butter, are $5.95 and $6.95.

Ah, but dinner's my favorite, and I simply could not resist the barbecued baby back ribs—absolutely delicious and served with frijoles covered with cheese and chunky french fries. What I could not finish I took home and it was just as good the next day. Conservative types might choose the boneless breast of plump chicken Mexicaine, marinated and topped with mushrooms, green chili salsa, diced tomato, and glazed Monterey Jack cheese.

Vegetarian customers will enjoy the café's beautifully fresh vegetables, steamed and served with cheddar cheese. Guayamas jumbo shrimps, Veracruz filet of sole, and broiled halibut steak amandine comprise the seafood offerings. For beef-lovers, the tournedos Taos—cooked the Zuni way, with broiled tomato, banana fritters, and horseradish sauce—is a dish large enough to satisfy any appetite and then some, as are the "Texas Cut" T-bone steak, the broiled New York–cut sirloin with mushrooms and fried onions, and the steak Tampico—a skirt steak marinated, broiled, and served with Spanish rice, frijoles de la olla, salsa, and flour tortilla. Entrees, served with salad or soup, potato or pasta, vegetable, and bread, range from $6.95 to $15.75.

The Santa Fe's late-night menu combines a number of the specialties from breakfast and lunch with its South of the Border pot of chili. Prices range from $2.95 to $7.95.

Sweet Santa Fe desserts expand from deep-dish apple pie for $2.45 to rich chocolate cake with fudge frosting (big enough for two) for $4.95.

And all this is served with warmth, thoughtfulness, and attention to detail.

The Café Santa Fe is open daily from 7 a.m. to 11 p.m. The bar is open all night. The café offers a good selection of beers and wines with dinner, as well as the usual alcoholic beverages.

SAVOY FRENCH RESTAURANT AND BAKERY AND SIDEWALK CAFE: 4149 S. Maryland Pkwy., at Flamingo Road in Tiffany Square (tel. 732-7373 or 733-9505).

Popular with Vegas show people, the Savoy is a bright and sunny little café done in brick and redwood with a Mexican tile floor. There are café curtains in the windows, and a few tables are placed outside for al fresco dining. As you enter, you'll pass a glass case filled with croissants, gâteaux, and pâtisseries. Since all baking is done on the premises, this is an ideal place to come for your morning croissants and coffee, not to mention your afternoon cappuccino and cheesecake. Everything (I tried to eat it all) is great! The country breakfasts are huge. Throughout the day you can order five-egg omelets, the largest in Las Vegas, with mix-and-match delights like ham and cheese, asparagus, corned beef hash, or shrimp, olives, and Créole sauce. If restraint is more in your nature, try the eggs Benedict or a variation thereof—a made-on-the-premises croissant à la Benedict with fluffy scrambled eggs, bacon, and hollandaise.

For lunch, French onion soup, sandwiches, and quiches are all in the $3 to $7 range. And the Savoy serves a half-pound hamburger that is one of the juiciest and tenderest in town. If your palate follows the esoteric, go for the homemade croissant stuffed with crab meat. The Savoy also offers salads—like the Neptune, a seafood delight—as well as homemade soups. All in all, everything is delicious and prepared to order. Wine and beer are both available, as are soft drinks and juices.

The Savoy has been run by the Seraccia family (just ask Joe) for over 12 years and was voted the number one bakery-café in Las Vegas for two consecutive years; it's evident in the quality, quantity, and price.

A lively little place at all hours, the Savoy is open Monday through Saturday from 7 a.m. to 6 p.m., Sunday till 3 p.m.

TONY ROMA'S A PLACE FOR RIBS: 620 E. Sahara Ave., near the Strip at Sixth Street (tel. 733-9914).

Tony Roma's is a popular place for ribs in Nevada, California, or any of its many other locations throughout the country. It's undoubtedly the most popular place for ribs in Las Vegas. The restaurant is simple yet pleasant, its wood-paneled walls hung with paintings. There's plenty of seating at booths and tables.

My favorite meal at Tony Roma's consists of their famous onion rings served in a half or full loaf, barbecued chicken, and baby back ribs with french fries and coleslaw. Selections are not limited to ribs and chicken, however. There's choice char-broiled rib-eye steak, London broil, and grilled swordfish steak brushed with lemon, as well as a half-pound Roma burger and salads, all for $6 to $13. In addition, each day brings a special, such as baked meatloaf on Monday, roast loin of pork on Wednesday, and sliced breast of turkey on Friday. Domestic and imported beer is served, wine is sold by the glass, and a variety of liqueur-laced coffees is available to finish your meal. At lunch a similar menu is offered, with smaller portions at lower prices—$5 to $10.

Tony Roma's is open daily until 2 a.m.: Monday through Friday from 11 a.m., on Saturday from noon, and on Sunday from 3 p.m. There's live music Thursday through Saturday from 8 p.m. to 1 a.m.

THE STARBOARD TACK: 2601 Atlantic Ave., off Sahara Avenue one block east of Eastern (tel. 457-8794).

Ruggedly nautical in decor, the Starboard Tack has unpainted or white brick walls covered with seagoing-theme photos and prints, tables made of highly polished, rough-hewn ship hatch covers, captain's chairs, lots of mast rope about, and a number of artifacts like a big ship's steering wheel. It's dimly lit (mostly by candlelight)—very atmospheric in a rustic-funky way. An oversize TV screen in the cocktail lounge is always tuned to sporting events, the action duplicated on a TV over the bar.

The Tack features "reef, beef, and booze"—steak and seafood dinners with entrees like sirloin teriyaki, roast prime rib with creamed horseradish, Alaskan king crab legs, and stuffed salmon steak. Included in the $12 to $30 price of your entree are offerings from the salad bar and fresh-baked bread and butter; a baked potato and corn on the cob are available as side dishes.

At lunch the menu concentrates on sandwiches, ranging from cold turkey to a bacon cheeseburger, as well as a few daily specials, and selections from the salad bar, all for $5 to $10. Homemade desserts are available throughout the day.

Open Monday through Friday for lunch and dinner from 11:30 a.m. to 6 a.m., on Saturday and Sunday for dinner only from 5 p.m. to 6 a.m.

The Starboard Tack has been a popular Vegas hangout for over a decade, and the owners branched out some years ago with the **Port Tack,** 3190 W. Sahara Ave., at Rye Street (tel. 873-3345). Also nautical in theme, this Tack is more sophisticated than the original, with diagonal cedar-paneled and exposed brick walls, and, when the weather warrants, three blazing fireplaces. Almost every table has a view of one of the fireplaces. Like the Starboard, the Port is very dimly lit.

The Port Tack keeps round-the-clock hours, and its menu is almost identical to the Starboard's. One innovation here is oysters flown in from New Orleans.

ALIAS SMITH & JONES: 541 E. Twain Ave., between Maryland Parkway and Paradise Road, in the corner of the Twain Plaza Shopping Center (tel. 732-7401).

Like the Starboard and Port Tack, Alias Smith & Jones is of the rough-hewn genre, a multilevel, woody (diagonal cedar paneling here too) setting filled with lots of flourishing plants and ferns (among the few nonplastic ones in town). Turn-of-the-century-style chandeliers attached to overhead rotating fans, stained-glass panels, antique cabinets, and spindle-backed oak chairs (interspersed with booths and an occasional comfy upholstered wing chair) complete the picture. A big stone fireplace makes things especially cozy. The bar, down a few steps from the main floor, has an oversize TV screen.

It's a relaxed, "civilized," easygoing kind of place, open long, uncivilized hours (11 a.m. to 6 a.m.) and dishing up a wide variety of victuals. The entire menu is available all day. You can design your own omelet by choosing from a possible 22 items; my favorite is the one stuffed with avocado, sautéed mushrooms, chopped tomato, bacon, and assorted cheeses. Omelets are served with cornbread and home fries. They're available, along with sandwiches, burgers, soups, and salads, for $5 to $12. More serious entrees like fried jumbo shrimp, beef ribs, and steak or chicken teriyaki are available for dinner for $10 to $20, complete with soup or salad, corn on the cob, and bread. Alias Smith & Jones also serves up a brunch on Sunday from 11 a.m. to 2 p.m. Entrees like eggs Benedict, steak and eggs, omelets, and strawberry french toast cost $7 to $12 and come with an unlimited flow of Bloody Marys, tequila sunrises, margaritas, or champagne. Desserts range from carrot cake to hot fudge sundaes.

MARIE CALLENDER'S: 600 E. Sahara Ave., at Sixth Street (tel. 734-6572).

The Callender family began making pies in 1948 when they sold their car for $700 and used the proceeds to start a small pie bakery. At first Marie baked about ten pies a day, but after two years she was baking 200 a day. When the orders reached into the thousands, the family opened their first pie shop in Orange, California. Today there are some 100 Marie Callender restaurants in the West, two of them in Las Vegas. They serve not only pies, but wholesome, home-style food.

Different soups—potato cheese, clam chowder, etc.—are featured each day by the bowl or tureen; they're accompanied by croissants or home-baked cornbread. Also available are selections from the salad bar, a Frisco burger (served on toasted sourdough bread and sprinkled with parmesan cheese), a tuna stack sandwich piled high with white albacore tuna salad, or an avocado and alfalfa sprout creation sprinkled with walnuts. All these delights fall in the $6 to $8 price range.

The menu is in effect all day. Dinner (or lunch) favorites range from shrimp linguine (served with salad and bread), to seafood pot pie, to a hamburger steak (with a trip to the salad bar), to chicken topped with cream, cheese sauce, and parmesan served with egg noodles. The restaurant grinds its own meat and makes its own pasta. Prices range from $7 to $10.

Do leave room for some pie. Apple, rhubarb, cream cheese, lemon, peanut butter, coconut, custard, banana, black bottom, blueberry, sour cream/apple, German chocolate, fresh strawberry, and peach pies, among others, are baked fresh daily, and all can be ordered with ice cream, whipped cream, or heavy cream.

Marie Callender's is open daily from 10 a.m. to midnight. I recommend it highly.

BATTISTA'S HOLE IN THE WALL ITALIAN RESTAURANT: 4041 Audrie St. (just east of the Strip), at Flamingo Road (tel. 732-1424).

This popular Italian restaurant is worth considering. A favorite of many celebrities, including Merv Griffin, Sergio Franchi, Dean Martin, Bill Cosby, Robert Goulet, and Tony Bennett, Battista's is famous for its full-bodied home-cooking and warm, inviting atmosphere. It's a festive place, the food is fresh, homemade, and terrific, and no one goes away hungry.

There are seven intimate dining rooms, all decorated unrestrainedly in Italian rococo. "Mooosolini" the moose hangs over the bar. The walls are plastered with celebrity photos, and clam buckets, fishnet, Chianti bottles, strings of garlic and peppers; a revolving barber's pole and an arbor of plastic grapes are among the many adornments. A collection of 2,800 miniature liqueur bottles is displayed in the bar, where you'll also find a few slot machines.

Dinners are priced at $13 to $24, and they all include the following abundant courses: an Italian salad with cheese and salami (sort of a mini-antipasto), all the homemade garlic bread you can eat, a homemade minestrone soup, your choice of about 30 entrees, and a pasta side dish (as much as you want of it). You also get all the wine you can drink to wash down these tasty victuals (they go through about 500 gallons a week!), and all the cappuccino you want—at no extra cost.

To enhance the very Italian ambience, Battista plays Italian music—grand opera, etc. in the background; he also sings for guests and sometimes gives away his own records. As a devoted fan, I could eat here every night just on the chance that he might perform.

Battista's is open for dinner from 5 to 11 p.m., seven nights a week. Reservations are essential. It's a not-to-be-missed experience.

RICARDO'S: 2380 Tropicana Ave., at the corner of Tropicana and Eastern (tel. 798-4515).

Ricardo's is a handsome brown ranch-like building you might easily mistake for a new mission. The interior is every bit as attractive as the outside. As you enter, ahead is what appears as a small Mexican plaza—pillars, tall cacti, a lovely fountain with a small balcony above, decorative tiles above and around the fountain, *Corrida de Toros* posters, and a beamed ceiling so high it's not readily noticed. A skylight adds to the feeling of being outside. This is the main dining room. Booths and tables are well spaced. The fabric covering the cushions on the bentwood chairs and booth seats is a pleasing rust, beige, brown, and blue Mexican design.

On your right is the Cantina, a large bar room with wooden booths and tables—mobbed, friendly. Two other dining rooms, La Sala and Hotel Aristos, carry through the Mexican decor with wrought-metal chandeliers, upright leather-covered chairs, dark-brown wood tables—more austerely Spanish than Mexican in feeling.

Ricardo's serves what I've found to be the best Mexican food in Las Vegas. It's delicious and the portions are huge—bring a big appetite. The corn chips alone are a quarter of the size of a corn tortilla, served with deliciously hot salsa.

Ricardo's serves both meat and seafood dishes, from $9.25 to $12 at dinner. The carne Ortega is a generous portion of broiled top sirloin, thinly sliced and smothered with steaming mild Ortega chiles and melted cheese. Those who enjoy seafood, a Ricardo's specialty the likes of which you won't find anywhere else this side of the border, should try their enchilada à la Puerto Vallarta—a seafood enchilada consisting of a flour tortilla filled with shrimp, crab, and whitefish sautéed with onions, mild chiles, wine, and spices. The enchilada is covered with Ricardo's ranchero sauce and garnished with guacamole and sour cream. Or there's the arroz con pollo, prepared from boned chicken breast over Mexican rice, topped with Ricardo's special sauce and melted cheese, and garnished with mild chiles and pimentos. Specialties of the house are served with cheese salad or soup, Mexican rice, and refried beans. The tostados entrees are truly an unforgettable experience—they're massive, delicious, and inexpensive at only $5.75 to $6.50. You can have all beef, or chicken, seafood, or diced pork. Whatever your choice, it's heaped on a crisp corn tortilla spread with refried beans, covered with shredded lettuce, tangy sauce, guacamole, two kinds of grated cheese, sour cream, and olives.

After several meals at Ricardo's (and I never reached the flan or deep-fried ice cream) I decided it's all delicious, and you'll never leave feeling as though you could eat more. To wash all this down, Ricardo's has a good selection of beers, wines, margaritas (small, medium, large, and by the pitcher), fruit margaritas, sangría, and piña coladas.

Service is attentive and prompt. Two strolling guitarists look, sing, and play as though Mexico were their home—not Tante Elvira's flamenco, but gentle music to dine by.

Reservations are essential for dinner, as the restaurant is usually full by 6:30 p.m., especially on weekends. Ricardo's is open Monday through Thursday from 11 a.m. to 11 p.m., on Friday and Saturday to midnight, and on Sunday from noon to 10 p.m.

THE VINEYARD: 3630 S. Maryland Pkwy., off Twain Avenue, in the Boulevard Mall (tel. 731-1606).

This is quite a production—a bustling indoor Italian street café with exposed brick and patinated walls, terra-cotta tile floors, street lamps, and shelves cluttered with wine barrels, crates of plastic grapes, etc. One wall is hung with shellacked-over Italian movie posters and ads for Cinzano, Alitalia, etc. Completing the festive ambience are high-backed rattan chairs at tables with checkered cloths and a huge salad bar, called the "Groceria," under a green-and-white-striped awning. There's more seating, as well as and similar decor, upstairs. The whole thing is quite charming, and the fare delicious. Fresh fruit and vegetables, homemade pasta, and fresh baked breads are served.

For openers, you can toddle up to the salad bar and help yourself to all you want of its abundant offerings. They're included in the price of your dinner entree. You can also opt for the salad bar as your entire meal: about $8 at dinner, $5 at lunch. When this fabulous smörgåsbord was last seen it included meatballs, baked spaghetti, greens, a wide choice of fresh fruits, many salads, brussels sprouts, marinated mushrooms, big chunks of provolone cheese, pepperoni, artichoke hearts, real roquefort, hard-boiled eggs, sausages, chick peas, bean sprouts, fresh-baked breads, and more—all of it delicious.

Should you want an entree as well, dinner fare ranges from $8 to $16 for pasta dishes like manicotti, cannelloni, and lasagne, or steak or shrimp scampi; sandwiches and pizza are also available. Lunch fare is mostly under $6. Prices on some items are reduced for children under 10.

The Vineyard is open daily from 11 a.m. to 11 p.m., on Friday and Saturday till midnight.

GINZA: 1000 E. Sahara Ave., between Maryland Parkway and Paradise Road (tel. 732-3080).

The best Japanese fare in town isn't at any of the Disney-esque extravaganzas in the major Strip hotels; it's at this simple and charmingly unpretentious little restaurant, and it costs about half the price of its dazzling counterparts. No waterfalls, thunderstorms, or jungles of plastic trees here—just shoji-screened windows, tables sheltered by shingled eaves, and a few Japanese prints, paintings, and fans adorning the pristine white walls. Nevertheless, knowledgeable locals, Japanese food aficionados, and Japanese tourists pack the place nightly. Kimono-clad ladies offer deft service.

Dishes priced from $13 to $15 are served with soup (miso or egg flower), sunomono (vinegared salad), steamed rice, and green tea. A choice of entrees includes sukiyaki, beef teriyaki, chicken teriyaki, salmon teriyaki, sashimi, yosenabe—a sort of Japanese bouillabaisse—and tempura shrimp and vegetables. A side order of nat-to oshitashi will make you wonder why anyone ever maligns spinach. As you might conclude, Ginza also has the very best sushi bar in town. You can order sushi by the piece or as a combination of tastes. Sake can be ordered to complement your meal.

Ginza is open for dinner nightly from 5 p.m. to 1:30 a.m.

GOLDEN WOK: 504 S. Decatur Blvd., at Alta Drive (tel. 878-1596).

This is your local Chinese restaurant, and the one most frequented by Las Vegas's Chinese population. It's not superb compared to the offerings in New York or San Francisco, but it is the best in town. (It's a fair distance away, about three miles—something to consider if you must take a taxi.) The decor is unpretentious, light and airy, with bamboo-patterned wallpaper, a beamed stucco ceiling, pale coral venetian blinds on the windows, and a number of plants here and there.

The menu encompasses Mandarin, Cantonese, and Szechuan cookery. I always begin a meal here by ordering pot stickers (Chinese dumplings) and/or, depending on the number of hearty eaters among the group, sizzling rice soup or hot-and-sour soup. If you like hot food, you might select a Szechuan entree like princess prawns (fresh jumbo shrimp sautéed with imported mushrooms, bamboo shoots, water chestnuts, hot pepper, soy jam, and a dash of Chinese liqueur) or tso tsung-tang chicken (diced chicken served with mushrooms and green beans in a hot sauce). Less spicy, but also very tasty, are the lemon chicken and moo shu pork served with Chinese pancakes. Should you feel like a filling dessert, there are banana fritters. Entrees, multicourse dinners, and combination plates fall in the $9 to $16.50 price range (duck dishes cost more). At lunch a terrific bargain is the $6.25 buffet where you can eat to your heart's content of eight different items, including eggrolls, fried rice, soup, and entrees. Beer and wine are available.

The chef here will usually prepare dishes not listed on the menu if you ask. Golden Wok is open weekdays from noon to 10 p.m., on Saturday and Sunday from 3 to 10 p.m.

RANCHO LUNA: 1800 S. Main St., between Oakey and St. Louis Boulevards (tel. 384-4422).

What's a Cuban restaurant doing in Las Vegas? Quite nicely, thank you. Owner Manolo Gonzalez is a long way from home; he left his native country years ago and lived in numerous locales around the United States before settling happily here. Now he and his wife operate an establishment that is very much a family enterprise, with friendly and competent waiters and a core of regulars, both Hispanic and non.

The restaurant (whose name, incidentally, means "Moon Ranch") occupies a storefront about half a city block north of Vegas World. Front and center is the well-stocked bar. The dining area is divided into small sections with mirrored and wood-paneled walls, gold tablecloths, and brown napkins and seat cushions. A single silk rose adorns each table. Vertical blinds on the storefront windows filter out the brilliant sunlight by day, so the place is always cool and pleasantly muted.

Cuban cuisine, which resembles Mexican not at all, relies heavily on steaks and seafood, as well as those old standbys, rice and beans. If you want an appetizer, there's a choice of shrimp or lobster cocktail. Entrees range widely from Moros y Cristianos ("Moors and Christians"—black beans and white rice) with pork and yucca to a variety of steaks, to mariscada or zarsuela de mariscos (a melange of seafood including scallops, oysters, crab, lobster, and fish, in tomato or red wine sauce). Meals come complete with salad and tasty Cuban bread, all for $8 to $15. Also on the menu is a variety of Cuban-style sandwiches for $3 to $6. For dessert, be sure to try Rancho Luna's out-of-this-world flan (caramel custard).

Rancho Luna is open weekdays from noon to 2 a.m., on weekends from 1 p.m. to 2 a.m. Reservations are advised. It's a terrific place to get an introduction to Cuban cuisine.

THE GARDEN EATERY/OMELET HOUSE: 2150 W. Charleston, near Rancho Drive (tel. 384-6868).

This eatery, a little bit away from the Strip, has to be one of the best breakfast/lunch establishments in Las Vegas in terms of quality, quantity, and price. As you walk up to the restaurant, you may feel that you're about to enter the neighborhood sports book—no windows and a rather simple, down-home exterior. The interior is very rustic, with a bare ranch-house feeling: simple, unpolished wooden booths and tables, wall lights, simple hanging lamps. But let's get down to the basics. You can just have eggs with the usual accompaniments, or you can have them with Vienna/Polish sausage. But why? There are 36 omelets to choose from, three varieties of quiche, all from $2.75 to $5.50, including a real barn-burner, the Rio Grande Surfer, with chorizo sausage, onion, and cheddar plus 14 available add-ons. Those with a strong stomach and a sense of humor should look for the Flatlanders Special.

You're a traditionalist? Try the old-fashioned buttermilk pancakes; you can even have them with apples, bananas, or blueberries and whipped cream (so much for tradition). For the super-hearty eater, there's a Flap Special with two pieces of bacon or sausage, pancakes, and two eggs—all for $3.45.

On the other hand, if you arrive just in time for lunch, there's an assortment of absolutely delicious hamburgers served on fresh onion rolls (with pickle and fruit garnish), salads, homemade soups (with pumpkin-nut bread or another of your choice), chicken fingers, or homemade chili. The chili size contains over a third of a pound of lean ground chuck sprinkled with mixed cheeses and onions for $3.95; a cup is also available for $1.50. The big Italian beef sandwich for $4.25 is a winner: tender roast beef chunks simmered in Italian sauce (gravy, to you purists) and served on Italian bread and sprinkled with Jack cheese. The top price on the menu for any single item is $5.50 (with the exception of the Flatlanders Special). All drinks are of the "soft" variety, including a good selection of teas. For a great refresher, have their Freshen-Up, a delectable combination of orange juice, Fresca, and "special secret ingredients."

The Garden Eatery/Omelet House is open daily (except Thanksgiving and Christmas) from 7 a.m. to 3 p.m.

FLAKEY JAKE'S: 2870 S. Maryland Pkwy., near Vegas Valley (794-0900).

Don't leave Las Vegas without going to Flakey Jake's for a huge half-pound "build it yourself" hamburger on a sesame-seed bun that's been baked right there. If a hamburger bun could ever be called a work of art, this is it—they're also the tallest I've ever seen.

Entering Flakey Jake's is much like going into a spotlessly clean produce market with a bakery and meat store to one side. Boxed tomatoes, purple onions, bags of hamburger-bun mix, and vegetables are neatly stacked on pallets around the inside of Jake's. If you weren't hungry before, the fragrance of freshly baked bread and cookies will surely send your salivary glands into ecstatic anticipation. To your left an island of carts contains every conceivable addition for a sandwich. Meat for the hamburgers is ground in a glass-enclosed room on your right. Go up a couple of steps. On your left are tables with blue-and-white-checked cloths, and behind them is the cookie and baked-goods counter. But this is no austere supermarket: many tall ficus trees and hanging plants as well as latticework separate the three dining areas, and old movie posters decorate the walls. To the rear of the restaurant is an open kitchen.

You can get a half-pound (Big Jake) or a third-of-a-pound (Butcher's Choice) hamburger and stack it yourself from the condiment carts. You can order any of the seven "enhancers"—grilled onions, onion rings, chili, guacamole, and on. There's also a good selection of other sandwiches and "features." The charbroiled chicken sandwich is delicious, either with the lemon-pepper or teriyaki marinade. Flakey Jake's also serves the ultimate hot dog—a one-third pounder, charbroiled and served open-faced on a sesame-seed bun. My weakness is for the taco salad—a four-ounce portion of spicy taco meat on a bed of lettuce in a crisp, deep-fried flour tortilla. Or you can order one of Jake's Platters, like the top sirloin cooked to order and served with a baked potato or fries, side salad, and a dinner roll—a great buy for $7.25. Sandwiches, hamburgers, or tacos will cost $2.95 to $4.50.

Flakey Jake's serves draft beer by the mug or pitcher, as well as a good assortment of bottled beers, wines, and the usual soft beverages.

You can buy cookies, pies, and hamburger or hot dog buns to go. Flakey Jake's is open from 11 a.m. to 10 p.m. daily.

CHAPTER IV

A BIT ABOUT GAMBLING

□ □ □

Almost everyone thinks he might make a fortune gambling if only luck stays with him. This elusive dream keeps people coming back, trying out elaborate systems, reading books on how to beat the odds, betting excitedly with the house when a craps table gets hot, or casually dropping spare change into slot machines in the supermarkets during daily shopping.

From relatively small beginnings, gambling in Nevada has grown to be an enormous operation with gross revenue in 1985 totaling almost $3 billion, an increase of almost 5% over the previous year.

BUNK: According to casino managers and pit bosses, all systems are bunk. Which is not to say that somebody who, say, consistently backs the same number at roulette, or who always stands pat with two cards at blackjack, won't occasionally strike it lucky. But, for the most part, *systems as such just don't work,* and the only one that gives the casino cause for alarm is some gamblers' habit of doubling their stake each time they lose. This, however, is countered very simply by imposing a limit on the amount of the stake, usually $1,000 or less.

Cheats, Thieves, and Slugs

Of course, some people's idea of a system is to cheat, and by now Las Vegas dealers feel they've seen almost everything. In fact, any casino that hired amateur dealers would probably be out of business within months. The most common dodge is for a player to try to slip a little extra onto his stake when the dealer's attention is diverted (sometimes a gambler's confederate will deliberately create a diversion). Specially marked cards with identifying lettering that can be read through tinted spectacles have occasionally been slipped into the blackjack games, and shaved or weighted dice can be substituted for the original ones by a smooth crook. Dice at Caesars Palace have a little "C" printed inside to avoid such plays. It's supposed to be a secret, but you can see them almost from the far side of the room, if you keep your eyes peeled.

Play at the tables is conducted almost entirely with casino chips, and almost all the currency taken in is ostentatiously pushed through a slot in the table to fall into a locked box below. This, of course, has occasionally been a target for thieves. The boxes are removed to the counting room at the end of every shift, while play continues, and at one time the replacement box used to sit under the table waiting for its time to come. This system was changed when somebody was caught substituting a box with a false back to it from which the dealer could extract the proceeds.

Dealers, naturally, are always under supervision, not only by the pit boss in their immediate area and various plainclothes security men wandering randomly through the casino, but by strategically placed television cameras or overhead mirrors. For anyone who appreciates style, watching an old-hand blackjack dealer, seemingly bored but actually always alert, is a study in professionalism. Flipping each player a card, noting his own, scooping up lost stakes, paying the winners, and filing the used cards without a wasted motion or change of expression are a graceful exhibition of manual dexterity that bears absolutely no relationship to the outcome of the game itself.

Changes have come, though, and younger-generation dealers are more prevalent. On occasion, some tend to be flippant, which is appalling to serious gamblers. But pit bosses watch dealers closely, dressing them down during rest periods (like Marine DIs chewing out new recruits) if they get out of line. Stern rules are enforced, and those who don't follow them are replaced. And that's *that*.

Obviously there have been dishonest dealers too. Some have been caught palming money; others have slipped chips into a slit in their necktie. (In some casinos only bow ties are allowed now.) But they're allowed to take tips, as long as they signal the pit boss when they tuck one away, and sometimes, especially from a big winner, the tips are exorbitant. Cocktail waitresses have also known the joy of being tipped more for a drink than a case of scotch might cost.

Slot machines have been a frequent target for cheats. The counterpart of the gambler who paints casino chips to represent bigger value is the slot-machine player who uses slugs or Mexican coins. It's a very serious offense in Nevada (as is bad-check writing) and leads almost certainly to jail.

In attempts to beat the house, slot-machine adventurers have taken films of the spinning reels (now cameras are barred in the casinos), drilled holes into the front and sides, slipped a plastic "spoon" into the coin slot to keep it operating without depositing coins, tried to manipulate the reels with magnets and to jam the jackpot mechanism.

Slot machines fixed with anticheat devices are a certain money-maker for a casino if only because they can be fixed to pay off as much or as little as possible. Most casinos adjust them to pay back up to 90% of what they ingest, because the constant tinkling of jackpots is presumed to be what keeps the players playing. The downtown casinos supposedly pay off the most often, and anyplace whose machines get only casual and unrepeated visits, the least. Reputed to be even better than the downtown slots are those in the restaurants and bars where locals hang out. Owners of these establishments claim that locals won't play unless the slots are "loose."

SLOT HISTORY: The jackpot slot machine has an interesting history, having been devised by a young German inventor named Charles Frey while operating a saloon along San Francisco's Barbary Coast. His first model, the Liberty Bell (now preserved in a Reno saloon of the same name), ostensibly paid off in drinks, candy, or bubblegum, but actually delivered to the winner one coin for two horseshoes all the way up to ten coins for three bells. Even in Nevada, gambling was still illegal in those days (it became legal in 1867, three years after statehood; it was banned from 1900 until 1931, when it became legal again).

Some idea of how the slot-machine business has grown since then can be gleaned from the fact that each machine now earns its operator over $6,000 per year—with about $500 per machine going to pay local and federal taxes. Various different models have been tried, including one that worked on a push-button basis rather than a handle; this model was never very successful because, even though slot players know that they have no control over the machine whatsoever, they still like to pull a handle—which gives them the illusion that they're influencing where the reels will stop. The latest models print out electronic messages every time you pull the handle: "Good Luck," "Easy Come, Easy Go," "Happy Days Are Here Again," "Columbus Took A Chance," etc.

If you're interested in antique slot machines, the Maxim Hotel, 160 E. Flamingo Rd., has a museum of them, mostly dating from about the turn of the century.

. . . AND WALK AWAY: Although all casinos impose limits for bettors, it's possible to get much more money down as a stake than at first appears possible, if all the different variations are used. Which illustrates the first lesson to be learned about gambling: learn as much as possible about the game you're going to play. For additional lessons, see the next chapter.

If you're lucky, you'll never need any of the Alka-Seltzer that pit bosses always keep handy on a nearby table.

The most popular games in Nevada, judging by the licenses that have been issued, are blackjack, craps, and roulette, in that order. Before you head off to play them, and before I tell you where to take in a show between rolls of the dice, here are some pointers on how to play them. *Then* you can walk away. And, finally, in looking for the most action for your money—downtown gambling has lower minimums than the Strip.

CHAPTER V

HOW TO BET

□ □ □

If you're going to try your luck at gambling, do your homework before you put your money down. Gambling with the slots —about a third of Las Vegas visitors do it—requires no headwork other than to be aware that "one-arm bandits" usually pay back 75% to 95% of what you pump in. It's hardly what you'd call a winning return. Slot machines have been called "mechanical licenses to steal and cause bursitis at the same time." About half of the gambling group gravitates to the blackjack tables, and most of the remainder to craps, roulette, or poker.

IMPROVING THE ODDS: You need timing and luck to beat the odds, but you can improve your chances of winning at blackjack or craps, or even baccarat, by learning the right way to play the game. You'll enjoy it more and so will the other players at your table. Here are the basics:

1. Learn the rules *before* you go to the table.
2. Set a daily betting limit and stick with it.
3. Leave the game when you're ahead—many good players hold out for a 50% profit.
4. Don't play when you're tired.
5. Raise your bet when you're winning, not losing. Some blackjack aficionados say if you lose three times in a row, try another table.

There are thousands of systems sold for beating the house odds. It *may* be that some of them work; the question is, Which ones do?

In Las Vegas, the **Gambler's Book Club,** now in its 25th year, can sell you a book on almost every system devised to beat the odds. They're at 630 S. 11th St. (just off Charleston Boulevard),

Las Vegas, NV 89101 (tel. 382-7555, or toll free 800/
634-6243). It's the most specialized bookstore of its type and has,
on hand, over 1,000 different titles on virtually every game. For
the collector or researcher, the store is a treasure trove of out-of-
print works—they have about 4,000 titles.

The Gambler's Book Club is not truly a club. It looks more
like a Left Bank bookshop. The name was chosen because Edna
and John Luckman, the owners, wanted a spot where gamblers,
writers, researchers, mathematicians, and computer specialists
could meet and exchange information. It's the type of store
Damon Runyon (and Harry the Horse) would have loved. There
are two clerks who can give you on-the-spot expert advice on craps
and blackjack (which does say something about odds and probabilities).

In 1986 the Gambler's Book Club mailed out its one mil-
lionth catalog. (Did you ever doubt a national interest in gambling?) The catalog lists several hundred publications, with a
description of the contents of each, and is free for the asking. Just
write to the club at the address above or call. Hours are 9 a.m. to 5
p.m. Monday through Saturday. The Gambler's Book Club motto
is "Knowledge Is Protection," and it's truer than ever when it
comes to gambling.

Never be too timid at the tables to ask questions of dealers at
the casinos; they're advised to be pleasant, helpful, and instructive
to all players. If you should encounter an unhelpful dealer, move
to a more congenial table . . . or take your business to another casino. For gambling should be fun. And all the experts will tell you
to indulge in gambling only as a pleasant pastime.

To gamble or to imbibe in Las Vegas, the minimum age is 21.
Such sports aren't for kids, and in-town activities are, primarily,
for adults.

Schools

Special systems aside, a basic way to improve the odds is to
know both the game and the rules. Many of the large hotels have
free "gaming schools" where you can learn the intricacies of craps,
blackjack, roulette, and baccarat. Some also have poker schools. If
you're interested, ask the hotel when you call for information or
when you register. Or you can simply review the list below. The
list is up-to-date as of this writing, but it continues to expand as
more casinos recognize the advantage of helping gamblers to increase their comfort and confidence.

Now why do you suppose a casino would spend its time and

money to teach you the intricacies of gambling and betting? You're right! The house always has the edge.

Below is a list of casinos that do offer instruction, and the times the classes are held. It's a good idea to check first before going, even though advance registration is not necessary.

Flamingo Hilton: There are sessions in craps, blackjack, and roulette. Days and times are posted in the hotel. Lessons are conducted at the tables in the casino.

Four Queens: One-hour sessions on craps are held in the casino at 4 p.m. daily. Poker lessons are at 2 p.m. daily.

Frontier: Instruction on the basics of poker is given at 10:30 a.m. daily, except Sunday, in the Poker Room. Door prizes are given at each session.

Hacienda: Instruction is given in craps, blackjack, roulette, and keno, Monday through Friday, in the casino from 11 a.m. till noon.

Imperial Palace: Now here's the way to do it—the Imperial Palace has a minicasino on the fourth floor where lessons are given daily at 9 a.m. and 1 p.m. for blackjack and roulette, 11 a.m. and 3 p.m. for craps. Classes usually last over an hour and mock chips are used.

Las Vegas Hilton: Lessons are given in craps, blackjack, roulette, and baccarat in a special area of the casino. Classes are conducted Tuesday through Saturday; for times, call the hotel.

Riviera: Classes are conducted Monday through Friday from 10 a.m. to noon in the Le Bistro Bar. You're given instruction and gambling hints on craps, blackjack, and roulette.

Tropicana: Tuesday through Saturday, separate sessions are held on the most popular casino games. Roulette instruction is at 9:30 a.m., baccarat at 10:30 a.m., craps at 11:30 a.m. and 3 p.m., and blackjack at 1 p.m. Signs in the main casino will direct you to the instruction area.

CRAPS

Since this game is played with dice, this is as good a time as any, perhaps, to look into the manufacture of the cubes with the dots. It's a fascinating process.

Although attempts have repeatedly been made to manufacture dice from more recently developed plastics, those used in casinos are still made of celluloid. Cotton is the primary base.

The ingredients are combined to create a viscous red mass that is strained to reject impurities and then pressed and baked and delivered in inch-thick slabs to the Nevada Dice Company. After this, the 60-pound cellulose nitrate slabs start a one-year processing that begins with four months in the curing chambers. All this special attention is necessary to eliminate any possible instabilities that might show up later in the finished dice.

Cut into cubes slightly bigger than the finished size, the dice are hardened, buffed, and finally drilled with the requisite holes. Then a white resinous compound is applied to the sunken dots with a special brush.

In the final process, the dice are shaved down to the exact measurements (with a variability of only one ten-thousandth of an inch), then embossed and packed into boxes for delivery to the casinos. Most dice are kept in play for one day only, sometimes less, and used sets may be sold as souvenirs in hotel gift shops.

THE TABLE: The craps table is divided into marked areas (Pass, Come, Field, Big 6, Big 8, etc.), where you place your chips to bet. Here are a few simple directions:

Pass Line
A "Pass Line" bet pays even money. If the first roll of the dice adds up to 7 or 11, you win your bet; if the first roll adds up to 2, 3, or 12, you lose your bet. If any other number comes up, it's your "point." If you roll your point again you win, but if a 7 comes up again before your point is rolled, you lose.

Don't Pass Line
Betting on the "Don't Pass" is just the opposite of betting on the Pass Line. This time, you lose if a 7 or 11 is thrown on the first roll, and you win if a 2 or a 3 is thrown on the first roll. If the first roll is 12, however, it's a stand-off, and nobody wins. If none of these numbers is thrown and you have a point instead, in order to win, a 7 will have to be thrown before the point comes up again. A "Don't Pass" bet also pays even money.

Come
Betting on "Come" is just the same as betting on the Pass Line, but you must bet *after* the first roll, or on any following roll. Again, you'll win on 7 or 11 and lose on 2, 3, or 12. Any other number is your point, and you win if your point comes up again before a 7.

Don't Come
This is the opposite of a "Come" bet. Again, you wait until after the first roll to bet. A 7 or 11 means you lose; a 2 or 3 means you win; 12 is a stand-off and nobody wins. You win if 7 comes up

DEALER   DEALER

BOXMAN

STICKMAN

THE CRAPS TABLE

before the point (the point, you'll recall, was the first number rolled if it was none of the above).

Field

This is a bet for one roll only. The "Field" consists of seven numbers: 2, 3, 4, 9, 10, 11, and 12. If any of these numbers is thrown on the next roll, you win even money, except on 2 and 12 which pay two to one.

Big 6 and 8

A "Big 6 and 8" bet pays even money. You win if either a 6 or an 8 is rolled before a 7.

Any 7

An "Any 7" bet pays the winner five to one. If a 7 is thrown on the first roll after you bet, you win.

"Hard Way" Bets

In the middle of a craps table are pictures of several possible dice combinations together with the odds the bank will pay you if you bet on any of those combinations being thrown. For example, if 8 is thrown by having a 4 appear on each die, and you bet on it, the bank will pay eight for one; if 4 is thrown by having a 2 appear on each die, and you bet on it, the bank will pay eight for one; if 3 is thrown, the bank pays fifteen for one, etc., etc. You win at the odds quoted if the *exact* combination of numbers you bet on comes up. But you lose if either a 7 is rolled, or if the number you bet on was rolled any other way than the "Hard Way" shown on the table. In-the-know gamblers tend to avoid "Hard Way" bets as an easy way to lose your money.

Any Craps
Here you're lucky if the dice "crap-out"—if they show 2, 3, or 12 on the first roll after you bet. If this happens, the bank pays eight to one. Any other number is a loser.

Place Bets
You can make a "Place Bet" on any of the following numbers: 4, 5, 6, 8, 9, and 10. You're betting that the number you choose will be thrown before a 7 is thrown. If you win, the payoff is as follows: 4 or 10 pays at the rate of nine to five; 5 or 9 pays at the rate of seven to five; 6 or 8 pays at the rate of seven to six. "Place Bets" can be removed at any time before a roll.

SOME PROBABILITIES: Because each die has six sides numbered from 1 to 6—and craps is played with a pair of dice—the probability of throwing certain numbers has been studied carefully. Professionals have employed complex mathematical formulas in searching for the answers. And computers have data-processed curves of probability.

Simplified, however, suffice it to say that 7 (a crucial number in craps) will be thrown more frequently than any other number over the long run, for there are six possible combinations that make 7, when you break down the 1 to 6 possibilities on each separate die. As to the total possible number of combinations on the dice, there are 36.

Comparing the 36 possible combinations, numbers—or point combinations—run as follows:

2 and 12 may be thrown in *1 way only*
3 and 11 may be thrown in *2 ways*
4 and 10 may be thrown in *3 ways*
5 and 9 may be thrown in *4 ways*

6 and 8 may be thrown in *5 ways*
7 may be thrown in *6 ways*

So 7 has an advantage over all other combinations, which, over the long run, is in favor of the casino. You can't beat the law of averages. Players, however, often have winning streaks—a proven fact in ESP studies, etc.—and that's when the experts advise that it's wise to increase the size of bets. But when a losing streak sets in, stop playing!

KENO

This popular game is one of the oldest known games of chance. Its origin is Chinese, and it dates back to the time before Christ, when it was operated as a national lottery in China. Legend has it that funds acquired from the game were used to finance construction of the Great Wall of China.

Keno first was introduced into the U.S. in the 1800s by railroad construction workers from China. Looking at a keno ticket, you'll notice that it's divided horizontally into two rectangles, and that the upper one contains the numbers 1 through 40; the lower half, the numbers 41 through 80.

Chinese tradition designates the upper area as Yin and the lower as Yang; and this, in Chinese lore, compares to other great opposites—night and day, for example, or heaven and earth, sun and moon, man and woman. Significantly, the Chinese believe that anything of importance occurring during the night should influence them to play in the first 40 squares, that any bad happening suggests that the lower rectangle be played.

Although the house percentage is greater than in any other game played in the casinos in Las Vegas, it's a sit-down game, offering a place to socialize with fellow players over a cool drink. Keno and Bingo are the only two casino games where people have a chance to strike up a conversation between plays.

You can also play keno while enjoying free casino lounge shows, most of which provide first-rate entertainment. If you're playing keno during the show, drinks are on the house, so you might as well spend your money on keno tickets; if you don't, you'll spend the same money on booze.

Keno is easy to play and you can win a maximum of $50,000. Each ticket consists of a series of numbered boxes and you can mark up to 15 of the numbers and bet anything from $1 up. Then the game begins, and you compare the numbers, as they light up on the keno board, with the spots you have marked on your ticket.

After 20 numbers have appeared on the board, if you're lucky, you may have won (depending on the number of spots you marked compared to those on the board—usually three or more will win). Winners must claim their winnings before the next game begins; if you're one of the winners, head for the cashier. A new game starts every few minutes, and helpful keno personnel will answer any questions you might have. They are also able to show you the best ways of marking a ticket and possibly improving your bet. (Every keno writer has his or her own "system.")

BLACKJACK OR "21"

The dealer starts the game by dealing each player two cards. In some casinos they're dealt to the player face up, or one down and one up, or both down, but the dealer always gets one card up and one card down. Everybody plays against the dealer. The object is to get a total of 21, or as close to it as possible. All face cards count as 10; all other number cards except aces count as their number value. An ace may be counted as 1 or 11, whichever you choose it to be.

Starting at his left, the dealer gives additional cards to the players who wish to draw (be "hit"), or none to a player who wishes to "stand" or "hold." If your count is nearer to 21 than the dealer's, you win. If it's under the dealer's, you lose. Ties are a stand-off and nobody wins. After each player is satisfied with his count, the dealer exposes his face-down card. If his two cards total 16 or less, he must "hit" (draw an additional card) until he reaches 17 or over. If the dealer's total goes over 21, he must pay all the players whose hands have not gone "bust" before him. It is important to note here that the blackjack dealer has no choice as to whether he should stay or draw. His decisions are predetermined and known to all the players at the table.

HOW TO PLAY: Here are eight "rules" for blackjack.

1. Place the amount of money you want to bet on the table.
2. Look at the first two cards the dealer starts you with. If your hand adds up to the total you prefer, place your cards *under your bet money*, indicating that you don't wish any additional cards. If you elect to draw an additional card, you tell the dealer to "hit" you by making a sweeping motion with your cards, or point to your open hand (watch your fellow players).
3. If your count goes over 21, you go "bust" and lose—even if the dealer also goes "bust" afterward. Unless hands are dealt face up, *you then turn your hand face up on the table.*
4. If you make 21 in your first two cards (any picture card or

10 with an ace), you've got blackjack. *You expose your winning hand immediately,* and you collect 1½ times your bet—unless the dealer has blackjack too, in which case it's a stand-off and nobody wins.

5. If you find a "pair" in your first two cards (two 4s or two 10s, etc.) you may "split" the pair into two hands and treat each card as the first card dealt in two separate hands. *Turn the pair face up on the table,* place the original bet on one of these cards, then place an equal amount on the other card. *Split aces are limited to a one-card draw on each.*

6. If your first two cards total 11 or under, you may, if you choose, double your original bet and make a one-card draw. *Turn your hand face up,* and you'll receive one more card face down.

7. Anytime the dealer deals himself an ace for his "up" card, you may insure your hand against the possibility that his hole card is a face card, which would give him an automatic blackjack. To insure, you place an amount equal to one-half of your bet on the "Insurance" line. If the dealer does have a blackjack, you do not lose, even though he has your hand beat, and you keep your bet and your insurance money. If he does not have a blackjack, he takes your insurance money and play continues in the normal fashion.

8. *Remember!* The dealer *must* stand on 17 or more, and *must* hit a hand of 16 or less.

PROFESSIONAL TIPS: Advice of the experts in playing blackjack is as follows:

1. *Do not* ask for an extra card if you have a count of 17, 18, 19, 20, or 21 in your cards, no matter what the dealer has showing in his "up" card.

2. *Do not* ask for an extra card when you have 13, 14, 15, 16, or more . . . *if* the dealer has a 2, 3, 4, 5, or 6 showing in his "up" card.

3. *Do* ask for an extra card or more when you have a count of 13 through 16 in your hand . . . if the dealer's "up" card is a 7, 8, 9, 10, or ace.

There's a lot more to blackjack-playing strategy than the above, of course. So consider this merely as the bare bones of the game.

A Final Tip

One more point: Avoid insurance bets; they're sucker bait!

ROULETTE

Roulette is an extremely easy game to play, and it's really very colorful and exciting to watch. The wheel spins and the little ball bounces around, finally dropping into one of the slots, numbered 1 to 36, plus 0 and 00. You can bet on a single number, a combination of numbers, or red or black, odd or even. If you're lucky, you can win as much as 35 to 1 (see the table). The method of placing single-number bets, column bets, and others is fairly obvious. The dealer will be happy to show you how to "straddle" two or more numbers and make many other interesting betting combinations. Each player is given different-colored chips so it's easy to follow the numbers you're on.

A number of typical bets is indicated by means of letters on the adjoining roulette layout. The winning odds for each of these sample bets are listed opposite. These bets can be made on any corresponding combinations of numbers.

Roulette Chart Key	Odds	Type of Bet
		Straight Bets
A	35 to 1	*Straight-up:* All numbers, plus 0 and 00.
B	2 to 1	*Column Bet:* Pays off on any number in that horizontal column.
C	2 to 1	*First Dozen:* Pays off on any number 1 through 12. Same for second and third dozen.
D	Even money	
		Combination Bets
E	17 to 1	*Split:* Pays off on 11 or 12.
F	11 to 1	Pays off on 28, 29, or 30.
G	8 to 1	*Corner:* Pays off on 17, 18, 20, or 21.
H	6 to 1	Pays off on 0, 00, 1, 2, or 3.
I	5 to 1	Pays off on 22, 23, 24, 25, 26 or 27.

BACCARAT

The ancient game of baccarat—or chemin de fer—is played with eight decks of cards. Firm rules apply and there is no skill involved other than deciding whether to bet on the bank or the player. Any beginner can play, but check the betting minimum before you sit down. The cards are shuffled by the croupier and then placed in a box which is called the "Shoe."

Players may act as banker or play against the bank at any time. Two cards are dealt from the Shoe and given to the player who has the largest wager against the bank, and two cards are dealt to the

ROULETTE CHART

croupier acting as banker. If the rule calls for a third card (see rules on chart below), the player or banker, or both, must take the third card. In the event of a tie, the hand is dealt over.

The object of the game is to come as close as possible to the number 9. To score the hands, the cards of each hand are totaled and the *last digit* is used. All cards have face value. For example: 10 plus 5 equal 15 (score is 5); 10 plus 4 plus 9 equal 23 (score is 3); 4 plus 3 plus 3 equal 10 (score is 0); 4 plus 3 plus 2 equal 9 (score is 9); etc. The closest hand to 9 wins.

Each player gets a chance to deal the cards. The Shoe passes to the player on the right each time the bank loses. If the player wishes, he may pass the Shoe at any time.

Note: When you bet on the bank and the bank wins, you are charged a 5% commission. This must be paid at the start of a new game or when you leave the table.

Player's Hand

Having	
0-1-2-3-4-5	Must draw a third card
6-7	*Must stand*
8-9	Natural. Banker cannot draw

Having	Banker's Hand Draws	Does Not Draw
	When giving Player 3rd card of:	When giving Player 3rd card of:
3	1-2-3-4-5-6-7-9-10	8
4	2-3-4-5-6-7	1-8-9-10
5	4-5-6-7	1-2-3-8-9-10
6	6-7	1-2-3-4-5-8-9-10
7	*Must Stand*	
8-9	Natural. Player cannot draw	

If the player takes no third card, the banker must stand on 6. No one draws against a natural 8 or 9.

BIG SIX

Big Six is a fun game and can be easily spotted by the giant vertical Big Six wheel and the carnival-barker patter of the person spinning it. The game provides pleasant recreation and involves no study or effort. The wheel has 56 positions on it, 54 of them marked by bills from $1 to $20 denomination. The other two spots are jokers, and each pays 40 to 1 if the wheel stops in that position.

All other stops pay at face value. Those marked with $20 bills pay 20 to 1; the $5 bills pay 5 to 1; etc.

SPORTS BOOKS

Most of the larger hotels in Las Vegas have sports book operations—looking much like commodities-futures trading boards. In some, almost as large as theaters, you can comfortably sit and watch ball games, fights, and, at some casinos, horse races on huge TV screens. To add to your enjoyment, there's usually a deli/bar nearby that serves sandwiches, hot dogs, soft drinks, and beer. As a matter of fact, some of the best sandwiches in Las Vegas are served next to the sports books.

Sports books take bets on virtually every sport, with the exception of the most fascinating sport of all—presidential elections. The majority of books I've listed below take bets on racing, but I've noted those that do not.

On the Strip there are sports books at the Aladdin, Bally's–Las Vegas, Caesars Palace, Circus Circus, Flamingo Hilton (sports only), Frontier Hotel, Holiday Casino (sports only), Las Vegas Hilton, Riviera Hotel, Sahara Hotel, Sands Hotel, Stardust Hotel, Tropicana (sports only), and Vegas World. Downtown, they'll take your bet at El Cortez Hotel, the Fremont Hotel, and Union Plaza.

TOURING THE STRIP CASINOS AND NIGHTSPOTS

□ □ □

The Las Vegas Strip is a postwar phenomenon, which means that the oldest structures are less than 45 years of age, and renovations, additions, and improvements are proceeding so constantly that, in actuality, even the original casino-hotels are among the sleekest and most modern to be found anywhere.

Structurally, most establishments on the Strip are very similar: a plush lobby opening off the street, with hotel reception desk tucked away to the left or right past the casino; a minuscule lounge; the open casino area encircled by various restaurants (always including a 24-hour coffeeshop); a theater/lounge offering almost round-the-clock entertainment; and the hotel gift shop, which is invariably stocked with such tourist-oriented merchandise as nudie playing cards, beer-stein radios, scrubbed decks of cards from the casino, slot-machine saving banks, clocks with dice as numbers, books on how to gamble, and the usual selection of cigarettes, candy, newspapers, and magazines.

THE CASINOS: The casino activities are almost identical in every hotel: banks of slot machines accepting both coins and, in some cases, dollar bills . . . a few roulette tables . . . three or more craps tables loosely linked together to form an enclosed area between them, where the "pit boss" stands watching the dealers . . .

many tables for blackjack . . . a keno lounge (keno is like Bingo) with rows of seats for the players . . . and, often in a roped-off corner with spectators, a baccarat game or two where thousands of dollars might change hands in a single play.

Cocktail waitresses circulate constantly; if you want service, ask the dealer to help you. It's the understandable policy of most casinos to bring gamblers free drinks, but do remember to tip ("toke") the waitress.

A Warning

However tempted you might be, don't start taking photographs of the gaming action. All casinos have strict rules about cameras, both for security and some guests' wish for anonymity, and the guards enforce them promptly. There are many aspects to security, incidentally, and as you'll soon discover, not only the men in uniform (some wearing sidearms) are keeping an eye on things. Informally dressed hotel employees wander around discreetly, and their observations are supplemented by overhead television monitors or one-way mirrors in the ceiling above the gaming tables.

THE LOUNGES AND SHOWROOMS: Surrounding the casino area are invariably at least a couple of bar-lounges, often with high-caliber entertainment. In the bigger hotels this may be a name star who inexplicably resents being described as a "lounge performer" despite the fact that he or she might be pulling in thousands of dollars per week for playing three or four shows a day, and despite the fact that these so-called lounges may accommodate as many as 600 or 700 people. The lounge policy in some hotels is to allow free admission but to insist on a two-drink minimum, with drinks costing from $2.50 to $4 apiece, depending on the show.

Most lounges keep their draperies open during the show so that nearby gamblers can play the slots and watch the show at the same time. The lounges that shut off the view are, of course, the ones with the top shows.

The big showrooms almost all have the same policy, which is to stage a dinner show at approximately 8 p.m., with dinner costing about $20 to $50 per person, minimum, depending on the performer. No tickets are issued, but reservations must be made. For the dinner show, arrive about an hour and a half early so you'll have time to finish eating before the entertainment begins. At the late show, generally starting between 11 p.m. and midnight, you get two to four drinks instead of dinner; in most cases, at either show, a tip to the maître d' is necessary if you want really good seats.

Occasionally, on weekends or holidays or when a superstar is booked, there might also be a third show at 2:30 a.m. In any case, there's always a late show playing in one of the lounges for people who like to stay up late. And in Las Vegas, visitors always do.

THE EXTRAVAGANZAS: Many major hotels have taken to staging or importing complete "extravaganzas"—either reruns of proven Broadway successes or lavish musicals such as the Tropicana's *Folies Bergère,* the Stardust's *Lido de Paris,* the Flamingo's *City Lites,* or Bally's *Jubilee.* Such shows cost a fortune to mount, but the costs are amortized over the two—and sometimes ten—years that such shows can run. Considering that a hotel offering regular talent changes might pay as much as $500,000 per week for performers' salaries, it's clear that even an initial investment of $5 million for a two-year show ends up as an economy!

The semipermanent productions, incidentally, are very imaginative with their theatrical effects: curtains of rain between audience and performers . . . film credits on giant screens onstage . . . artificial fog drifting into the proscenium . . . galloping horses . . . live camels and elephants parading through a desert oasis and nude nymphs swimming in a "mirage" pool . . . fountains and waterfalls . . . fires and hurricanes . . . and bare-breasted chorines with safety belts who descend smoothly from the ceiling on circular pedestals.

Veteran producer Frank Sennes is an outstanding name in local show-business circles. After two decades of planning Strip productions, in 1958 he started the trend to foreign imports by booking the *Lido de Paris* show and combining it with sound-and-light effects that the French edition had never dreamed of. Frederic Apcar has gone even further, imaginatively, in this direction.

THE HOURS: The gambling, unlike the entertainment—which takes a breather for a few hours a day!—continues all the time. It's just as easy to find action at four or five in the morning as it is at five in the afternoon. The hotels and casinos are open 24 hours a day.

AN EXPLANATION: What follows is a rundown on the establishments along the Strip; it's basically a nightlife guide, of course, but because most of the lounge acts start early in the afternoon, the concept of nightlife per se almost doesn't exist in this town without clocks.

LAS VEGAS
DOWNTOWN HOTELS

1. Union Plaza
2. Nevada
3. Mint
4. Horseshoe
5. Golden Nugget
6. Fremont
7. Four Queens
8. Gold Spike
9. Fitzgerald's
10. Ogden House
11. El Cortez
12. Western
13. Showboat

Bear in mind that while most people think of the Strip first for entertainment, the Golden Nugget (downtown) features some of the greatest headliners in show business—Dolly Parton, Dionne Warwick, Kenny Rogers, Harry Belafonte, Melissa Manchester.

Please keep in mind that I've already described most of these famous hotels in Chapter II. There, however, my interest was in finding a place to stay. Here I'll deal with the "hotel-as-sightseeing-attraction-in-itself," with its casinos, theater nightclubs, and other entertainment facilities.

NIGHTSPOTS ON THE STRIP

BALLY'S–LAS VEGAS: Bally's–Las Vegas, on the Strip at 3645 Las Vegas Blvd. (tel. 739-4111), as befitting its super-colossal image, has not one but two major showrooms: the plush 1,400-seat **Celebrity Room** for superstar entertainment, and the **Ziegfeld Room,** an 1,100-seat entertainment palace used for the super-spectacular *Jubilee.*

The Celebrity Room's opening-night mega-star was Dean Martin, who played to a full house of VIP invited guests. He's still among Bally's stable of stars, along with Tom Jones, Frank Sinatra, Sammy Davis, Jr., and Jerry Lewis, among others.

In the Ziegfeld Room, Donn Arden's *Jubilee* replaced the famed *Hallelujah Hollywood.* The latter ran from 1974 to 1981 with a full house every night, and so far *Jubilee* is equally popular. In fact, it's a good idea to reserve your tickets when you reserve your room. *Jubilee* has a cast of more than 100 gorgeous showgirls, many of them ostrich-plumed, bespangled, and often bare-breasted. It glorifies Hollywood movies and entertainers of the last 50 years, pays a tribute to Elvis, re-creates the scene from *Samson and Delilah* in which the temple falls, shows the sinking of the *Titanic,* and includes a World War I dogfight in the air. The theater is equipped with every known theatrical device and moving stages. The costumes were designed by Bob Mackie.

Dinner shows in the Celebrity Room cost about $30 to $50 (depending on what you order), $25 to $40 for midnight shows (depending on the performer), those prices including three drinks.

Jubilee has cocktail shows only at 7:30 and 11 p.m.; there are three shows on Saturday, none on Wednesday. They're priced at $27.50 and include three drinks.

Bally's also offers a nostalgic trip into cinema history at the Bally's Theatre, where Hollywood classics are screened; viewers enjoy the comfort of lounge seating and love seats. It's like seeing a movie in the comfort of a Hollywood screening room.

CAESARS PALACE: From its opening over 20 years ago, Caesars Palace, on the Strip at 3570 Las Vegas Blvd. (tel. 731-7110), has been a tremendous hit. And the most illustrious of stars have appeared regularly in its 1,200-seat showroom, the **Circus Maximus**. In the past the room has been used for long-running Broadway hits like *Fiddler on the Roof* and *The Odd Couple*. These days it's one of the few places still offering big-name entertainment only.

The galaxy of stars at Caesars includes Wayne Newton, Diana Ross, Joan Rivers, Julio Iglesias, Willie Nelson, George Burns, Paul Anka, Tom Jones, Rodney Dangerfield, and the Pointer Sisters. The room is decorated in Roman motif (natch), its plush royal-purple booths fashioned after ancient chariots. Every seat in the tiered room, which has no pillars or posts, affords a clear view.

There are no dinner shows at the Circus Maximus, only cocktail shows at 8:30 and 11:30 p.m.; closed Tuesday. Admission is usually $25 to $50, depending on the performer; drinks are often included in the price.

Another entertainment facility at Caesars is **Cleopatra's Barge,** which floats on the "Nile," five feet deep, drawing 3½ feet of water when loaded. It's off one of the hotel's wide corridors. The barge has oars (though no galley slaves man them), ostrich-feather fans, statues of the ancient pharaohs, sails (furled), and a canopied royal box where the queen supposedly entertained her Roman friends. There's a seating on the main barge, aboard two adjacent lesser craft, and on the dock. Hydraulic mechanisms rock the barge and attendant craft gently; you board via gangplanks. A small legion of Nubian-inspired waitresses—in diaphanous minitoga costumes—are on duty. A dockside fence had to be constructed, though, to keep awestruck sightseers from falling into the "Nile."

There's a live band for dancing playing nightly from 9:30 p.m. to 4:30 a.m., and they're really good. No reservations are required and there's no cover, just a two-drink minimum.

Newest entertainment facility at Caesars is the innovative **Omnimax Theatre,** housed in a geodesic dome with 380 seats that recline 27° and a wrap-around screen for thrilling special effects. Omnimax films allow the viewer to travel in space, under the sea, inside an atom, or through time itself. The screen explodes with glorious color and movement; you'll find yourself gripping your seat and actually feeling dizzy, though you haven't moved at all. The awesome visual effects are enhanced aurally by a six-track stereophonic "sensaround" sound system emanating from 16 behind-the-screen speakers and 56 additional speakers under the theater seats. At night, the exterior of the Omnimax dome is used to project a light show visible from the Strip. Recent offerings have included *Niagara—Miracles, Myths, and Magic,* featuring everything from a wild ride down the rapids to a high-wire crossing above the Niagara Gorge. The film also takes a historical look at the legends and tourism long associated with the Niagara River and the falls. The story of Niagara has alternated with *Speed,* an Omnimax production about man's attack on velocity, from primitive times through to supersonic jets and space travel. Caesars Omnimax Theatre has also been home to the magnificent story of the *Grand Canyon—the Hidden Secrets;* and to *To Fly,* a paean to the exhilaration of flight.

There are continuous hourly showings from 11 a.m. to midnight. Admission is $5 for adults, $4 for kids under 12. Don't miss this unique entertainment.

LAS VEGAS HILTON: With the construction of the International Hotel, which later became the Las Vegas Hilton, 3000 Paradise Rd., at the Convention Center (tel. 732-5111), millionaire Kirk Kerkorian opened up what still is, even with name change and new management, a "Strip" unto itself. So huge is the 3,174-room hotel, in fact, that it almost seems a separate town all on its own.

Barbra Streisand was hired to kick off the first couple of weeks of the Hilton's 2,000-seat **Hilton Showroom** for something around $100,000 a week. An eye-popping variety of superstar headliners adds to the hotel's reputation for top-drawer entertainment. Current stars in the Hilton galaxy include Bill Cosby, Wayne Newton, Engelbert Humperdinck, Dionne Warwick, and Gladys Knight.

An unusual aspect of the showroom is a 400-seat mezzanine cocktail lounge, which for the first time in Vegas allows patrons to watch dinnertime shows even if they've eaten earlier or intend to dine later. The 8 p.m. show will set you back about $25 to $40 per person; the 11:30 p.m. show, including two drinks, costs $20 to $25.

There's more nightly entertainment in the Hilton's **Casino Lounge,** featuring live entertainment and dancing from 8 p.m. to 3 a.m.

And then there's the spectacular **Hilton Center Amphitheatre,** which hosts world-championship fights and very special concert appearances. The multitalented Eddie Murphy made his first Las Vegas appearance at the Hilton Amphitheatre and packed them in. As you might expect, prices at the Amphitheatre vary considerably, depending on the event and the performer.

THE DESERT INN: The Desert Inn, on the Strip at 3145 Las Vegas Blvd. (tel. 733-4444), was totally revamped some years back. Today it's the classiest hotel on the Strip, with a glamorous casino and first-rate facilities of every kind.

Its showplace is the **Crystal Room,** where Frank Sinatra once played in the early days; Danny Kaye, Phil Harris, and Noël Coward were also associated with DI shows. Later, the hotel followed the trend to spectaculars, featuring advanced lighting effects, dazzling feathered and sequined costumes, etc.

Beginning in 1985 the DI went back to big-name entertainment with stars like Sammy Davis, Jr., Bobby Vinton, Tony Orlando, Juliet Prowse, the Smothers Brothers, and Crystal Gayle.

There are cocktail shows (with two drinks) only at 8 and 11 p.m. Tickets usually cost $25 per person every night except Friday and Saturday, when they are $30. Prices depend on the performer. The Crystal Room's moderate size (it seats over 600) affords the entire audience a reasonable view of the show. There is no show on Monday.

There's high-quality entertainment, too (a pianist or combo from 2 p.m. to 4 a.m.), in the **Raffles Bar,** a deluxe Victorian/British Colonial lounge with rattan furnishings, red velvet curtains suspended from brass posts, potted palms, and slowly rotating fans overhead. No cover or minimum.

THE STARDUST: The Stardust, on the Strip at 3000 Las Vegas Blvd. South (tel. 732-6111), was responsible for the first big show to be brought intact from abroad—the *Lido de Paris* revue, imported by veteran Las Vegas producer Frank Sennes in 1958. The show is full of beautiful dancers, and artifices such as a live elephant onstage, dozens of doves released over the audience's heads, a fire, ice-skating rinks, and waterfalls worked into the plot. Now joining the *Lido* is the award-winning comedy of Bobby Berosini and His Orangutans. These apes have appeared on stage, screen, and TV.

More than 13 million people have seen the *Lido* show at the Stardust's 1,300-seat **Café Continental** so far, and, with annual changes, it looks as if it might run forever. Two shows nightly are at 7 and 11 p.m. All are cocktail shows, with two drinks, priced at $25. No shows on Tuesday.

In addition, the **Starlite Lounge** provides live entertainment from 8 p.m. to 2 a.m.

THE FLAMINGO HILTON: The Flamingo Hilton, on the Strip at 3555 Las Vegas Blvd. South (tel. 733-3111), has presented some of the all-time greats over the years—among them Judy Garland, Louis Armstrong, Jack Benny, and Lena Horne—and provided an early showcase for such up-and-coming performers as Richard Pryor, the Smothers Brothers, Charo, Flip Wilson, Wayne Newton, and Tom Jones. In the 1950s the opening act for Mickey Rooney was the Will Mastin Trio, which featured a young multitalented dynamo named Sammy Davis, Jr. Since Jimmy Durante's name christened its marquee in 1946, the Flamingo's vocal offerings have ranged from Don Ho to Ray Charles, its comedy acts from Harpo Marx to Lenny Bruce. The late Totie Fields made her Las Vegas debut at the Flamingo as an opening act for Trini Lopez. It's a hotel with an impressive entertainment history, of which the above is only the tiniest glimmer.

In recent years the Flamingo, like many Vegas hotels, has gone the spectacular route with *City Lites,* a show packed with gorgeous showgirls, singers, dancers, and ice skaters. It offers a parade of music from *Over the Rainbow,* ice ballet to rousing country songs, an Oriental fantasy segment, and a grand finale featuring show tunes from *New York, New York* and *42nd Street.* Tickets for the dinner show (at 7:45 p.m. nightly) start at $22.95. The 11 p.m. cocktail show is $17.95, including two drinks. There's no show on Sunday.

There's also continuous entertainment nightly 8 p.m. to 4:30 a.m. in **Casino Lounge,** where disco alternates with lounge acts. No cover; there's a two-drink minimum on weekends only.

THE TROPICANA: When the Tropicana, on the Strip at 3801 Las Vegas Blvd. South (tel. 739-2222), first opened in 1957, it competed with everyone else for the superstars, but in 1959 it imported the famous *Folies Bergère,* and this lavish show, with annual changes, has filled the hotel's **Tiffany Theatre** ever since. (Its Paris counterpart has been going for over a century!) The show never fails to dazzle audiences with its magnificent costumes and splendor, ambitious technical gimmicks, and the semi-nude chorus line that extends around three sides of the vast theater. The 32nd anniversary edition of the *Folies* celebrates American music, with numbers featuring such all-American products as blues and boogie.

The dinner show, with entrees priced from $27.50 to $40,

starts at 8 p.m., the late show ($22.50, including two drinks) at 11 p.m. There is no performance on Thursday.

Another Tropicana entertainment facility is the **Atrium Lounge** overlooking the shopping plaza. Here singers perform from 4:30 p.m. to 3:30 a.m. in a glittering marble-and-brass gazebo fashioned after a Parisian bandstand.

THE RIVIERA: The Riviera, on the Strip at 2901 Las Vegas Blvd. South (tel. 734-5110), has long offered top-flight entertainment in its vast and elegant **Versailles Theatre.** Liberace, candelabra and all, was on hand for the gala opening of the Riviera on April 18, 1955. (In 1960 his opening act was a new singer named Barbra Streisand.) Appearances have also been made by top stars like Dolly Parton, Barry Manilow, Kenny Rogers, Liza Minelli, Joan Rivers, Shirley MacLaine, and Diana Ross.

Currently running at the Versailles Theatre is *Splash,* an aquacade spectacular with the guest comedy star, Joey Villa. It's a great family show with diving and swimming stars, mermaids, dancers, and showgirls.

The dinner show begins at 8 p.m. nightly, with prices ranging upward from $24.50, including a buffet and two drinks. There's also an 11 p.m. cocktail show, which costs $19.50. Closed Wednesday.

At the **Mardi Gras Plaza** is a brilliant and long-running revue, *An Evening at La Cage,* starring a bevy of female impersonators. It's clever, hilarious, and thoroughly enjoyable. The production is spectacular with its beautiful costuming and dance numbers. Shows are at 7, 9, and 11 p.m., and the $15 admission includes a buffet or two drinks. Closed Tuesday.

THE DUNES: Until recently, the Dunes, on the strip at 3650 Las Vegas Blvd. South (tel. 737-4110), like many other hotels, had forsaken star entertainment for one show.

Currently, the **Casino Theatre** features *The Comedy Store,* a riotously funny revue from its Los Angeles namesake.

There are two cocktail shows nightly, at 9 and 11:30 p.m. (closed Monday), on Saturday at 8, 10 and midnight. They cost $14.50 per person, including two drinks.

There's also nightly entertainment in the **Casino Lounge** from 8 p.m. to 3:30 a.m. No cover or minimum. And at the **Oasis,** musical groups perform from noon to 4:15 a.m.

THE SANDS HOTEL & CASINO: The Sands, on the Strip at

3355 Las Vegas Blvd. South (tel. 733-5000), represents glamour to thousands of people who've never even been to Las Vegas. Maybe it's because of Frank Sinatra's long-time association with the place—now ended—and maybe it's because of the shrewd promotion and advertising all over the world. And to add to the glamour, the Sands is now reported to be owned by the legendary Kirk Kerkorian.

At the hotel's famed **Copa Room,** Dionne Warwick, Shecky Greene, Alan King, Jerry Vale, Doc Severinsen, Rita Moreno, Wayland Flowers and Madame, Foster Brooks, Anthony Newley, Joan Rivers, Tony Bennett, David Brenner, and Debbie Reynolds have all appeared.

There are cocktail shows six nights a week in the Copa Room; it's closed Monday. The times of the show and the price (with cocktails) vary with the featured entertainer. Obviously, the best idea is to call well in advance of the date you might like to go.

The Sands also has live entertainment nightly in the **Winners Circle Lounge,** just off the casino, from 5 to 11 p.m. Sunday, 6 p.m. to midnight Monday, 5 p.m. to 1 a.m. Tuesday through Thursday, and 4 p.m. to 3 a.m. Friday and Saturday.

THE SAHARA: When the Sahara, on the Strip at the corner of Las Vegas Boulevard and Sahara Avenue (tel. 737-2111), was first built in 1952, it was regarded as being out of town. Today it's at the top of the Strip, at a major intersection between the Convention Center, downtown Las Vegas, and the remainder of the Strip hotels.

The Sahara's **Congo Theatre** combines hits from Broadway with headliners. Currently, *Ain't Misbehavin'* is featured. The Congo Theatre offers two cocktail shows nightly, usually at 8 and 11 p.m. Prices vary, depending on the show. And quite a variety it is—appearances have been made by Don Rickles, George Carlin, Redd Foxx, and Mel Tillis.

The Sahara's **Casbah Room** has been famous for star lounge shows. Entertainment is from 6 p.m. to 4 a.m.

THE HACIENDA HOTEL: The Hacienda, on the Strip at 3950 Las Vegas Blvd. South (tel. 739-8911), is either the first hotel on the Strip or the last, depending on which direction you're coming from. When the Hacienda first opened in 1956, its gambling license was still pending—manager Dick Taylor estimated that the wait was costing the stockholders $70 per minute—and original owner Bayley, something of a promotional genius, began to formulate plans to bring the customers in. Car drivers were handed discount folders as they paused at streetlights in neighboring cities, a DC-4 was fitted with a piano bar and used to fly customers in free from West Coast cities, and a 19th hole was built onto the golf course offering a $5,000 prize for any golfer who could achieve a hole in one (four people did it, but the deal has been discontinued). The hotel was also the first to add helicopter service from its own heliport. The casino license was eventually granted, but the Hacienda has continued many of its package plans, adding a daily free champagne party. The hotel claims to be the world's largest user of domestic champagne—150,000 bottles every year.

Currently, *Minsky's Burlesque* with Jimmy Mathews and Lynn Chase is the hit of the strip at the **Fiesta Room.** There's a dinner show at 8 p.m. and a cocktail show at 11 p.m. The 8 p.m. dinner show costs $19 to $28, depending on what you order; the late show, which includes two drinks, costs $15. Closed Thursday.

There's also entertainment nightly in the **Bolero Lounge** from 9:15 p.m. to 2:15 a.m. Closed Wednesday.

THE FRONTIER HOTEL: Million-dollar hotels have been commonplace for a long time, but the Frontier Hotel, on the Strip at 3120 Las Vegas Blvd. South (tel. 734-0110), may be one of the only hotels to erect a million-dollar neon sign. It is 200 feet high and billboards the various entertainment attractions currently playing.

The 800-seat **Music Hall** was best known in the past for featuring singer Wayne Newton (a tremendously talented local boy whose enormous popularity here turned him into a national celebrity). Other stars who've played here include Nipsey Russell, Sergio Franchi, Joan Rivers, Steve Lawrence and Eydie Gorme, Lola Falana, Bobby Vinton, Glen Campbell, Roy Clark, and Juliet Prowse.

Entertainment runs from dusk till dawn (3:30 p.m. to 3:15 a.m.) in the intimate **Wild Horse Lounge,** located in the center of the Frontier's casino. No cover charge here, but there is a two-drink minimum.

IMPERIAL PALACE: The pagoda-roofed Imperial Palace, on the Strip at 3535 Las Vegas Blvd. South (tel. 731-3311), houses a 869-seat showroom called the **Imperial Theatre.** Presentations here vary from dance extravaganzas, to *Legends in Concert,* a musical re-creation of legendary superstars in a multimedia laser extravaganza. It's a great family show. There are two cocktail shows nightly, except Sunday, at 8 and 11 p.m. Admission is $15.95.

HOLIDAY INN HOTEL AND CASINO AT CENTER STRIP:
The Holiday Inn, on the Strip at 3473 Las Vegas Blvd. South (tel. 369-5000), presents a great new revue called *The Roaring Twenties Revue* twice nightly at the **Holiday Theatre**. Shows are at 8 and 10:30 p.m. except Sunday. Admission, including two drinks, is $12.95.

MAXIM:
When it opened in January 1977, the Maxim, 160 E. Flamingo Rd. (tel. 731-4300), got off to a hot start with *Minsky's Burlesque,* a name that has been lighting up theater marquees since the turn of the century. In their heyday, the Minskys (Abe and his son, Harold) developed such comedy stars as Abbott and Costello, Phil Silvers, Red Buttons, and Pinky Lee. The famed naughty revue came to Vegas in 1950 and played at various hotels for over two decades. It featured gorgeous showgirls, exotic dancers, comedy routines, sketches, etc.

The Minskys are no longer at the Maxim; these days the hotel has Playboy's *Girls of Rock 'N Roll.* Two shows nightly take place Sunday through Friday in the **Cabaret Showroom,** at 8 and 10:15 p.m., with a third show on Saturday at 12:30 a.m. All are cocktail shows, including two drinks, and admission is $12.95.

There's also live musical entertainment Monday through Saturday from 7 p.m. to 6 a.m. in the **Cloud Nine Lounge** off the casino; no cover or minimum.

CIRCUS CIRCUS:
The pink-and-white-striped concrete "tent" of the $12-million Circus Circus, on the Strip at 2880 Las Vegas Blvd. South (tel. 734-0410), has been a hit since the day it opened. Almost 4 million visitors filed through in the first year to gamble and/or watch the continuous circus acts taking place overhead. Ed Sullivan once did a CBS show from here, and several movies have used it as a setting.

Bulgarian-born Alexander Dobritch, innovator of the circusy show—who also booked talent for "The Ed Sullivan Show" and even operated his own touring circus—has died, but his policies have continued. Daring and talented circus artists, performing continuously overhead from 11 a.m. to midnight, include aerialists performing on painted carousel horses, stunt cyclists, jugglers, high-wire acts, trapeze artists, tumblers, clowns, acrobats, etc. Kids love it, and so do their parents.

Any or all of these acts can be seen free while you're playing electronic games and pinball machines or sipping cocktails in the revolving Horse Around Carousel Bar.

DOWNTOWN NIGHTS

Most people head straight for the glamorous Strip when they hit Las Vegas. Until the new Golden Nugget (downtown) was created by Steve Wynn, the Strip got the most publicity and the biggest spenders. Now you don't overlook the downtown area— glamour has arrived, accompanied by the superstars of show business.

THE GOLDEN NUGGET: For your entertainment at the Golden Nugget, 129 E. Fremont St. (tel. 386-8100), there is a veritable roster of headliners who appear at the magnificent new **Theatre Ballroom,** and at the intimate, informal **Cabaret.** This is where you go to see the superstars light up the sky—David Brenner, Dolly Parton (her debut engagement was in the Cabaret), Kenny Rogers, Dionne Warwick, Harry Belafonte, Melissa Manchester, Paul Anka, and Alan King, among others. Whoopi Goldberg made her Las Vegas debut in the Theatre Ballroom. There are two shows nightly, except Monday, at 8 p.m. and 11 p.m. The cost is $25 and up, depending on the performer and whether or not dinner is served, so it's best to call first.

THE UNION PLAZA: The major entertainment facility at the Union Plaza, 1 Main St., at Fremont Street (tel. 386-2110), is the 650-seat **Plaza Theater Restaurant,** in which Broadway-style musicals and comedies are featured. In the past they've presented *Oklahoma!* and Cole Porter's *Anything Goes* (based on a book by P. G. Wodehouse), *Fiddler on the Roof,* and *The Odd Couple.* There are two shows nightly, except Monday, at 8 and 11:30 p.m. The former costs $13.95 to $15.95 and includes dinner; the latter is $9.50 with two cocktails.

The Union Plaza also offers entertainment from 3 p.m. to 3 a.m. in the **Omaha Lounge** off the casino. On Monday from 8 p.m. to 2 a.m. there's a talent showcase. No cover or minimum. There's also a piano bar within the Center Stage Restaurant.

AND OTHER ACTIVITIES

Generally, nightlife in Las Vegas means attending one or more lavish shows at various Strip hotels, with possibly a bit of gambling squeezed in at whatever casino happens to be handy.

Many tourists start out at an 8 p.m. dinner show, hop over to somebody else's midnight offering, and sometimes, if it's a weekend, take in a third show at 2:15 a.m.

But there are a few other things to do.

MOVIES: Las Vegas isn't a big town for movies because of the wealth of live entertainment available, and a fair number of the theaters that exist show "adult" movies only. There are some conventional movie houses hereabouts, however (consult their ads in local papers), including a dozen drive-ins, among them: the **Sunset,** 3800 Cheyenne Ave., off Tonopah Highway (tel. 648-7550); and the **Nevada,** 3873 Las Vegas Blvd. North (tel. 644-0988).

The biggest theater complex in town is the grouping of 11 **Red Rock Theatres,** 5201 W. Charleston Blvd., one block west of Decatur Boulevard (tel. 870-1423).

CULTURE IN LAS VEGAS: The city's hub of cultural activities is the campus of the **University of Nevada, Las Vegas,** on Maryland Parkway, between Flamingo Road and Tropicana Avenue. Among the regular daytime and evening activities are concerts by various music and dance groups, including the award-winning Jazz Ensemble, the Las Vegas Symphony, the University Dance Theatre, and the Nevada Dance Theatre.

The Department of Theater Arts, also an award-winner, stages productions of both contemporary and classic plays in two theaters—the 550-seat **Judy Bayley Theatre** and the 180-seat **Black Box Theatre.** Recent offerings have included Tennessee Williams's stirring drama *The Night of the Iguana;* the popular British musical *Stop the World—I Want to Get Off;* and Shakespeare's comedy *The Merchant of Venice.*

The **Donna Beam Fine Arts Gallery** displays works by artists of national and international reputation in a spacious area with natural lighting and a loft. Among the notable exhibits that have received considerable acclaim are the *Smorgon Family Collection of Contemporary American Art* and *The Monumental Image.*

The **UNLV Museum of Natural History** features traveling exhibits as well as permanent displays on the Mojave Desert, the Navajo Indians, and pre-Columbian pottery.

Lectures by prominent national speakers and leading academic experts are offered in the prestigious Barrick Lecture Series and the University Forum Lecture Series.

The university also boasts a 2,000-seat concert hall, an impressive facility that showcases many of the world's greatest classical musicians in the Master Series concerts. Among the great performers who have been featured are Aaron Copeland, Isaac Stern, Itzhak Perlman, and Andrés Segovia.

For details on university cultural events, call the Performing Arts Box Office (tel. 739-3801 or 739-3131) for a recording of weekly campus events.

SPORTS IN LAS VEGAS

□ □ □

Take your sports gear to Las Vegas or you may regret it. Las Vegas has devoted more space to more sports than almost any city I know, except San Diego. Although Las Vegas has no in-town beaches, there's swimming at nearby Lake Mead and in uncounted swimming pools at almost all the Strip hotels and motels. Golf courses are among the country's finest, and there are supposed to be more tennis courts (almost all of them lit for night play) open to the public here than in any other American resort.

Bowling, rodeos, basketball, table tennis, boating, boxing, shuffleboard, horseback riding, fishing, hunting, skiing, and football are among other sports for spectators or participants, either in the city or within a short drive.

Camping, horse- and mule-packing trips, hiking and backpacking in wilderness areas in nearby Zion and Bryce Canyon National Parks (Utah) and in Grand Canyon National Park (Arizona) have increasingly been attracting entire families. Accommodations at the parks are comfortable and reasonably priced. Also appealing to families are river-float trips. Departures for adventurous white-water float trips on the Colorado and other wild western rivers can easily be arranged from Las Vegas.

The almost endless outdoor opportunities in the Lake Mead National Recreation Area, which covers 5½ million acres, and on 12,000-foot Mount Charleston, only an hour's drive from Las Vegas, are worth consideration too.

TENNIS: Many hotel tennis courts are open to public use in Las Vegas. And that's not to mention a dozen night-lit tennis courts at the University of Nevada, Las Vegas (tel. 739-3150). They're open from 6 a.m. to 9:45 p.m. Monday through Friday, 8 a.m. to 8 p.m. on Saturday, 10 a.m. to 6 p.m. on Sunday. The charge is $2 per hour for nonuniversity people (students and faculty have priority). Call before you go to find out if a court is available. Guest passes are obtained at the Physical Education Building, Room 306 or 312.

Rates are generally quite reasonable at the various courts around town. Some places charge a small fee for each player using the locker rooms. It's best to telephone in advance for rates and reservations.

The **Tropicana Hotel,** 3801 Las Vegas Blvd. South (tel. 739-2222), has four outdoor courts lit for night play. With so many possible play hours, you can usually line up a partner. Courts are for hotel guests only.

Another likable feature at the Tropicana is the cocktail lounge overlooking the courts. Those who'd rather watch than play can enjoy themselves and observe the goings-on to their heart's content. The mezzanine lounge is attractive, with wood paneling, thick wall-to-wall carpeting, comfortable chairs, and good service. The tennis pro in charge at the Tropicana is Steve Drappo.

The **Riviera Hotel,** 2901 Las Vegas Blvd. South (tel. 734-5110), has four night-lit tennis courts, open from 6 a.m. to 10 p.m. Riviera guests have preference, then other hotels' guests.

Caesars Palace, 3570 Las Vegas Blvd. South (tel. 731-7110), has eight outdoor courts, and two are lit for night play. Patrick Du Pre is the tennis pro and tournament consultant. The courts are open from dawn to 11 p.m. for hotel guests and the public.

Bally's—Las Vegas, 3645 Las Vegas Blvd. South (tel. 739-4111), along with every other imaginable facility, has ten courts, four lit for night play. Bally's guests have preference, then other hotels' guests. The resident pro is Jim Prisock.

The **Las Vegas Hilton,** 3000 Paradise Rd., adjacent to the Las Vegas Convention Center (tel. 732-5111), has six courts for hotel guests only. The courts are located on an immense rooftop, stories high. Four are illuminated for night action. There are several teaching pros.

The **Desert Inn,** 3145 Las Vegas Blvd. South (tel. 733-4444), has ten courts, and all are lit—including five new courts adjacent to the Desert Inn Spa. Marty Hennessey is the teaching pro. The Desert Inn courts are often used by celebrities and political figures. They're open from dawn to 10 p.m. for all, but hotel guests have priority.

The **Sands,** 3355 Las Vegas Blvd. South (tel. 733-5000), has six courts, all lit, and the teaching pro/tennis director is Matt McDougall. The courts are open from 9 a.m. to 10 p.m. for all, but hotel guests have priority.

At the **Hacienda Hotel,** 3950 Las Vegas Blvd. South (tel. 739-8911), there are six courts, with two lit for night use; they're open from 8 a.m. to 11 p.m. for hotel guests only. Lou Petro is the resident pro.

The **Frontier Hotel,** 3120 Las Vegas Blvd. South (tel. 734-0110), has two outdoor courts, both lit for night play. They are reserved for hotel guests only; open from 8 a.m. to 10 p.m.

The **Aladdin Hotel,** 3667 Las Vegas Blvd. South (tel. 736-0111), has three outdoor courts, all lit for night play. They are open to the public, but priority is given to the Aladdin's guests. The courts are open from dawn to 10 p.m.

The **Union Plaza,** 1 Main St. (tel. 386-2110), has four courts, all lit for night play, located on the hotel's sports deck. Open to the public, these courts are especially handy for those staying downtown; the hotel's location is convenient to all. The courts are open from 9 a.m. to 10 p.m. The pro is Tony Gurovsky.

Apart from tennis facilities at the hotels, courts are also available at the clubs listed below. Reservations are necessary.

The **Center Court Racquet Club,** 3890 Swenson St. (tel. 735-8153), has four outdoor courts, three lighted, and ten indoor courts. Hours are 7 a.m. to 10 p.m. on weekdays, to 6 p.m. on weekends.

The **Las Vegas Racquet Club,** 3333 W. Raven Ave. (tel. 361-2202), has six outdoor courts lit for night play. Hours are 10 a.m. to 10 p.m.

The **Sports Club–Las Vegas,** 3025 Industrial Rd. (tel. 733-8999), has two indoor tennis courts. Hours are 9 a.m. to 10:30 p.m.

RACQUETBALL: Courts can be found in several locations around town.

Caesars Palace, 3570 Las Vegas Blvd. South (tel. 731-7110), has courts open daily from 10 a.m. to 5 p.m.

The **Center Court Racquet Club,** 3890 Swenson St., between Flamingo and Desert Inn Roads (tel. 735-8153), has two courts open daily from 7 a.m. to 10 p.m. on weekdays, to 6 p.m. on weekends.

The **Las Vegas Athletic Club East,** 1070 E. Sahara Ave. (tel. 733-1919), has ten courts, open 24 hours a day, seven days a week.

The **Las Vegas Athletic Club West,** 3315 Spring Mountain Rd. (tel. 362-3720), has 12 racquetball courts, as well as Nautilus equipment, basketball, volleyball, an outdoor pool, and aerobics classes. The club has free child supervision. Hours are 6 a.m. to 10 p.m. on weekdays, 8 a.m. to 6 p.m. on weekends.

The **Sports Club–Las Vegas,** 3025 Industrial Rd., behind the Stardust Hotel (tel. 733-8999), has 12 racquetball courts and 2 squash courts open 24 hours a day, seven days a week. (See the description of all the Sports Club's facilities, below.)

Eight courts at the **University of Nevada, Las Vegas,** 4505 S. Maryland Pkwy. (tel. 739-3150), are open Monday to Friday from 6 a.m. to 9:45 p.m., on Saturday from 8 a.m. to 8 p.m., and on Sunday from 10 a.m. to 6 p.m. There's a $2-per-hour charge for nonuniversity people (students and faculty have priority). Call before you go to find out if a court is available. Guest passes are obtained at the Physical Education Building, Room 306 or 312.

GOLF: Golf has reigned as the most popular outdoor sport in Las Vegas for years. Tennis enthusiasm has grown so fast, however, that golf soon may be in second place. At any rate, many major courses cater to visiting golfers. In alphabetical order, they are:

The **Black Mountain Country Club,** at 501 Country Club Dr. in nearby Henderson (tel. 565-7933), is semiprivate, requiring reservations four days in advance. It's 18 holes, par 72. Yardage: 6,307 regular, 5,666 ladies. There are also a driving range, coffeeshop, cocktail lounge, and dining room. The greens fee, including golf cart, is $21 on weekdays, $22 on weekends and holidays. The course opens at 5:30 a.m.

The **Craig Ranch Golf Club,** located at 628 W. Craig Rd. (tel. 642-9700), is public. It's 18 holes, par 70. Yardage: 6,001 regular, 5,221 ladies. A driving range, pro shop, and snackbar complete the picture. The greens fee is $9, plus $6 for a cart, for 18 holes. The course opens at 6 a.m. and you can book tee times up to seven days in advance.

The **Desert Inn Country Club & Spa,** 3145 Las Vegas Blvd. South (tel. 733-4444), also gets the nod from champions. It's an 18-hole, par-72 course. Yardage: 7,108 championship, 6,508 regular, 5,754 ladies. The Desert Inn is a PGA and LPGA tour stop. It has a driving range, pro shop, restaurant, and cocktail lounge. The golf director is Dave Johnson, and Rick Seven is the head pro. This is an excellent driving course, with undulating greens. The greens fee is $70 for hotel guests, $110 for visitors, including mandatory cart. The course opens at 6 a.m.

The **Desert Rose Golf Club,** 5483 Club House Dr. (tel. 438-4653), is 18 holes, 6,511 yards, par 71. There are a driving range, pro shop with rental clubs, restaurant, and cocktail lounge.

The greens fee is $16 on weekdays, $27 on weekends. This is a county course, well managed, with good hybrid Bermuda greens.

The **Dunes Country Club,** 3650 Las Vegas Blvd. South (tel. 737-4747), is an 18-hole championship course, 6,571 yards, par 72. There are a clubhouse, locker room, pro shop with rental clubs, coffeeshop, and cocktail lounge. The greens fee is $45 for hotel guests, including a mandatory cart, $55 for nonguests. The Dunes course is interesting, with its long par 5s, and par 3s that have quite a few well-placed traps.

The **Las Vegas Municipal Golf Course,** 4309 Vegas Dr. (tel. 646-3003), is 18 holes, par 72. Yardage: 6,335 regular, 5,734 ladies. There are a lighted driving range, pro shop, coffeeshop, and cocktail lounge. The course is a good test, especially on the back side. Greens have been remodeled. The greens fee is $12. The course opens at 6 a.m.

The **Sahara Country Club,** located at 1911 Desert Inn Rd. (tel. 796-0016), is a public course. It has 18 holes, par 71. Yardage: 6,815 championship, 6,418 regular, 5,761 ladies. It's a tough driving course with some water. Greens have been remodeled. There are a pro shop and a full-service restaurant and bar on the premises. The greens fee is $42, including the mandatory cart-rental fee. The course opens at daylight.

The **Showboat Country Club,** 1 Green Valley Pkwy. (tel. 451-2106), has an 18-hole, par-72, championship golf course. Yardage: 6,967 championship, 6,473 regular, 6,134 ladies. Other club facilities include a pro shop, putting green, driving range, and a clubhouse with a coffeeshop and cocktail lounge. The greens fee is $45 on weekdays, $55 on weekends, including mandatory cart. This is a challenging course; it has been the site of the U.S. Senior Open. The course opens at 6 a.m.

The **Tropicana Country Club,** 66 E. Tropicana Ave. (tel. 739-2579), is located across Tropicana Avenue from the hotel. It has 18 holes, par 70. Yardage: 6,647 championship, 6,107 regular, 5,787 ladies. The Tropicana has more character than most desert courses. It's hilly, with many traps and trees. The country club building, lined with imposing columns, faces Tropicana Avenue. The coffeeshop and cocktail lounge are located there. There are also a pro shop and driving range. The greens fee, including the mandatory cart rental, is $45 for hotel guests, $55 for visitors. The course opens at 6 a.m.

BOWLING: After you've seen the bowling alleys at the **Showboat Hotel,** 2800 E. Fremont St. (tel. 385-9153), you'll never want to bowl anywhere else. The hotel expanded the number of lanes to 106, and they're the most modern and best-equipped in the world. They're kept busy day and night, and there's a snackbar at the alleys, as well as a free kiddie playroom with a full-time attendant.

RODEO: Top rodeo stars compete for the prize money at rodeos in Las Vegas. Check local papers for events and dates, but the National Finals are usually held in December. It's a shame that most big rodeos don't schedule their Las Vegas meets far enough in advance to list them here. They're exciting western shows that appeal to everyone, a combination of carnival antics and cowboy grit.

The **Helldorado,** rated the 13th most important rodeo in the world by the Pro-Rodeo Cowboy's Association, is an annual event; it takes place in late May or early June.

A HEALTH CLUB: Though many of the Strip hotels have health clubs, none offers the amazing range of facilities you'll find at the **Sports Club–Las Vegas,** 3025 Industrial Rd., right behind the Stardust Hotel (tel. 733-8999). Opened in 1978, this posh club for men and women is the best-equipped, best-run, and most luxurious I've ever seen. It has 12 racquetball/handball courts; two squash courts; two tennis courts; a full gymnasium for basketball, volleyball, and free exercise equipment; an outdoor pool; a 60-foot-long indoor swimming pool; indoor and outdoor jogging tracks; saunas, steam rooms, Jacuzzis, and siesta rooms; sunbathing areas; a pro shop; men's and women's skin care and hair salons; a tanning salon; an excellent babysitting service; a restaurant, bar, and social lounge. Aerobics classes are held at frequent intervals throughout the day. There's even a masseur on the premises. And it's open 24 hours a day.

Many celebs work out here—I've seen Susan Anton, Engelbert Humperdinck, Mike Tyson, Jerry Lewis, and J. J. Walker pumping iron at the Sports Club. The cost for a single visit is $17.50; reduced weekly and monthly rates are available.

HORSEBACK RIDING: About 30 minutes by car from midtown Las Vegas is **Bonnie Springs Ranch** in Old Nevada, Nevada, 1 Gun Fighter Lane (tel. 875-4191), which actually is only 18 miles from the city line, straight out of town on West Charleston Boulevard (next to the "wild west" attraction, Old Nevada). Lots of animals—pigs, goats, sheep, cows, turkeys, a buffalo, coyote, racoon, skunks—are kept in a petting zoo at this rustic desert oasis, and horses are available for riding. Horse rental costs $13 per hour for a one-hour guided ride. There's a good restaurant and bar. The restaurant overlooks a small duck pond, cedar tables are hand-hewn and rugged, and the menu is written on whisky bottles. The menu is surprisingly gourmet, offering mostly steak and seafood entrees—everything from frogs' legs to T-bone steak—as well as sandwiches, and homemade pies for dessert.

OTHER ADVENTURES: If you'd like to know all the out-of-Vegas options for adventure tripping, the experts are **Adventure Guides, Inc.,** 36 E. 57th St., New York, NY 10022 (tel. 212/355-6334). You can send for their 256-page book, *Adventure Travel North America* by Pat Dickerman ($14 postpaid). It tells not only about rafting trips but about mountaineering, cycling, four-wheel drive trips, cattle drives, you name it. There are special trips geared to young people, as well as ranches you can stay at, in Dickerman's other book, *Farm, Ranch, and Country Vacations* ($14 postpaid). The folks at Adventure Guides can also help you plan adventure trips using Las Vegas as a departure point.

CHAPTER VIII

LAS VEGAS MISCELLANY

□ □ □

There are always useful bits of information that aren't "big" enough for a special chapter—or they don't fit a particular category. Hence, this Department of Miscellany:

SHOPPING: There are shops in most of the big hotels, but for resort fashions, at boutique prices, the most complete shopping places in Las Vegas are the Boulevard Mall, the Meadows, and the Fashion Show.

The Malls

The fully air-conditioned and enclosed **Boulevard Mall,** Maryland Parkway, between Twain Avenue and Desert Inn Road, has stores arranged in arcade fashion along a central walk of tile and carpeting. Plentiful benches are placed throughout the mall, and there's a big central fountain beneath a domed skylight set in high, vaulted ceilings. Potted plants and trees add a bit of charm.

Over 70 stores, snackbars, and restaurants are located at the Boulevard, and they occupy a total of a million square feet. A movie theater installed by the American Broadcasting Company shows first-run movies. Parking is provided for 5,800 automobiles.

Broadway, Sears, and Penney's are the largest stores in the mall. Each carries the wide range of products usually sold in department stores. You can also purchase a turtle, parrot, or guinea pig at the Docktor Pet Center; smoked cheese, fish, etc., at Hickory Farms of Ohio; and wonderful, sexy, skimpy bits of almost nothing at Frederick's of Hollywood. Those are just a few of the Boulevard stores; whatever you want—fabrics, clothing, hardware, shoes, automotive supplies, trophy engraving—you'll find it here.

There's also a B. Dalton bookstore; bookstores—except those selling X-rated adult literature—are scarcer than ice water in hell in this town.

From the Strip the Boulevard Mall is a short bus ride away. It's open weekdays from 10 a.m. to 9 p.m., on Saturday to 6 p.m., and on Sunday from 11 a.m. to 5 p.m. The Boulevard Mall also has valet parking.

One of the largest of the Vegas malls, the multi-million-dollar **Meadows** opened its million square feet of shopping area at 4300 Meadows Lane several years ago. It has over 140 shops, restaurants, snackbars, etc., including four major department stores— the Broadway, Dillards, Sears, and J. C. Penney's—and parking space for 4,500 vehicles. Fountains and trees ameliorate the starkness of the ultramodern, high-ceilinged architecture.

You can get just about anything you can afford to pay for at the Meadows—from jogging shoes to maternity clothes, from children's toys to adult games, from health food to chow mein, burgers, and pizza. There are over 20 restaurants and snack and food stores on the premises. It's also a good place to look for shoes; you have a choice of 16 shoestores plus the department stores.

The Meadows is open weekdays from 10 a.m. to 9 p.m., on Saturday to 6 p.m., and on Sunday from noon to 5 p.m.

The **Fashion Show,** 3200 Las Vegas Blvd. South, at the corner of Spring Mountain Road just across the street from the Frontier Hotel, is a newer addition to the world of Las Vegas shopping. The doors opened February 13, 1981, giving the city an early Valentine gift. It was quite a celebration—a black-tie gala, highlighted by a fashion show of one-of-a-kind couture creations. Many of the world's leading designers—including Adolfo, Geoffrey Beene, Bill Blass, Bob Mackie, and Pauline Trigère—were on hand to show their interpretations of the "Las Vegas look." (Bill Blass described his ruffed creations for Vegas as "haute glamour and pulsating heat.") And since no event in Vegas would be complete without celebs, the Fashion Show borrowed a page from Hollywood and had the entertainers put their handprints and signatures in wet cement. The result is the mall's Promenade of Stars, which includes the prints of Danny Thomas, Doc Severinsen, Johnny Carson, Juliet Prowse, Tony Bennett, Anthony Newley, Wayne Newton, Steve Lawrence, and Eydie Gormé.

This totally enclosed and air-conditioned mall, the largest in the city, also has valet parking. It is a most luxurious environment in which to shop. There are multitiered planters filled with mature trees, flowering plants, bushes, and ground cover. A unique ramp-staircase system was designed to showcase fashion shows in the central court, and clerestory skylight windows provide natural light while conserving energy.

The 34-acre site is home to 140 shops and services. Some of the finest retailing names are represented here. Major department stores include Neiman-Marcus, Saks Fifth Avenue, Bullock's, Goldwaters, and Dillards. There are designer boutiques like Uomo, Cache, and Lillie Rubin. And there's even a branch of Abercrombie & Fitch. Other services include four airline ticket counters: TWA, Eastern, Western, and United Airlines.

Of course, there are numerous eating places. Fast food is represented by Orange Julius, Hot Dog on a Stick, and Herbie Burgers. Fajitas, Renzios, Magelby's Muffins, Le Croissant Shoppe, Ice Cream Shoppe, Yang's Wok, Schlotzskys, and the Sbarro Italian Eatery add an international note. And for dessert, there's Häagen-Dazs ice cream, Heidi's Frozen Yozurt, Cinnabon, and Mrs. Fields Cookies.

The Fashion Show is open weekdays from 10 a.m. to 6 p.m. (on Thursday and Friday till 9 p.m.), on Saturday till 6 p.m., and on Sunday from noon to 5 p.m. There's free parking for 3,500 cars.

Until the above was completed, the only mall that had the advantage of being right in the center of the Strip was **Las Vegas Plaza,** 3025 Las Vegas Blvd. South (across the street from the Stardust), with about 40 tenants. Most stores here are open Monday to Saturday from 9 a.m. to 5:30 p.m., and on Sunday from noon to 5 p.m.

For Gifts

For jewelry, first try **M. J. Christensen's,** 856 E. Sahara Ave., between Paradise Road and Maryland Parkway (tel. 732-0136). It's open Monday through Saturday from 9 a.m. to 5:30 p.m. Christensen's has two branches, one in the Meadows Mall (tel. 878-7832) and a second at a new location in the Renaissance West Shopping Center at Flamingo and Decatur (tel. 365-1211).

For silver and furniture, **Bertha's,** a few doors away at 896 E. Sahara Ave. (tel. 735-3711), is open Monday through Saturday from 9:30 a.m. to 5:30 p.m.

Very good for gifts (and perhaps a briefcase or handbag for yourself) is **El Portal Luggage and Gifts,** in the Fashion Show Mall at 3200 Las Vegas Blvd. South (tel. 369-0606). It's open Monday through Friday from 10 a.m. to 9 p.m., on Saturday to 6 p.m., and on Sunday from noon to 5 p.m. El Portal also has a shop in the Boulevard Mall at 3574 S. Maryland Pkwy. (735-6433).

For handsome turquoise and silver Indian jewelry in Navajo

and Zuni motifs (among others), try **Trader Bill's,** 324 Fremont St., at Fourth Street (tel. 384-4408), open daily from 9 a.m. to 6 p.m. You can also buy Las Vegas souvenirs here. A special feature is a complete line of authentic moccasins for men, women, and children.

Also be sure to stop at the **Desert Indian Shop,** 108 N. Third St., between Fremont Street and Ogden Avenue (tel. 384-4977), especially notable for its authentic and imaginative collection of both Navajo and Hopi work. Artifacts of the "Old West" are a specialty here. Open Monday through Saturday from 10 a.m. to 5 p.m.

Another gift shop at the **Alpine Village Inn** has select pewterware, cuckoo clocks, and such (details in Chapter III).

ETHEL M. CHOCOLATES: At the turn of the century Ethel Mars and her husband began making fine chocolates in a little candy kitchen. This small enterprise developed into some very familiar names in the world of candy: Milky Way, 3 Musketeers, Snickers, Mars Almond Bars, and M & M's. With all this success, it was still Ethel Mars's dream to make the finest boxed chocolates in the world.

Ethel M. Chocolates are made only in Las Vegas in an ultra-modern factory. It's open daily from 9 a.m. to 5:30 p.m. for self-guided tours. Over 1,000 people a day visit the factory to watch candy being made. The best time to go is on weekday mornings when most of the activity goes on. Guests view the process through large glass windows and video monitors. All equipment is marked to aid in the understanding of the process. If you can't time your visit for the morning, the video shows do follow the process, and people are always at work doing something. Your tour ends in the beautiful new chocolate shoppe done in pinks and mauve with etched-glass and brass touches. This is where you can decide for yourself if these are the world's best chocolates. The candies, alcoholic (including the great liqueurs) and nonalcoholic, are on sale here for $11.95 a pound.

The chocolate factory is located at 2 Cactus Garden Dr., just off Mount Vista and Sunset Rd. in the Green Valley Business Park, six miles from the Strip (tel. 458-8864). It's just a 15-minute drive from the Strip; take Tropicana Boulevard east, and follow the signs.

An additional benefit of visiting the chocolate factory is the adjoining two-and-a-half-acre cactus garden. Designed and land-scaped under the direction of Gary Lyons, curator of the Desert Garden of the Huntington Library and Botanical Gardens in California, it features cacti and succulents from all over the world. It's a photographer's paradise. Both attractions are free.

FUN BOOKS: Many of the casinos—especially those downtown—give out fun books full of coupons for free nickels, meals, double-your-money bets on blackjack, Bingo cards, etc. One place to find coupons to get the fun books is newsletters like *Today in Las Vegas, Vegas Visitor, Marquee,* and *What's On in Las Vegas;* you'll usually find them free at your hotel. They're often chock-full of additional discount coupons—sometimes so many you could eat and gamble free for a week off one issue. Fun books are also given out at car-rental places.

LAS VEGAS WITH CHILDREN: It wasn't uncommon in the old days to see children kicking their heels on the sidewalk, their noses virtually pressed to the outside windows of the glittering casinos while their parents gambled away indoors.

This wasn't so bad when their parents were having a short fling, but it bordered on child neglect when a winning (or losing) streak forced the gamblers to make a day of it.

One of the most far-reaching projects for handling children is the **Hilton Youth Hotel**—a $2-million facility built specially for children, with supervision, popular activities, and even dormitories. Guests at the Las Vegas Hilton can leave children with experienced counselors for about $4.50 per hour or $25 for an overnight stay (calculated from midnight to 8 a.m.). The Youth Hotel is open from 8 a.m. to 10 p.m. all year round. It's open for overnight stays seven days a week from mid-June until Labor Day, and during weekends and holidays during the rest of the year. There's a playground for the younger kids, and instruction in fencing, baseball, arts and crafts, photography, etc., for subteens and teenagers. The children are encouraged to become involved in what interests them most, even if it's only listening to the jukebox or reading. Closed-circuit television supervises the dormitories at night.

Another excellent choice for families traveling with kids is the **Circus Circus,** where so many activities are geared toward youngsters that I dare any child to ask the proverbial "What can I do?" First, of course, there are the continuous circus acts under the Big Top from 11 a.m. to midnight—clowns, acrobats, aerialists, tightrope walkers, and other thrilling attractions. The circus acts can all be seen from the mezzanine, a huge area filled with arcade and midway games, a veritable junior casino where the winnings are stuffed animals and the like. There are electronic games, balloons to shoot at, skeeball, pinball machines galore, etc.

One very good thing about the mezzanine is that it overlooks the casino—a very secure feeling for kids who can look down and wave to mom and dad.

Bally's–Las Vegas has a game room for kids—an arcade of about 54 machines with skeeball, pinball, electronic games, air hockey, etc. They also offer a babysitting service (tel. 737-4111) from 8 a.m. to 8 p.m. Sitters read stories and play games with the kids. Rates are $3.50 an hour ($4 an hour for the non-potty-trained).

The **Omnimax Theatre** at **Caesars Palace** is a great place to take—or send—the kids. There are continuous showings from 11 a.m. to midnight, and children under 12 pay $4 (adults pay $5) for admission. Details are in Chapter VI.

Kids love **Ripley's Believe It or Not Museum** at the **Four Queens Hotel** downtown. There are over 1,000 exhibits and 54 wax figures on display. Various rooms cover nature's oddities, as well as those in art and music. The squeamish might prefer the interesting Oriental gardens to the torture cave. The exhibit is open from 9 a.m. to midnight on weekdays, to 1 a.m. on Friday and Saturday. Admission is $6 for adults, $3 for children under 12; it's free for those under 5.

Most kids, over and under 21, are fascinated by the **Imperial Palace Auto Collection,** at the hotel of the same name. You can ogle, or drool over, 200 vintage and special-interest cars, including those I've described in detail under the hotel listing in Chapter II.

You can also take the kids bowling at the 106 lanes at the **Showboat Hotel,** open round the clock. And if you'd like to bowl yourself, but your children are too young for the sport, you can leave them at the Showboat's free playroom (with attendant) for up to three hours.

If these aren't enough places to amuse the kiddies, consider the above-described **Ethel M.**—the chocolate factory paradise, with free tour. Then there's the **Las Vegas Museum of Natural History,** 3700 Las Vegas Blvd. South (tel. 798-7757), with its life-size moving (yes, I did say "moving"), roaring dinosaurs, and skeletons of prehistoric creatures in a life-like setting. It's open daily from 9 a.m. to 9 p.m. And finally, **Bonnie Springs Ranch/Old Nevada,** with its petting zoo, Old West villains, shoot-outs, opera show, and even an old mine, is detailed below.

The **Sports Club–Las Vegas,** a 24-hour health club with 12 racquetball courts, also has babysitters on hand to take care of your children while you work out. (See Chapter VII for details on the Sports Club).

If you're not staying at or visiting any of the above establishments, you might inquire about babysitting at your hotel. Otherwise, you can avail yourself of the services of one of the numerous babysitting agencies around town:

The **Las Vegas Babysitting Agency,** 1900 Ginger Tree Lane (tel. 457-3777), charges $6 an hour for up to three children from one family, with a four-hour minimum.

Reliable Babysitting, 4301 Avondale Ave. (tel. 451-7507), charges $4.50 an hour for up to two children in one family, 50¢ more for an extra child from one family, with a minimum of $22 for one or two kids, $24 for three or four, and $26 for five or six.

Both of these agencies provide adult sitters only, all of whom have been cleared with the Health and Sheriffs Departments. They also arrange their own transportation.

SIGHTSEEING TOURS: Several tour companies offer tours of the Las Vegas area. The **Gray Line,** 1550 S. Industrial Rd. (tel. 384-1234, or toll free 800/634-6579), offers a 5½-hour City Tour for $25 per person; it covers downtown Casino Center, the Liberace Museum, the Boulevard Mall, the University of Nevada campus, plush residential areas (past some of the stars' homes), the Ethel M. chocolate factory, and Strip attractions. Lunch is included.

The Gray Line also offers several trips to Hoover Dam, ranging in price from $21.50 to $33.30 per person. Some of these tours include lunch, a narrated boat cruise on Lake Mead, as well as a tour of historical museums and Sam's Town Western Emporium. There are daily tours to Red Rock Canyon, Valley of Fire, and Laughlin, Nevada.

Overnight trips to the Grand Canyon ($91 per person, double occupancy; $120 per person, single occupancy) and Zion/ Bryce ($100 per person, double occupancy; $127 per person, single occupancy) are also available through the Gray Line. Other tours offered are Mount Charleston, Lee Canyon, a Grand Canyon Land/Air Tour, and a Colorado River Raft Tour—not a dull one among them. The Colorado River Raft Tour is an exciting float trip (without rapids) on a Coast Guard–approved river raft. It takes you through the majestic Black Canyon, where you'll see, among other things, warm water springs bubbling out of the cliffs, and perhaps a bighorn sheep. Lunch is served at Willow Beach, and your trip takes you down past the Willow Beach trout hatchery. A Gray Line bus takes you back to your hotel and the glitter of Las Vegas. The tour price is $63 per person.

There are several nighttime tours offered by the Gray Line. One such is the nightclub tour, which begins with dinner and show—*Folies Bergère* at the Tropicana. This dazzling extravaganza includes French can-can acts, a Rolls-Royce onstage, live monkeys, a horse, acrobats, magicians, and elaborately costumed beauties in all their sequined and feathered or birthday-suit splendor. In between shows, you tour the glittering Strip. Then it's on to the Flamingo's 11 p.m. show, the lavish *City Lites,* in the Flamingo Showroom. You get two drinks at the latter show; all tips and gratuities are taken care of at both shows, and round-trip transportation to and from your hotel is also included. Price per person is $65.50. This tour does not operate on Thursday.

All the tour services operate pickup systems and will collect you in time for the particular tour. Arrangements can be made either through the bell captain at your hotel or by making a direct call to them by phone.

PARK IN THE DESERT: With infinite wisdom, Las Vegas has created a park in a cool oasis about ten miles out of town in the desert. This is the **Floyd R. Lamb State Park** (tel. 486-5413) at 9200 Tule Springs Rd., a shady grove of lawns and trees off U.S. 95 to the northwest.

Floyd R. Lamb State Park represents a part of the Las Vegas area's history, first as Tule Springs, an oasis and a watering stop for the Indians, and later as a working and dude ranch. The Indians who first came to the oasis called themselves the "tudini" (desert people); these were the ancestors of the Southern Paiutes. During the early 1900s, Tule Springs became a major watering hole for travelers going to and from the gold fields. The town subsequently went through several incarnations from a bootlegging center to a ranch housing gals and dudes waiting out residency requirements for divorce.

The park was the site of the Tule Springs Archeological Expedition, which found evidence of the presence of man dating back over 11,000 years; it was thus one of the oldest confirmed sites of human habitation in Western North America. Most important were findings of the remarkable fossil remains of mammoths, bison, camels, and other Pleistocene fauna.

Today the park offers a variety of daytime activities in tree-shaded groves nestled next to four small lakes. There are barbecue grills, picnic tables, and a casual collection of chickens, ducks, geese, and peacocks (none for the eating) who wander the lawns and park grounds.

Fishing is permitted in the lakes, provided you have a valid Nevada fishing license (children under 12 do not need one). The lakes are stocked with catfish and bluegill. A trapshooting range concession open to the public is also located inside the park.

Apart from eating, fishing, and taking a break from the rigors of the gaming tables, there are lots of other things to do at the park. In the morning you can take a bird walk around the ponds to look for yellow-headed blackbirds, great blue herons, and an elusive pair of wood ducks. Or you might want to go on the Tule Springs Ranch tour, or even the arboretum walk. But above all, be sure to call and ask about the Special Events. In the past these have included demonstrations of dressage and free-style riding, games on horseback, horse-and-cart demonstrations with Morgans, and square-dancing demonstrations, among other enjoyments.

The park is open year around (closed Christmas and New Year's) from 8 a.m. to sunset. Entrance fees are $3 per vehicle from March 1 to October 31, and $1 per vehicle from November 1 to the end of February.

MUSEUMS: Right on the campus of the University of Nevada, Las Vegas, 4505 Maryland Pkwy., at University Road, is the **UNLV Museum of Natural History** (tel. 739-3381), which has an interesting collection of live animals from the surrounding desert area. You can view specimens representative of the geology, biology, archeology, and ethnography of the southern Great Basin/Upper Mohave Desert natural regions. Exhibits include pre-Columbian pottery, Navajo rugs, Indian silver and turquoise jewelry, and photographs of early Las Vegas. The museum also features a large desert garden. The museum and gift shop are open Monday through Friday from 9 a.m. to 5 p.m. and on Saturday from 10 a.m. to 5 p.m. Admission is free.

Much more typical of Las Vegas is the **Liberace Museum,** 1775 E. Tropicana Ave., just east of Paradise Road (tel. 798-5595). The museum is a collection of memorabilia spanning Liberace's entire career. Guests to the Spanish-style structure are greeted at a piano-shaped desk, and marble floors reflect the sparkle of the ever-present candelabra, crystal, and jewels. Included among his many costumes are a Czar Nicholas uniform with 22-karat-gold braiding and a blue velvet cape styled after the coronation robes of King George V (it's covered with $60,000 worth of rare chinchilla). As one would expect, there are many pianos in the collection, including a French Boulle, a Chickering concert grand once owned by George Gershwin, and a piano played by Chopin. And a fleet of classic, customized cars features a red, white, and blue Rolls-Royce used in a 1976 Bicentennial salute. It all provides a peek into the world of "Mr. Showmanship," who performed to SRO audiences whenever he appeared in Las Vegas.

The Liberace Museum is open daily from 10 a.m. to 5 p.m., on Sunday from 1 to 5 p.m. The tax-deductible entry fees of $4.50 for adults, $4 for seniors, and $3 for children 6 to 12 (who must be accompanied by an adult) furnish 28 American colleges and universities with scholarship money.

BONNIE SPRINGS RANCH/OLD NEVADA: Some 20
miles west of Las Vegas is a group of attractions that afford a variety of enjoyable experiences. Bonnie Springs/Old Nevada is a combination ranch and Old West town that can be reached by driving due west on West Charleston Boulevard. As you leave Las Vegas proper, it's fascinating to see how the terrain changes. About 16 miles out of town, you enter the **Red Rock Canyon Recreation Lands,** an area of unusual red-and-yellow sandstone hills (you can see them on the horizon from Las Vegas) surrounding flatter lands full of desert flora such as yucca, cactus, and Joshua trees. Just off the main road there's a **Visitor Center** run by the Bureau of Land Management (tel. 362-1921), which is open Friday through Monday from 9 a.m. to 4 p.m. Here you can get information on the numerous attractions in the canyon. You might enjoy taking in the scenery on the 13-mile loop drive that starts here. (It's open daily from 7 a.m. to 6 p.m.)

About five miles beyond is **Old Nevada.** It's open daily from 10:30 a.m. to 5 p.m. from November through April (until 6 p.m. the rest of the year); admission is $5 for adults, $4 for seniors, and $3 for children. There's plenty of parking; on weekends and during the summer a little train acts as a shuttle between the car lot and the entrance.

Old Nevada is a microcosm of an old western town. The main "street" is lined with weathered wood buildings fronted by covered verandas. There are country stores, an old photography shop, an ice cream parlor, and a restaurant. You can view tableaux of the Old West in the Spirit of Old Nevada Wax Museum, and peek into a replica of an old barbershop. Every hour or so there's an amusing oldtime melodrama acted out in the saloon, complete with mustache-twirling villain and heroic-but-helpless "maiden"; and the square in front of the Sheriff's Office (where some very unsavory characters languish in jail) is the scene for frequent "shootouts" and "hangings." The Golden Queen Mine is a bit of a fun house; also available are a horseshoe pitching and a shooting gallery. All in all, there's a lot of fun to be had by kids and adults.

Next door is the **Bonnie Springs Ranch.** Here you can go horseback riding (see Chapter VII for details), visit the petting zoo, and enjoy a drink or dinner at the bar and restaurant.

For those without transportation, Bonnie Springs Ranch/ Old Nevada runs a shuttle bus to and from the city. Call 875-4191 for information on this and any other aspects of the attraction.

OUT FROM LAS VEGAS TO A FASCINATING WONDERWORLD

□ □ □

Nevada is a most beautiful state, well worth a day's, five days', three weeks' exploration. Matter of fact, the more time you have, the more adventure awaits you. You can venture just out of Las Vegas, or all the way to the Grand Canyon; either way, you'll have a marvelous western experience.

How? If you don't have your own car, you can rent one. If you don't want to do it on your own, take a guided tour by bus. . . or by plane!

SOME SIGHTSEEING HISTORY: Back in the 1840s when the gold-hunters headed west hoping to make a strike, most of them were too preoccupied to notice more than the barren deserts, though even these enthrall some people. But as disillusionment set in, and as the California mines began to peter out, some of the erstwhile prospectors remembered Nevada's wide-open spaces, the majestic grandeur of its rocks and canyons, and the lush greenness of its oasis-like valleys.

The people who settled here first were pioneers: Mormon farmers, miners, horsemen, gamblers . . . gradually supplemented by the bankers, merchants, lawyers, and businessmen that give every community its necessary stability. Gambling, which was outlawed officially for a while, was always taken for granted in the state, and most people were relieved when it was finally legalized in 1931.

A ROUND-UP OF WHAT TO SEE AND DO: You can find slot machines, roulette tables, and craps games all over Nevada, but 90% of them are in the Reno, Lake Tahoe, and Las Vegas areas.

AN EMPHATIC WARNING: The U.S. Department of the Interior has printed advice to those who plan to drive throughout the area, and it should be heeded.

"A word of caution to desert travelers is advisable. Many parts of Southern Nevada are accessible only by rocky dirt roads, seldom traveled by anyone. When venturing into these areas, always advise the local sheriff or someone else of your destination and when you expect to return. Always carry extra water, food, gasoline, and clothing or blankets. A breakdown or accident in these areas could mean several days of hardship before you are rescued."

As a rule, too, "desert buggies" are the only sort of vehicle that will hold up in more rugged terrain; regular passenger cars are not suited for unpaved roads. Flares and other signal devices are suggested for those venturing into remote regions, which can be hazardous. Such expeditions are not for individuals who have had no special training or preparation for desert exploration.

About 100 miles south of Las Vegas and a stone's throw from the metropolis of Bullhead City, Arizona, is the fastest-growing gambling town in the U.S.—**Laughlin,** Nevada. Its main attraction? Gambling on the Colorado River.

For all but the compulsive gambler, though, it's worth taking a look at some of the other things around the state. Nevada's capital, **Carson City,** with its old homes and absorbing state museum, is about 200 miles to the northwest, in the same direction as the **Lake Tahoe** resort area and **Reno** (448 miles distant). The very lively "ghost town" of **Virginia City** is also in this area, in the northwest corner of the state.

Almost as accessible from Las Vegas is Arizona's **Grand Canyon**—225 air miles away, but reachable by one-day excursion trips—or the mysteriously bizarre **Death Valley** on the California/Nevada border.

Less than one hour's drive southeast of Las Vegas is the magnificent **Hoover Dam,** whose construction back in the 1930s finally brought prosperity to all the regions within reach of the once-rampaging Colorado River. **Lake Mead,** which is becoming saltier with silt and evaporation processes, rose behind the dam. **Boulder City,** created as a home community for the thousands who labored on the building of the dam, is one of the state's few towns that bans gambling.

Yet another man-made "wonder," 70 miles northwest of Vegas, is what's come to be known as the **Nevada Test Site**—more than 1,300 square miles of proving ground dominated by the Atomic Energy Commission, which employs 10,000 people in the state's second-biggest "industry," after gambling. The AEC a while back was working on a deep-space nuclear rocket for manned travel to Mars and beyond. The area is desolate and forbidding, and not only because of the physical terrain: top security prevails, and visitors are discouraged. (The AEC maintains a public information office in Las Vegas; tel. 295-1000.)

Nevada abounds in outdoor recreation opportunities. For a complete listing of camping sites, write to the **Nevada Commission on Tourism,** Capitol Complex, Carson City, NV 89710. Some of the more popular spots in the Las Vegas area are Lake Mead National Recreation Area, Valley of Fire State Park, and the Mount Charleston Area. At Lake Mead there is Boulder Beach and Las Vegas Bay (off Rte. 41); Callville Bay, Echo Bay, and Overton Beach (off Rte. 12); and Eldorado Canyon, Cottonwood Cove, and Davis Dam (off U.S. 95). Valley of Fire is located off U.S. 15 on Rte. 40 about 45 miles from Las Vegas. Going north of Las Vegas (off U.S. 95) is the Mount Charleston Area. There you'll find the Charleston Recreation Area (on Rte. 39) and Lee Canyon Recreation Area (on Rte. 52).

INTO THE MOUNTAINS

In summertime, the mountains that encircle **Toiyabe Park,** about 40 miles northwest of Las Vegas, are as much as 30° to 40° cooler than the sweltering desert city, and a visit to this national park is a popular daytime trip. Two ravines provide access to the Spring Mountains, in which the park is situated—Kyle Canyon and Lee Canyon—and both of them lead westward off U.S. 95, about 15 miles apart.

Nevada Rte. 39 winds up for about 20 miles through **Kyle Canyon,** beginning its climb through sparse scrubland, the cactus and Joshua trees gradually giving way to pine and fir trees and

THE MAJOR
ACCESS ROADS

pleasantly wooded slopes. The gorge is narrow to begin with, but gradually widens, and near the mountains several summer homes are located among the trees.

The road eventually dead-ends where the woods become thicker, a small road leading to the lovely **Mount Charleston Restaurant and Lodge** (tel. 872-5408), which is open every day of the year, 24 hours a day (food is served from 7 a.m. to 10 p.m. Sunday through Friday, to 11 p.m. on Saturday). The restaurant has one of the biggest fireplaces in the West, heaped high with enormous logs, and the atmosphere, notwithstanding the cluster of slot machines, is pleasantly homey and comfortable.

It's a twilight-zone feeling to come from hot and air-conditioned Las Vegas to this sometimes snowy region. When you're sitting before a blazing fire with hot buttered rum, it's a mite disorienting. And speaking of hot drinks before the fire, although they do serve hot buttered rum, they also have a not-to-be-missed house specialty drink. Called Mount Charleston coffee, it's a concoction of coffee (a special Jamaican blend), brandy, Drambuie, and rich, homemade vanilla ice cream, topped with real whipped cream, a touch of nutmeg, and a cherry.

Of course, you'll probably want to dine before sitting around the fire with drinks. (Reservations are suggested for dinner on weekends.) The food is excellent, lovingly prepared and served. You might begin with a shrimp cocktail. The house specialty is prime rib, and with your entree you get a salad, a stuffed or baked potato, homemade rolls, and butter. For lighter fare, there's a half-pound cheeseburger with french fries. Entrees range in price from $9 to $20. For dessert there's also homemade pie for $2.50.

Mount Charleston has entertainment in the lounge—a combo on Sunday and a pianist Thursday to Saturday nights. There are special menus for breakfast and lunch.

Campgrounds with tables, fireplaces, and toilets are located farther up the woods along an undeveloped track, and a short walk will bring you to some falls.

About 15 miles farther up U.S. 95 is the turnoff to **Lee Canyon,** where a simple ski area (see below) has been developed. However, it isn't necessary to go back to the highway, because a splendid road winds through the mountains between the two canyons, connecting Rte. 39 with Nevada Rte. 52. The drive is a positively beautiful one.

One stop along the road: **Robber's Roost** is a mountain cave about half a mile from the road up a narrow gorge—it must be traversed on foot—which may or may not have been used by fugitives. At any rate, the isolated cave today is a popular spot with young Las Vegans, who like to go there and play guitars in the peace of the mountains.

Lee Canyon Ski Area (tel. 872-5462) has a cafeteria offering breakfast, lunch, and dinner during the ski season. A ski-rental shop, and a 3,000-foot chair lift and T-bar are the sum total of the development so far. The ski area and its facilities are open from Thanksgiving (if there's snow) to Easter.

The road back down from Lee Canyon to the main highway, U.S. 95, is 20 miles of sheer delight. Starting amid the coniferous trees of the mountain slopes, it soon traverses a barren but beautiful semi-moorland of cactus and Joshua trees. The contrast between the greenery and coolness of the mountains and the desolate brown sand and scrub of the valley floor is quite startling. To the right of the road, gently undulating foothills look as though they have been carved and smoothed by a giant sculptor, while in the distance the sun brings out the shades and colors of the different strata of rock in the surrounding hills.

Las Vegas is 28 miles away when you rejoin U.S. 95; the round-trip to both canyons, therefore, is about 94 miles. For a skier, the best plan would be to spend the day at Lee Canyon and then finish at Mount Charleston for dinner.

VISITING HOOVER (BOULDER) DAM

Until the 1930s much of the southwestern United States shared two natural problems—parched, sandy terrain that lacked irrigation for most of the year; and extensive flooding in spring and early summer, when the mighty Colorado River, fed by melting snow from its source in the Rocky Mountains, overflowed its banks and destroyed crops, lives, and property.

Finally, prodded by the seven states through which the river runs during the course of its 1,400-mile journey to the Pacific, Congress authorized construction of what came to be known as Hoover Dam. Completed in 1935, it not only stopped the annual floods, but became one of the world's major electrical generating plants, providing power to a score or more of surrounding communities.

Together with **Lake Mead** (the world's 16th-largest manmade lake), the dam has become a major recreation area whose boating, swimming, and fishing facilities attract more than three million visitors each year.

It's possible to take a bus from downtown Las Vegas to Boulder, about 25 miles southeast, and then on to Hoover Dam. Or you can take one of the sightseeing tours offered by the Gray Line, 1550 S. Industrial Rd. (tel. 384-1234). Their $24.50, 6½-hour tour takes you not only to Hoover Dam—where you'll tour the plant and see a movie about the dam's construction—but also to Old Vegas and the Southern Nevada Museum. Lunch is included. Another tour, this one six hours and priced at $34.35 (lunch included), visits Hoover Dam and Lake Mead. An excursion on the lake aboard the tour cruiser *Echo* is part of the trip.

What many people do, however, is drive. The best route is southeast, along Hwy. 93/95 through the industrial city of Henderson, past the new Las Vegas Downs racetrack and on into Boulder City. If you do drive, try to avoid Saturday and Sunday.

BOULDER CITY: Although the city limits embrace an area of 33 square miles and shelter a population of about 10,000, Boulder appears to be little more than a main street to transient visitors driving through. Actually, it's a pleasant, well-planned town—built only half a century ago as a construction town for the building of the vast dam. Located here are laboratories of the University of Nevada's Desert Research Institute, as well as similar facilities for the U.S. Bureau of Mines, the headquarters of the National Park Service for Lake Mead, and the regional headquarters of the Department of Energy. The city rose up in just a year, turning a desert waste into a community of 6,000, with homes, four churches, stores, restaurants, hotels, and even a 700-seat theater. The workmen came from all over the country.

Today it harbors a dozen or so motels, tennis courts, swimming pools, and a park with picnic facilities. One of the most interesting spots is the Gold Strike Inn, where there's a lobby display of oldtime slot machines, all in mint condition. Drop by the **Hoover Dam Visitors Bureau,** 1228 Arizona St. (tel. 293-1081), to see a free showing of the 28-minute movie, *The Story of Hoover Dam* (screened from 9:30 a.m. to 4:15 p.m.), which was made during construction.

ONWARD TO THE DAM: Some 200 or 300 yards past Boulder City, at the top of a slight incline, Lake Mead comes into view. It's quite eerie-looking, surrounded by sandy-colored rocky hills on which nothing seems to grow, sloping down to the water's edge.

You'll pass the Alan Bible Visitor Center, outlet for information about the Lake Mead National Recreation Area (about which more later). And so on to the dam (which, curiously enough, crosses a state line and a time zone: it's an hour later on the east than it is on the west!). Hoover Dam is a magnificent project whose $175-million cost is gradually being repaid by the sale of

inexpensive power to cities (Burbank, Glendale, Pasadena, Los Angeles), states (Arizona and Nevada), and the water and electrical utilities of southern California.

A massive, horseshoe-shaped wall, more than 600 feet thick at the bottom and tapering to 45 feet thick where the road crosses it at the top, it acts as a plug between the canyon walls to hold back the millions of gallons of water in Lake Mead. Four concrete intake towers on the lake side drop the water down about 600 feet to drive turbines and create power, after which the water spills out into the river and continues south.

Because it was a product of the WPA period, all the architecture is on a grand scale: even the rest rooms and the exhibition hall reflect an ornateness more typical of Radio City Music Hall than an engineering project.

The best way to understand the dam is to take one of the 35-minute tours ($1 for adults; children under 16, free) which are conducted at regular intervals daily between 7:30 a.m. and 7:30 p.m. Memorial Day to Labor Day (9 a.m. to 4:15 p.m. the rest of the year), and this is preceded by a free ten-minute orientation in the exhibition hall—a taped explanation of the course of the Colorado River and why it was necessary to dam it in the first place.

In addition, the exhibit building, open to the public, houses a model of a generating unit and a scale model of the Colorado River, with further information about the river and the workings of the dam. Over 22 million people have toured the dam and its immense power complex since guided tours were instituted in 1937. Last year over half a million visitors took the conducted tour through what has been called one of the Wonders of the World.

The tour begins with a one-minute elevator ride that drops you 44 stories (528 feet), almost to the level of the river on the Nevada side. Here the rocky cliffs are honeycombed with over seven miles of tunnels, but the tour takes you along only half a mile of them (all that space and not a slot machine to be seen!), a guide pointing out the seven-story-high turbine generators, each of which contains 800 tons of rotating units. The turbines are so complex and so enormous that each takes almost three years to manufacture and assemble.

The heroic scale of the dam is reflected in the art around it. On one side (Nevada) there is a magnificent pair of 30-foot-tall seated figures, the *Winged Figures of the Republic,* cast in bronze by sculptor Oskar Hansen. The sculptures are on black diorite bases.

When the dam was first being built, almost all the incredibly heavy pieces of equipment had to be lowered 600 feet to the river level from a cable railway at the road level overhead, and looking up now you can still see the control room for this cable operation overhanging the steep cliffs. The heads of people standing on the road and peering over look from here like the tiniest specks.

Across the river and through another long tunnel the tour pauses in a hollowed-out chamber above a section of one of the 30-foot-wide pipes that carry the water down to the turbines.

LAKE MEAD: Most of the lake's major attractions lie along its western shore, adjoining Nevada Hwy. 166; easiest access is from **Alan Bible Visitor Center,** maintained by the National Park Service. At the center, Hwy. 93 and Lakeshore Road (tel. 293-8906), overlooking the lake, you can pause to watch an educational movie and pick up a folder that lists nearby facilities and also carries safety tips both for wilderness areas (hiking and camping are popular in this region) and those using boats on the lake. Two miles from here is Boulder Beach, with good swimming, a boat dock, and restaurant three miles from the Visitor Center, motels, trailer court, store, and camping facilities.

Waterskiing is an almost year-round sport on the lake, with complete equipment available for rent. And boats are also much in demand by fishermen, who came to fish by day or night in its clear, blue waters. Bass (largemouth and striped) is the most popular fish, with channel catfish and rainbow trout also numerous.

Farther up the lake, a mile or two north of Boulder Beach, is **Lake Mead Resort and Marina,** 322 Lakeshore Rd., Boulder City, NV 89005 (tel. 702/293-3484), departure point for boat tours and locale of a floating restaurant. It's open Monday through Friday till 9 p.m., on Saturday and Sunday to 10 p.m. There's live music occasionally in the summer, and the bar stays open nightly until the action winds down.

You can also rent boats here. There are boats of all sizes available, from a 16-foot 15-horsepower fishing boat that rents for $10 per hour with a two-hour minimum ($45 per day) to a 19-foot 140-horsepower ski boat that costs $40 per hour with a two-hour minimum ($110 for four hours, $175 per day). Ski equipment and more sedate patio boats can also be rented. For example, you can rent a pontoon boat (with a gas barbecue and cooler) for $24 per hour (two-hour minimum), $70 for four hours, or $120 for the day. This marina is run by Seven Crown Resorts Inc., which also operates the Echo Bay and Temple Bar marinas on Lake Mead. At **Echo Bay** (tel. 394-4000) you can even rent houseboats that sleep six to ten people, from $430 to $1,055 for a three-day weekend or $800 to $1,800 for a week. For information and advance reservations, you can call Seven Crown Resort's toll-free number, 800/752-9669.

Down the road apiece, and under the same management, the **Lake Mead Lodge**, 322 Lake Shore Rd., Boulder City, NV 89005 (tel. 702/293-2074), offers 44 remodeled units with lake views. Facilities include a swimming pool, a steak-and-seafood restaurant, a coffeeshop, and barbecue. Rates are $42, single or double occupancy, and $49 for a room with two queen-size beds. Additional persons pay $6 per night. All units have bath but no phone or TV.

Lake Mead Yacht Tours operated by the Lake Mead Ferry Service, 2200 E. Patrick Lane, Suite 21 (tel. 736-6180), has daily sightseeing cruises from Lake Mead Marina, 23 miles from Las Vegas. They depart four times daily, year round, except Christmas, at 10:30 a.m., noon, 1:30 p.m., and 3 p.m. Cost of the cruise is $8.50 for adults; children under 12 pay $5.50.

Lake Mead Yacht Tours also offers a 5½-hour bus-and-boat trip for $35 per person. On this tour, a bus picks you up at your Strip hotel. A stop is made at Hoover Dam, and lunch is included. En route to the Marina, your tour bus goes through **Henderson,** Nevada. With a population of 33,000, this industrial town is the sixth-largest city in Nevada. Except for the hundreds of Chinese elms, which decorate the streets and the yards of practically every home, Henderson has very little of tourist interest. But after a few days away from trees and lawns, the greenery seems wonderful.

From Henderson, you continue on a good highway through a barren and gullied moonscape, where flash floods erode the bleak terrain a couple of times a year. This territory is reminiscent of parts of southern Spain or of lower California. Some refer to it poetically as "beige beauty," and it is raw and strangely compelling.

You'll also go through Boulder City and have time to take the Hoover Dam tour ($2 additional).

Once you reach the Lake Mead Marina, you board the yacht *Echo* for a 1¼-hour cruise to the dam and back.

The average depth of Lake Mead is 250 feet. Different levels of the surrounding mountains expose layers of civilization. Precambrian rock on one island, for example, is estimated to be 750 million years old.

Wild burros, cougars, big-horn mountain sheep, golden eagles, deer, and wild horses all roam the surrounding Sierra Madre ranges.

The entire 550-mile perimeter of Lake Mead is dotted with

campsites, eight of them equipped with running water, picnic benches, and stoves. These are administered by the National Park Service, and rangers are on call (tel. 293-4041) 24 hours a day in case of emergency or for information. Camping is restricted to 30 days. A small charge of $5 per night (per campsite) is exacted at the entrance to each campsite.

Wildlife is very prevalent in the area and hiking and exploring are popular, except in the middle of summer, when daytime temperatures top 100°. Sunglasses and a hat are strongly recommended for summer visitors, warm clothing for those visiting in winter.

Park rangers and naturalists present evening programs at the **Boulder Beach Amphitheater** in spring, summer, and fall, and in fall, winter, and spring all-day conducted hikes leave from the Alan Bible Visitor Center.

LAUGHLIN/LAKE MOJAVE

LAUGHLIN: If you drive just about 100 miles south of Las Vegas (Hwy. 95 south to 163 going east), you'll find it hard to believe that just 25 years ago, in 1964, Don Laughlin bought a down-at-the-heels motel and bar in South Point. He parlayed his purchase into the Riverside Resort Hotel and Casino and, in the process, changed the name South Point to Laughlin. This up-and-coming town is currently reminiscent of Las Vegas 35 years ago.

At this writing, the Riverside Resort Hotel and Casino is one of seven such establishments situated along the Colorado River. Harrah's Hotel and Casino is scheduled to be completed shortly, just south of Sam's Town Gold River Casino on Laughlin's Casino Drive. The 49-acre development will feature a 468-room hotel, with a Mexican theme to be carried throughout the rooms, the four restaurants, the entertainment lounge, and the casino.

Another major contender in the burgeoning Laughlin gaming market is Ramada, building a $60-million Ramada Station Hotel/Casino across from the Colorado Belle. The Ramada resort will be designed along the lines of a Victorian-era railroad station. The first phase in the development of the 28-acre resort will be the completion of 406 rooms; ultimately, the resort will total 1,194 rooms. The Ramada intends to have five restaurants and lounges, parking facilities for 1,500 cars, and a narrow-gauge railroad to carry guests from parking areas to the hotel.

As for the Colorado Belle, it's a 608-foot landlubber replica of a Mississippi paddlewheeler. At seven stories high, it's substantially larger than any such vessel that ever plied Mark Twain's river. The Belle has 200 rooms, and there are 1,000 in the adjacent six-story hotel.

As of this moment, Laughlin's hotel/motel/casino strip is little more than a mile long on a road called Casino Drive. On a busy weekend, gamblers outnumber the residents by about 20 to 1. Odds are that with the remarkable growth of the town, that ratio will shortly be changing in favor of the locals.

On an average, hotel rates in Laughlin run less than those in Las Vegas. Double rooms currently range from $38 to $45. In general, too, Laughlin costs less than Las Vegas, although dinner in a few of the fancier restaurants (like the New Orleans Room in the Colorado Belle) will run about $80 to $90 for two, with wine. But let's face it—there aren't the big-name star shows with the likes of Frank Sinatra, Dolly Parton, Tom Jones, and Wayne Newton. The coming of the larger and perhaps splashier hotel/casinos may well begin to raise the average tab for the new gambling crowd.

One of the big draws in Laughlin is the **Colorado River,** but like most of the visitors to the town, it's fast-moving. One does not spend dreamy hours on its banks. The brownish Colorado bursts by, carrying water taxis ferrying passengers to hotels and casinos, or taking them across the river to Bullhead City in Arizona.

Swift-moving and cold (about 58°F), the Colorado is not the place to take a dip. But if you'd like a fun break from gambling, there are daily river cruises—and even a moonlight cruise—downriver or up to Davis Dam. And if you've always wanted to see the famous London Bridge, the Colorado River King will take you on an 8-hour, 60-mile round-trip voyage south to Lake Havasu, where you can lunch at the London Bridge Resort.

For more information about river tours, call 800/228-9825. And if you'd like to know more about Laughlin itself, the Chamber of Commerce is always available to help (tel. 800/227-5245).

While you're at Laughlin, make the short drive to **Lake Mojave,** about ten miles north of the gaming tables. It's a beautiful place to swim, sail, sunbathe, or fish. Almost any water sport is especially enjoyable here because during the summer the water warms up to about 80°F.

At Katherine Landing on the lake, there are 50 hotel rooms, RV spaces with full hookups, and slips for boats. Double hotel rooms are $38 per day Sunday through Thursday, $58 per day Friday and Saturday. Kitchen units are sometimes available. Nonlandlubber types can take to the water and rent a houseboat for a few days and tour the lake. In low season, from September 15 to June 15, you can move about for three days on a fully equipped houseboat for $430—complete with instructions on how to handle it. The boat is suitable for sleeping six: this amounts to less than $24 per person per day. Assuming that you plan to eat and sleep during the voyage, you will need to bring your own food and linens.

If you prefer to take a seven-day trip in low season, the cost will be $790. From June 15 to September 15, the three-day rate increases to $775; for seven days, it's $1,260. It's still a bargain, though: the seven-day excursion amounts to $30 per person per day, assuming that you have a full complement of six people. Beyond seven days? How well do you think you all can get along in a confined space for that period of time?

Lake Mojave is part of the Lake Mead Recreation Area, and the Park Service manages two campsites—one at the northern end of the lake, toward Lake Mead, and the other at Katherine Landing. Campsites are $6 per night for one vehicle and no more than eight people. The Park Service does not take reservations—it's strictly "first come, first served."

If you haven't been to Lake Mojave before, bear in mind that the water temperature at the upper end of the lake is about 55°F in the summer, while that near Katherine Landing is more like 80°F. Equally important, during the summer the air temperature can rise to 115°F; even though it's dry desert heat, that's still hot. A final note relative to beaches, swimming, and generally lazing around: starting about Memorial Day and throughout the summer, there is high water on the lake, which is to say that there's very little beach for you to use. This can obviously limit your activities.

For information on Lake Mojave boat rentals and hotel reservations at Katherine Landing, call Seven Crown Resorts (tel. 800/752-9669). The Lake Mead National Recreation Area is a most helpful source of information on the one million acres they oversee (tel. 702/293-8907).

VALLEY OF FIRE

Most people's conception of desert is of the **Lawrence of Arabia** variety—countless wastes of undulating sand broken only by an occasional ridge of dunes or oasis of palm trees.

The desert of America's Southwest bears hardly any resemblance to that romantic image. It stretches for hundreds of miles around Las Vegas in every direction—a seemingly lifeless tundra of reddish earth, shaped by time, climate, and subterranean upheavals into a million canyons and ridges. In fact, it is far from lifeless:

deserts are natural homes for many fascinating species of plant and animal life.

In the distance, always seeming but a short walk away, the rugged cliffs and crags punctuate the irregular terrain as though in a giant's rock garden, changing through the color spectrum as the day gets shorter and the viewer gets nearer.

The **Valley of Fire State Park,** about 60 miles northeast of Las Vegas, is the major example of bizarrely colorful rock formations in this part of the country. It's a popular one-day trip for visitors to the city, and can be combined with a visit to Lake Mead, whose northwestern shore almost skirts it, or made the subject of a separate excursion. This is the largest state park in Nevada—46,000 acres.

By car, the most interesting route is to take Las Vegas Boulevard north, then go eastward along Lake Mead Boulevard. This will take you along North Shore Road through part of the Lake Mead National Recreation Area. Facilities for camping, fishing, picknicking, and swimming are available along this route. Visitors can stop for a meal at Callville Bay, Echo Bay, or Overton Beach. No concession facilities are available in the Valley of Fire.

The turnoff into the Valley of Fire is about four miles beyond the Overton Beach exit. A small interpretive station at the entrance has a display of maps and helpful information for park visitors.

The most scenic aspects of the Valley of Fire are the dominant Aztec sandstone formations. Wrinkled, etched, and scoured by time, these ancient rocks were formed in the Jurassic period, 135 to 150 million years ago.

Photographers, naturally, find the intricately shaped and brightly colored rocks fascinating, and in recent years Hollywood movie producers have begun to exploit this intriguing landscape. Burt Lancaster, Lee Marvin, Eva Marie Saint, Claudia Cardinale, and Gregory Peck have all shared starring roles with the natural wonders. The park is noted for its many diverse and whimsical formations—a duck, beehives, the "Rock of Gibraltar," the "Seven Sisters," and as many varied creatures as imagination can create. Most of these features are the result of chemical erosion aided by natural breakage of the brittle sandstone.

Fascinating Indian petroglyphs pecked into the rock walls and boulders can be seen throughout the park. These ancient rock writings are dramatic reminders of earlier cultures who traveled through this area on food-gathering and hunting expeditions. Fine examples of this rock art are found at **Atlatl Rock and Petroglyph Canyon**—both easily accessible from the main park roads.

At several park locations you can see petrified wood—the remains of ancient forests that washed into the area some 225 million years ago!

The many plants and animals seen in the park have developed elaborate strategies to survive the desert temperature extremes. Plant life includes creosote bush, numerous types of cactus, primroses, and other vegetation. Desert animals such as kit foxes, jackrabbits, ground squirrels, lizards, and snakes avoid extreme desert conditions by venturing out only in the cooler evening hours. Often the only evidence of these mammals and reptiles is delicate tracks left in the fragile sand dunes. A lucky visitor, however, might even get to see a desert tortoise. Birds are also common within the park, and a great number of species can be observed.

A good place to begin your visit to the Valley of Fire is the air-conditioned **Visitor Center** on Hwy. 169 six miles west of North Shore Road (tel. 397-2088). It's open seven days a week from 8:30 a.m. to 4:30 p.m. Exhibits explain the origin and geologic history of the park's colorful sandstone, describe the ancient people who carved their cryptic rock-art panels on the canyon walls, and identify the plants and wildlife you're likely to see. Postcards, books, slides, and film are on sale here.

Hiking trails, several picnic sites, a group-use area, and two campgrounds are available in the park. Most sites are equipped with tables, grills, water, and rest rooms. A fee ($4 per night per vehicle, $2 from June through August) is charged for use of the campground.

Although it is possible to drive right through the park and rejoin the main highway at the other side, an alternative route is to double back and visit the tiny town of **Overton,** in a surprisingly fertile valley replete with trees, vegetable crops, horses, and herds of cattle. You might find it a welcome contrast after the topography of the last 60 miles. Here you can obtain gas, food, and lodging.

Now primarily a residential area, Overton, settled in the late 1800s, once produced excellent lettuce, radishes, onions, melons, tomatoes, and alfalfa in quantities sufficient to supply large markets in southern California, Utah, and Las Vegas.

About one mile south of Overton (which is little more than a main street and a couple of bars and cafés) is the **Lost City Museum** (tel. 397-2193), commemorating the ancient Indian village that was discovered in 1924. The city's population reached one of the highest levels of Indian culture in the United States. Artifacts dating back 12,000 years are on display here, and exhibits tell the story of the ancient Lost City settled and inhabited by prehistoric dwellers of this area.

The museum's main display is of the ancient Pueblo culture that inhabited this area between A.D. 300 and 1150. Old clay jars, dried corn and beans, arrowheads, necklaces of tiny seashells, and straw baskets—all are displayed, as are a few macabre skulls and bones. A large case full of local rocks—petrified wood, fern fossils, iron pyrites, green copper, red iron oxide—together with manganese blown bottles, turned purple by the ultraviolet rays of the sun, occupies most of the rear room of the Lost City Museum.

Admission is $1 for those 18 and over. The museum is surrounded by reconstructed Indian pueblos. It is open daily from 8:30 a.m. to 4:30 p.m.

DEATH VALLEY

It's barely possible to drive from Las Vegas to Death Valley and back in the same day, but it wouldn't make much sense. The nearest entrance to this famous national park is about 140 miles to the northwest (take U.S. 95 and turn off at Lathrop Wells).

In winter, spring, and fall, the only times when it's cool enough to be comfortable, the few accommodations in the valley itself are usually booked up several weeks ahead—so advance reservations are a must. These are the resort hotels at **Stovepipe Wells** and **Furnace Creek.**

The Furnace Creek Ranch, Hwy. 190, P.O. Box 1, Death Valley, CA 92328 (tel. 619/786-2345), is rustic and very "western" in feel, with accommodations in sprawling cabins, fairway-view and pool-view units. A green desert oasis, it offers an astounding number of facilities in addition—of course—to horseback riding. There are an 18-hole golf course, a large swimming pool, Ping-Pong, shuffleboard, bicycling, volleyball, basketball, two tennis courts, even movies and Bingo. For dining there are a steakhouse, a coffeeshop, and a cafeteria. As for the horseback riding, there are two escorted two-hour rides a day, which cost $10 per person.

The ranch is open year round, although some activities are not available in summer. During the summer all accommodations are $65 per night (cabins are not available in the summer). The rest of the year you pay $65 for a redwood cabin with tub and shower, $84 for a pool-view room, or for what they call Fairway deluxe rooms, which are like modern hotel rooms and overlook the golf course. Rates are for one or two people.

Up the road apiece (a mile to be exact) is the luxurious and exclusive **Furnace Creek Inn,** P.O. Box 1, Death Valley, CA 92328 (tel. 619/786-2345), with its own supper club, the Oasis, offering nightly entertainment and gourmet fare. Typical entrees range in price from $25 to $35, and include filet mignon béarnaise and breast of capon Marengo; flambé desserts are a specialty. The Oasis is justly famous for its $12 champagne Sunday brunch, served from 11 a.m. to 2 p.m. Other facilities include four tennis courts, a restaurant/cocktail lounge, a swimming pool, and very lovely rooms. Of course, guests can also avail themselves of all the facilities back at the ranch.

The tile-roofed inn was built of adobe bricks by Panamint Indians over half a century ago in the opulent pre-Depression days. These days it's owned and operated by the Fred Harvey Company, about which more later in this chapter. (The ranch was established even earlier—in the 1880s—originally to provide accommodations for men working in the borax mines.)

The inn is open from mid-October to mid-May only. Rates are on the Modified American Plan, which means breakfast and dinner are included. They range from $190 to $210 a day, single or double occupancy. An extra person is $50; children aged 5 to 11 can stay in their parents' room for $25 each.

Needless to say, Death Valley must be seen in daylight, and the jagged mountains with their subtly changing tones . . . the rippling sand dunes . . . snowy-looking salt flats . . . and endlessly undulating flatland, all hold their special beauty for the visitor who has time to appreciate it.

The best starting point is actually the Visitors' Center at **Furnace Creek,** a quarter mile north of the ranch on Hwy. 190 (tel. 619/786-2331). The center functions as a combination information area, auditorium, museum, and camping ground (trailers are very popular around here, and there are facilities for camping), which is open November 1 through Easter from 8 a.m. to 8 p.m. seven days a week, to 5 p.m. the rest of the year. There is an 18-minute orientation film shown hourly.

In 1988, Death Valley began charging a fee for entry into the National Monument. The fee per motor vehicle for a seven-day visit is $6, for a bicycle or pedestrian, $2.50. An annual area pass good for the calendar year is $16.

Big-horn sheep (stuffed), burros, hummingbirds, and kangaroo rats can all be inspected in the museum, which is probably the only place visitors do see them. There are many explanatory displays about the valley's geological evolution—how numerous flash floods over the ages have covered the floor with water, only to be dried out again throughout long centuries of baking sun.

In some places, salt is many feet thick on the valley floor, and a salty creek that runs north to south, disappearing underground and reemerging from time to time, actually contains a tiny species of fish whose ancestors can be traced back to the Ice Age. Although streams run down from the surrounding mountains at some times of the year, the valley receives less rainfall—less than two inches a year—than anywhere else in America. (By comparison, New York City receives 43 inches each year; Los Angeles, 15; and San Francisco, 22.) There have been occasions when Death Valley's entire annual supply of rainfall has been dumped from the clouds within one hour's storm—not in summertime, though, when temperatures of 110°F and 120°F are fairly common.

Roughly speaking, temperatures rise by 5½° for every 1,000-foot drop in elevation, and the heavy, cool air that drops down between the mountains is compressed (and heated), rising to make room for more cool air to take its place (so glad you asked). All you need to know about this is that if you're going to wander around the valley in summertime, be sure to have plenty of water with you, and if your car breaks down, stay—sheltered—as close to it as possible.

Some things can live in the desert with little or no water—creosote bushes and mesquite trees, which put down deep, spreading roots, and the kit fox, which gets its moisture from other animals (it catches and eats sidewinder snakes, lizards, and bats).

The museum's evidence that the mastodon stalked across the land was removed as the track area was closed to the public. A cast of a Titano skull, an ancient rhino-like mammal, is displayed, however. Other milestones of history are uncovered in the different layers of rock—twisted and distorted from their geological sequence by the earthquakes that shattered the region eons ago.

The various living conditions that exist for plant life in the valley are defined poetically as "shady streamsides, mountaintops, sunbaked slopes, and salty flats."

Indians have always lived here, and still do; they are believed to have been around when the luckless prospectors ("the 49ers") on their way to California were trapped by the valley's hostile environment and soon died of thirst and starvation. Indian beads, baskets, arrowheads, and cornhusks are on display, side by side with old prospectors' tools and supplies. Many adventurers have tried their luck for gold and silver, and the northeast edge of the valley nearest Las Vegas is still dotted with ghost towns, such as Rhyolite (near Beatty), which were once thriving communities. Borax, a salty white mineral used for chemicals, paint, gasoline, glass, detergents, and as a preservative and water softener, has been mined extensively in Death Valley for years, and another small museum, devoted to this activity, is located next to the Furnace Creek Ranch.

One of the most interesting attractions in Death Valley is an elaborate, man-made, $2,000,000 structure, **Scotty's Castle.** It was built in the early 1920s by a Chicago millionaire, Albert Johnson, in association with a notorious pseudo-prospector, storyteller, and publicity seeker, Walter E. Scott, better known as "Death Valley Scotty." Their story is one of a unique friendship that lasted for almost a half century.

The structure was originally called **Death Valley Ranch,** but Scotty publicized it—and the press always touted it—as Scotty's Castle. Spanish and Moorish in style, and lavishly furnished in antiques and custom-made pieces, the castle stands in the northern section of Death Valley. It's about an hour's drive from either Stovepipe Wells or the Monument's headquarters at Furnace Creek.

Scotty was a frequent guest of Johnson's and is credited with suggesting the site for his desert home. After Johnson's death in 1948, Scotty lived on here until the end of his own life. No one has ever been able to discover whether Scotty, an ex-performer with Buffalo Bill's Wild West Show, actually had a gold mine in the desert or not. He did spend almost half a century prospecting in Death Valley, supported by various grubstakes, the most famous of them being from Albert Johnson. Up until his death in 1954, Scotty was frequently trailed into the desert, but no one ever located his mysterious mine. It appears now that there never was a mine, and that Scotty's real gold mine was Johnson.

The castle and grounds are open to visitors every day of the year, and there are regularly scheduled 45-minute tours of the interior. The tour is $5 for adults, $3 for children.

Near the castle is a volcanic crater, **Ubehebe Crater,** 490 feet deep, and two hours' drive from there is a fascinating mud playa called the "racetrack" because of the heavy stones that have been moved across it by strong winds, leaving clear tracks behind.

Another attraction in the extreme north section of the valley (starting just outside the old ghost town of Rhyolite with its house made of bottles and its abandoned mineshafts) is the 26-mile **Titus Canyon,** so narrow that traffic is one way throughout its entire length from Rhyolite to the northbound highway through the valley.

Near Furnace Creek is **Zabriskie Point,** a fascinating area of badlands and multicolored rock that was the scene of an Antonioni movie of the same name. A 1½-hour round trip will take you to **Dantes View,** which is the only place accessible by road from which you can view the entire panorama of the 130-mile valley.

There are, of course, numerous other sightseeing spots for visitors with the time to spare. A comprehensive map of the valley can be obtained at the Furnace Creek Visitors' Center, from which various expeditions are regularly conducted.

GHOST TOWNS

The shadowy phenomenon of ghost towns—once-flourishing areas, later deserted and abandoned—has always been an intriguing and romantic image to just about everyone.

Many began with a lone traveler who serendipitously stumbled on mineral-rich rocks while out on another pursuit—perhaps tracking game, strayed livestock, or criminals. He would mark off his area, stuff his pockets and knapsack with specimens, and rush off to the nearest mine with his claim. If there was anything to it, adventurers, drifters, and raggedy prospectors would soon flock to the area, set up meager lodgings, break out picks and shovels, and set to work.

Ofttimes this initial feverish effort would quickly prove fruitless, but if the yield seemed in the least bit promising, word would spread and entrepreneurs would arrive with provisions. Soon a main street would develop around a general merchandise store, followed by other shops and the inevitable mining-camp saloons, gambling houses, and red-light district. A camp newspaper would come into being, more stores and more permanent buildings of stone, brick, and concrete would be erected. Eventually a real town would evolve, with schools, churches, perhaps electricity and even a railroad station.

But then the mines would begin to dry up. Little by little businesses would fold and the population dwindle. Vandalism, wind, and fire would ravage the remaining structures, leaving only ghost-inhabited remnants of what had been. And so the towns died.

Nevada has at least 40 such towns, ranging from those that still (or again) have a small population centered around a store, a bar, and perhaps a post office, to those that are now merely relics and rubble. The latter are perhaps the more mysterious and evocative.

A third category are the Disney-esque artificially revived-for-tourism towns, often with rides and attractions, not to mention cutesy misspelled "olde" signs. One of these, Calico (in California), is actually owned by Walter Knott of Berry Farm fame.

The following listings run the gamut. To some you need to bring a vivid, and perhaps visionary, imagination. Others, like

McDonald's, "do it all for you." These are the ones you should probably seek out if you're traveling with kids.

All are within driving distance of Las Vegas, most in Nevada, but some in accessible areas of adjoining states.

GOODSPRINGS: To reach this ramshackle town 35 miles from mid-Strip Las Vegas, follow Rte. 15 for 28 miles almost straight south toward the California border, then turn onto Rte. 161 (at the sign that indicates Jean-Goodsprings). The road is good all the way.

There are two specific reasons for mentioning Goodsprings: first, it's close to Vegas; second, the **Pioneer Saloon** in the center of town (tel. 874-1484), open daily from 10 a.m. to midnight, is an authentic leftover from time past. It's the only complete metal building still standing anywhere in the United States.

As you enter Goodsprings, you'll pass the cemetery first. It's down-at-the-heel, not the sort of place where perpetual care has been a big thing. The graves appear to be only shallow mounds in some cases, but I was assured that "coffins are set just as deep as anywhere, even if they have to dynamite to get down six feet." A couple of markers are wood, weathered almost to the point of no identification. The only standard headstones are in a segment of the yard that has been fenced off by a low rail. These stones all belong to the Fayle family, who were top brass in Goodsprings for some years. In the area near the cemetery, you can search for Indian arrowheads, spearheads, and other artifacts. They're difficult to recognize, however, unless you've had some experience studying them in museums.

"Slots—Cocktails—& Booze" says the painted sign on the side of the building as you approach the Pioneer Saloon. The saloon is a metal building with pressed-tin walls and ceiling on the inside, more metal (which almost looks like cement or stone blocks until you inspect it and feel it cold to the touch) on the exterior. There are a potbelly stove, linoleum so worn that it no longer has a pattern, drapes (they never were *draperies)* that don't match, a swamp cooler, and a long, saloony bar.

The Pioneer Saloon has been in business since at least 1913. There's a 1916 copy of the *Goodsprings Gazette* that carries an advertisement for the saloon. And the Goodsprings Hotel was advertised in New York newspapers as "the finest in the West." In those days Goodsprings had a population of 2,000 (which had shrunk to 62 by 1967; today it's about 100), and people from Las Vegas went to Goodsprings "to shop, gamble, dine out, drink, go to the theater, and to live it up." The thriving metropolis had nine bars, several restaurants, a theater, churches, other businesses and homes, and it was a regular stop for Barnum & Bailey. It was the biggest town in Nevada in its time. A narrow-gauge railroad carried ore from the surrounding mines to the Union Pacific tracks at Jean.

On January 16, 1942, Goodsprings made headlines because it was the closest town to Potosi Mountain (25 miles distant, but it seems nearer in the clear desert). A flight, lost in a storm, crashed there with Carole Lombard, the famous movie star, aboard. There's a piece of the wreckage on top of the potbelly stove, and people who drop in at the saloon remember details as if the tragic event had occurred only yesterday. Clark Gable, the actress's husband, stayed at the Goodsprings Hotel. Later the hotel burned to the ground, and the last big blow to Goodsprings occurred when the old General Store was torn down and used to construct part of the Long Branch Saloon in Las Vegas.

Surrounding Goodsprings, you can see the rotting remains of mining companies such as the Argentine and Yellow Pine Zinc & Lead, and discarded wrecks of old, abandoned cars on the far outskirts of town.

NELSON: Like Goodsprings, Nelson has the advantage of proximity to Las Vegas. Head south along U.S. 95 and turn off at Rte. 60.

The Spaniards, in the 1770s, were the first to discover gold in this region; they called it Eldorado, but did little about mining the area's riches. The gold remained unextracted till about 100 years later, when good old American know-how took over. Unfortunately, the consequent Techatticup Mine was riddled with violence from the start. Disagreements between labor and management, not to mention heated ownership disputes, led to so many killings that the town of Nelson was among the West's most notorious.

Nevertheless, several millions in gold, lead, silver, and copper were mined successfully. Today huge cyanide vats (cyanide was used in processing gold ore), all that is left of the old settlement, remain an imposing sight.

MINERAL PARK, ARIZONA: Mineral Park, Arizona, is less than 90 miles from Las Vegas, five miles from U.S. 93 near Kingman, Arizona. It was a thriving town in 1877, when it was designated as county seat of Mohave County. And in those days, a good-sized emporium, blacksmith shops, attorneys' offices, an assayer's building, an apothecary, and several bars were kept busy by seekers and finders of gold in the surrounding hills. Silver was known in the 1860s, but marauding Indians got in the way of any serious attempts to mine. It wasn't too long until miners established a foothold, however, and Mineral Park had "made it" when the first post office was opened there in December 1872. But the town fathers of Mineral Park put too many hopes into "the railroad" to keep things humming. Their prediction went bust. In 1887 the Mohave County seat was switched to Kingman, and the only newspaper in the town and county closed shop and moved to Kingman too. The railroad, alas, never came closer to Mineral Park than 12 miles.

Today Mineral Park is dominated by a mining venture of the Duval Copper Division. It's a relatively clean and neat setup, but much that had survived of the lean-to town is buried under heaps of rock and by new buildings put up by Duval. Still, a few things from the past may be seen.

An old edifice with a cupola houses a kiln that must have been used to evaluate ore samples, and it continues to hold its own, somewhat awry and out of kilter. Verbena blooms in the yard. And the remains of a wan but sturdy adobe brick house of some substance valiantly struggle against time. Outside walls had been whitewashed—you still can see that—and faded flowers bloom from the tattered wallpaper inside, peeling from the walls in sheets. Vandals have done their work, and windows and doors and floors have been damaged. The roof is still intact, though, and the fireplace (also of adobe brick) stands proudly.

The road from U.S. 93 is kept clean, and it isn't a bad drive. For those interested in the ecology of copper mining, Duval provides a look toward the problem of getting rid of tin cans. They're used in the extraction of copper from the ore! You'll probably also see rock blasting. The smelting, incidentally, is performed not in Mineral Park but in El Paso, Texas.

About 15 miles away is **Kingman,** where the **Mohave Museum of History and Arts,** 400 W. Beale St. (tel. 602/753-3195), was opened in April 1968. Ancient Indian carvings and stone implements, and a superb collection of carved turquoise, are on display here along with pioneer wagons, mine equipment, and other implements that the early people of Kingman used. Well-known artist Roy Purcell did much of the artwork in the museum, including a fascinating mural that adorns the front lobby. However, one of the most popular exhibits is that including portraits of the Presidents and First Ladies by Laurence Williams. There's a restored 1926 pipe organ, and a room devoted to actor Andy Devine, who grew up in Kingman. A gift shop on the premises features Indian craft articles. The museum is close to two nice parks, at the junction of U.S. 93/Historic Route 66, and I-40.

It's open weekdays from 10 a.m. to 5 p.m., and on Saturday and Sunday from 1 to 5 p.m.; closed on most major holidays. Admission is free but contributions are appreciated.

CALICO, CALIFORNIA: Calico, California, is 160 miles from Las Vegas off sleek Interstate 15, on above-average roads all the way. You turn from I-15 between Yermo and Barstow onto a paved side road when signs point to Ghost Town Road. As you enter Calico, you'll go between the old Boot Hill Cemetery and a trailer camp that's been planted with trees. (I've never quite understood why so many ghost towns located their cemeteries on the approach roads.)

Calico has had a silver lining. Silver made it big in 1881 and kept the town humming for 15 years while associated businesses that go with a boom town thrived. Silver from coffers of Knott's Berry Farm was poured into restoration of the sagging town more recently, and the town was deeded by the Knott family to San Bernardino County. It's now maintained by the regional parks system of San Bernardino County, and you can enjoy it as a restoration (if a somewhat touristy one) that approximates Calico during its heyday.

Calico's vast riches were discovered by chance when a Panamint Indian stole a horse from one Lafayette Mecham. Mecham pursued the thief across miles of desert into the Calico Mountains. He never did catch the Indian, but he did observe what looked like indications of silver in the mountains. There had been talk of silver in Calico before this, and Mecham's sons, Frank and Charles, upon hearing their father's story, decided to investigate. They assembled a group, and grubstaked by John C. King, sheriff of San Bernardino County, they set out in the spring of 1881.

Charlie made the first important find in September of 1882. Silver King (named in honor of the expedition's sponsor) was for a time the richest mine in California.

By 1885 the mine had yielded about $1 million worth of silver bullion. Word spread, and soon the Mechams' lone tent was joined by hundreds of lean-tos, sun-bleached adobes, shanties, and rustic frame houses.

It became a thriving mining community of some 3,500 men, women, and children, including 40 Chinese residents who set up a small Chinatown at the eastern end of the town, complete with a

Chinese restaurant. Their town boasted two hotels, a church, a one-room schoolhouse, and 13 saloons! During the boom years they extracted close to $20 million in silver ore from the Calico Hills. (Some estimates say $86 million is closer to the true figure, and there are old miners who claim another $86 million in silver ore is still buried in them thar hills.)

The entire town was totally devastated by fire twice, in 1884 and 1887, and completely rebuilt. But a more important disaster to the inhabitants was the continuing drop in the price of silver. When Charlie found his first lode the price of silver was $1.13 an ounce; by 1894 it had dropped to 64¢ an ounce, and many prospectors had already begun to abandon Calico to search elsewhere for something more lucrative—gold.

By 1896 the price of silver was a mere 53¢ an ounce, and the stamp mills were shut down. The discovery of borate (Twenty Mule Team Borax originated in Calico) kept things going until 1907, after which the swift exodus began, and desert winds and sands began to claim the town.

The legendary folk of Calico included many colorful characters. Wyatt Earp was a frequent visitor, though the town was notably law-abiding and peaceful compared to its counterparts elsewhere. As on TV's "Gunsmoke," there was the town physician, Dr. Goodenough, dubbed by local wags "Dr. Drunkenough," and Diamond Lil (known as Madam de Lil), Calico's answer to Kitty. And then there was old Quartz Davis, so tough that when a black scorpion bit him, it died.

Perhaps the most intriguing legend concerns an unlikely pair, a miner, Pat Hogan, and his Chinese friend, Wong Lee, a Calico cook. They arrived in town together in the early 1880s, and every night, after work, they would go to watch the gambling and revelry at Lucky Joe's Palace. Lee never betted, but he would always study a certain roulette wheel. He also studied the stars from an old Chinese astrology text. Finally, the auspicious night arrived. He stepped up to the wheel with a silver dollar of Hogan's and a $5 gold piece of his own. He won and kept winning, wiping out the owner and then politely refusing further play. An argument ensued and Wong was killed, but Hogan escaped with the winnings. He soon turned up in Vegas, where, several days later, he was shot in a drunken brawl. His last words were "the gold—it's buried in Calico three feet from the big rock." But he never said which rock, and people are searching for Hogan's gold to this day.

Or so the story goes.

Legends were all that remained of Calico until Walter Knott

decided to purchase the town and surrounding areas in 1950. Knott had a sentimental interest in the preservation of Calico. He was the nephew of Sheriff John King, who had grubstaked the original mining expedition, and as a young man he had even spent a summer working one of the mines.

He rebuilt Calico over a period of about 15 years, trying to reflect the spirit of the town as he remembered it, although adding such necessary conveniences as modern plumbing, piped water, and parking lots. Several oldtimers were called in as consultants in the reconstruction.

Although Calico now bustles with activity during the day, without the large number of tourists it is still a ghost town of just a few residents.

If you prefer to explore Calico on a more-than-one-day trip, and don't wish to use the trailer park, several motels are located within reasonable distances, and nearby towns offer nighttime recreation. There are also camping sites ($10 per night per camper, plus $1 for off-road vehicles) located in shaded canyons; call 619/254-2122 for information. A parking lot is located just below the town, and a fee of $3 per car for daytime-only parking helps pay for maintenance. From the parking lot, you can either climb flights of stairs to Main Street or ride up the steep incline on a tramway ($1 to $1.50 for adults, 50¢ for kids, round trip).

Shops that retain the atmosphere of Calico have opened on Main Street and along some of the short side streets. You may dine in several places.

Fees are charged for several of Calico's attractions, but not for all of them. The ones that do charge—such as oldtime melodramas at the Calikage Playhouse—are reasonably priced, and most are worth it. Calico also features the Maggie Mine tour, the Calico-Odessa R.R. Museum, and a shooting gallery. In this regard, visitors should remember that Calico is not supported by taxes. So anything you may drop into the coffers to help keep up the town is encouraging, and perhaps an incentive toward preservation and restoration of other such places. At any rate, while other ghost towns fade and sag in sad disrepair, Calico plays host to thousands of visitors every year. Annual celebrations include Calico Days in October, the March Hullabaloo, and the May Spring Festival.

Nearby Mohave Desert Sights

While you're in the area, you might want to take in some other Mohave Desert attractions. One is an archeological dig, the **Calico Early Man Site** (tel. 619/256-3591), located 15 miles northeast of Barstow via Interstate 15, then 2½ miles north on Minneola Road (the last two miles the road is unpaved, but it's quite passable by car).

Excavations since 1964 have unearthed over 11,500 artifacts. Lab and field analyses have established man's presence in North America for more than 50,000 years. It's the oldest site on the continent, and unique as the only site in the Americas ever worked by famed anthropologist Louis S. B. Leakey. The site was developed by the National Geographic Society and the San Bernardino County Museum and is significant as a "stone tool" workshop. The area is open for tours Wednesday at 1:30 and 3:30 p.m., Thursday through Sunday every two hours from 9 a.m. to 3:30 p.m. (major holidays excepted). Admission is free.

Visitors may enter the excavations on guided tours, observe tools and methods of excavation, visit the small museum to handle stone tools, casts, and replicas, and view photographs of work.

Detailed desert recreation information, maps, and brochures, are available at the **California Desert Information Center,** at 831 Barstow Rd., one block north of Interstate 15 (tel. 619/256-8617). It's open from 9 a.m. to 5 p.m. daily. The center is managed by the Bureau of Land Management and the Barstow area Chamber of Commerce. It houses displays on the high desert's natural history, its wildflowers, and its wildlife. The staff can tell you about area lodgings, camping, hiking, and driving in the desert; they're also a great resource for information on canyons, petroglyph sites, things to see and do in the Barstow area, and local services. All in all, the California Desert Information Center is well worth a visit if you plan to explore the area.

As long as you're here in Barstow, there are several points of interest you might want to investigate for some historical and geological background on the area. First of all, stop at the California Desert Information Center and pick up their folder called *Begin in Barstow with 5 One-Day Adventures.* Directions and maps in the folder are more detailed and helpful than any other maps you may have.

Note, then, that Barstow is home to the **Mojave River Valley Museum,** at 270 E. Virginia Way (tel. 619/256-5452), open daily from 11 a.m. to 4 p.m. The museum is dedicated to the preservation of the heritage of the Mojave River Valley, and has artifacts and displays relating to the area, a number of them from the famous Calico Early Man Site. The museum also displays a variety of materials from Paleo-Indian sites found throughout the desert. Specimens of local gemstones on exhibit present a selection of the minerals still being mined in the Mojave Desert. You might want to check into the field trips the museum conducts to local sites of historical interest.

And while you're in Barstow, stop at the **Barstow Station,** 1611 E. Main St. (tel. 619/256-0366), open daily from 9 a.m. to 9 p.m. This unique early-1900s railroad station and complex has a wide variety of interesting shops.

If you'd like to peruse a portion of the nearby foothills of the Calico Mountains on horseback, the **Pan McCue Ranch** would be the place to begin. Pan McCue is not the name of the ranch's owner but of a stallion—one the founding sires of the American Quarter Horse Association. The ranch conducts western trail rides for both the novice and the more experienced rider, taking them through the high desert with its magnificent scenery and varied terrain. You might also want to join in on one of the ranch's old-fashioned cookouts or hayrides. The Pan McCue Ranch is eight miles east of Barstow via I-15 (tel. 619/254-2184), and is open daily from 7 a.m. till sunset, later by reservation.

About 20 minutes north of Barstow lies **Rainbow Basin/Owl Canyon** (tel. 619/256-3591). This area was formed a bit before our time, perhaps between 10 and 30 million years ago. It contains fossilized remains of insects and animals, said to be among the best-preserved specimens found anywhere. Erosion has revealed richly colored sedimentary layers of remarkable beauty. The four-mile loop into and out of the area is narrow but passable for small vehicles. If you have an RV, the Owl Canyon campground, one mile east, accommodates 31 units and has picnic tables, grills, fire rings, drinking water, and trash receptacles for $4.50 per night.

The Rainbow Basin area is frequently visited by university groups interested in the fossil remains found here. In 1972 the Rainbow Basin was designated a "National Natural Landmark" by the Secretary of the Interior. Its sediments are textbook examples of folds, faults, and other disruptions of the earth's crust. And because of the quantity and quality of fossils found at the Rainbow Basin, the locality is a reference standard for the age of Barstovian land mammals who lived 12 to 16 millions years ago in North America. Hiking through the Owl Canyon wash, next to Owl Canyon Campground, you will pass through three different geologic formations, evidencing a time span of millions of years.

In a more contemporary vein, and if you're a careful observer, you may see a variety of wildlife, including the kit fox, desert tortoise, and bobcat. The barn owl, the red-tailed hawk, and the turkey vulture frequently are sighted in this area. Bear in mind that all species are protected by the State of California, unless designated as game animals; therefore, desert tortoises and birds of prey may not be removed or harassed. Furthermore, hobby collection of fossils is restricted and all significant fossil finds must be reported to the Bureau of Land Management. As noted above, the California Desert Information Center in Barstow has a wealth of information on this area and guidelines for its use, including a map that outlines roads, trails, campsites, viewpoints, and the natural area boundary.

When you run out of archeological sites, and the children are beginning to squirm, head for **Lake Dolores** (tel. 619/257-3315 or 254-2009), about 20 miles northeast of Barstow via I-15. The area is open from Palm Sunday weekend (the weekend before Easter) through Labor Day weekend from 8 a.m. to 5:30 p.m. The water park has the West Coast's first and biggest high-speed water slide—80 feet high and 200 feet long; you can reach speeds of up to 50 miles per hour. For the Tarzan in you, there's a 350-foot-long cable extending over one of the lakes; aspiring circus performers can trapeze into the middle of a 15-feet-deep lake. Once that excitement dies down, there are skeeter boats to whip around a half-mile course, or the gentler wet-and-wild bumper boats. Kiddies can play in a shallow lake with teeter-totters, swings, and slides. When you come out of the water, you can enjoy a leisurely game of miniature golf, have a picnic, or use the snackbar facilities. Showers are also available. Admission to Lake Dolores is $6 for those 9 years old and up, $3 for kids 3 to 8; no charge for those under 3.

GOLD POINT:
You have to turn off a good highway and cover about seven miles of graded gravel to get to Gold Point, about 180 miles from Las Vegas. But it isn't overly rugged. The town is located between Beatty and Goldfield. You take U.S. 95 most of the way, then turn onto Nevada Rte. 3.

The weathering of the years is the only real debilitation that Gold Point has suffered. It's been saved from the depredation and disgrace of vandals, mostly because the vigilant postmistress stayed on to serve the population of eight. (It takes only one strong-willed individual to save a town in some Nevada precincts.) The number of residents in Gold Point recently jumped somewhat, because of a new glimmer of interest in mining. Now there's some consternation about the newcomers, who have a bright chance to do more harm than good—parking their trailers among the old buildings, digging all over the place. "They're not environmentalists interested in preservation," snorted one state official.

I won't suggest that you attempt to drive a regular passenger car out into the rough desert from Gold Point. But if you have access to a desert buggy, which can stand more rigorous terrain, you might look into both Oriental and Gold Mountain, nearby mining centers that have fallen into sagging relics since their prime days in the 1870s and 1880s. Plenty of old diggings can be seen in the weathered hills.

Funny thing about Gold Point: it started out as Hornsilver, after an earlier metallic lure, and even had a newspaper, the *Hornsilver Herald,* an accomplishment that gave towns of that era a certain cachet.

During the good old days, the population zoomed to 2,000. Silver turned to gold and so did the town's name, in 1929, but that's "way back in history" in these parts of Nevada. The year 1929 is when some mine operators started digging again and stayed on through several ensuing years. And it's probably why the town hasn't given in as much as most of its less recently occupied contemporaries. Good points about Gold Point: it's about 60 miles beyond Rhyolite, one of Nevada's most famous ghost towns, and also within a reasonable distance of Death Valley, for an entirely different travel sensation.

GOLDFIELD: Returning to U.S. 95 from Gold Point, you might want to continue north a bit and explore two more ghost towns, Goldfield and Tonopah.

The first you'll reach is Goldfield (182 miles north of Las Vegas). It's now boarded up and abandoned, but in the early 1900s it was a thriving community of 30,000. When prospectors Billy March and Harry Stimler first staked their claim in 1902, the town was called "Grandpa," but the region's vast resources suggested the name change.

It was a rip-roarin' town, with all the shoot-outs, labor disputes, and other disorders so typical of turn-of-the-century mining settlements. Of course, there were numerous flourishing saloons, the best known run by Tex Rickard. Rickard had made a fortune in the Klondike and lost it. In addition to running a bar so huge that it required 80 bartenders to handle it, Rickard moonlighted as a fight promoter. A nationally publicized bout for the lightweight championship of the world in 1906 between Gans and Nelson ran 42 rounds, with Rickard offering the largest purses in fight history—$20,000 to the champ, Nelson, and $10,000 to the challenger.

In the beginning years the abundant Goldfield mines produced between $5 million and $11 million worth of ore annually, but by the early 1920s production had dwindled to a fraction of that amount.

Today Goldfield is one of the more interesting of Nevada's ghost towns, since so many structures are still standing intact— despite a flash flood and a huge fire. The boarded-up Goldfield Hotel, once a beautifully appointed showpiece, remains at the center of town. Its lobby is still furnished under layers of dust, its dining room set up for an evening meal that never took place. And there are old mines and dumps to see at the foot of the Columbia Mountain.

You can also see Tex Rickard's home, but like the hotel, it's not open to visitors.

TONOPAH: Proceeding about 25 miles farther north, you'll reach Tonopah, where, during the boom years of 1905 and 1913, $250 million worth of gold and silver was mined.

There are quite a few stories about the discovery of mineral wealth in Tonopah. According to expert Lambert Florin, author of a series of books about western ghost towns, the most likely version concerns two prospectors, Jim Butler and William Hall, who were en route to a mining camp called Southern Klondyke in 1900. They camped overnight at Tonopah, and the ornery Hall, unable to waken Butler from a sound slumber the next morning, went on alone. Butler finally woke, tracked down the party, and was just on the point of flinging an angry stone at the burros when he noticed that the stone showed signs of valuable ore.

Butler's wife, upon hearing the story later, called in expert Tasker L. Oddie, who estimated that the area could produce $350 per ton of rock. She then staked a claim in one of the richest-producing mines in the region—the Mizpah Mine.

The town was laid out, grew, prospered, and diminished, but never completely. Some mining is still in progress today, though mostly for semiprecious stones. Hence, Tonopah is not, strictly speaking, a ghost town. It has a thriving main street of shops and restaurants centered around the five-story Mizpah Hotel. An unusual feature of the town is its high curbs designed to channel the floodwaters that occasionally rush through the town.

RHYOLITE: As the crow flies, Rhyolite is about 118 miles from Las Vegas, off Rte. 58, close to Death Valley. You can reach it in about 2½ hours. Because of its proximity to Death Valley, most vacationers prefer to combine a trip to both places.

Two buildings stand out in Rhyolite today—the **Bottle House,** built entirely of bottles, and the **railroad depot** without a railroad on Golden Street. (Nearest railroad is no closer than 100 miles.) Both buildings are in fair states of preservation, and both warrant a look-see.

At the Bottle House, logically, bottles are sold. They are empty ones—bottles hauled in from the desert. Some have turned amethyst in color, a change wrought from the original hues by blazing sun. They're collectors' items, these bottles.

Originally, the Bottle House was built by a bartender. The materials were used partly in fun, I understand, but the bottles proved to be practical; they were available in quantity (miners imbibe in the desert!), and they cost the builder nothing. The house has outlasted more pretentious buildings that once graced the city of 10,000. (Of course, it helped that it was restored for a movie setting in 1925 by Paramount.) In addition to bottles, they also sell books about the desert, postcards, and suchlike. Open daily from 7 a.m. till sunset.

The depot serves current traffic too, selling beer and soft drinks to visitors across the old bar, once a fashionable place to line up for healthier firewater.

A third enterprise in Rhyolite is the **Red Barn Antique Shop,** which sells glassware, Lenox china, and hand-cut crystal; you can also buy coffee and doughnuts here.

Rhyolite began with the Bullfrog Mine. Gold was dug there at a fantastic clip, and speculation ran high. The precious metal was discovered by Frank (Shorty) Harris and Ernest L. Cross in August 1904. As Shorty later described it in the *Rhyolite Herald:* "The quartz was full of free gold. . . . Talk about rich! Why, gee whiz, it was great! . . . The very first boulder was as rich in gold as anything I had ever seen. . . ."

As the news traveled, scores of rainbow-chasing prospectors poured into the camp; by September there were already 75 residents.

H.D. and L.D. Porter arrived with an 18-mule team laden with merchandise and set up the town's leading store. By mid-March the population was 200, most of them lodged in tents and other ramshackle affairs.

In the course of time a gentleman named Pete Busch showed up. As he shivered through the winter on the uncomfortable slopes of the mining camp, he dreamed of promoting a livable town. He liked the idea of wide streets and good buildings. Apparently a lot of other miners liked the idea, for Rhyolite blossomed into a city within a matter of months. Miners who had been paying $5 for a barrel of water, men who had lived in drafty tents, now lavished their golden bounty trying to outdo each other with grand houses. The miners were rip-roaring men, free with their new wealth.

Water was piped into Rhyolite, a new post office was built, and a school building was constructed for the (then) outrageous sum of $50,000. In 1906 three railroads fell over each other to reach the city first. The Las Vegas and Tonopah Line arrived first, connecting Rhyolite with the famous Union Pacific tracks. In its hey-day Rhyolite had electric light and power, a telephone system, three newspapers, and a stock exchange. There were banks, office buildings, churches, a hospital, a jail (much needed), restaurants, hotels, an opera house, many stores, and, inevitably, over 20 saloons and a thriving red-light district.

Unlike other mining towns built of canvas, adobe, and thrown-together wood structures, Rhyolite was built of stone and concrete—it was built to last. Its population peaked at over 10,000. A real town, Rhyolite offered its citizens not just the usual boom-town saloon/gambling-hall entertainments, but such genteel activities as Sunday school picnics, church socials, dances at the opera house, a tennis court, and concerts—even the circus came to Rhyolite.

But by 1907 financial panic had begun to sweep the nation, and Rhyolite was hard hit. The railroads, so hungry to be in the city only a year earlier, were as anxious to leave as they were to get there. They ripped up their tracks, sold the metal and the ties, and deserted the depot.

After three frustrating years, only about 700 people remained in the city. By 1911 the Montgomery-Shoshone Mine, the last working mine, had overextended. It, too, closed shop. The remaining 700 workers lost little time in packing up their belongings and moving out.

It must have been discouraging for those remaining 700 people to see what had happened to their town. They had watched, helpless, as friends and neighbors hightailed it to other places, watched as thousands abandoned their businesses, paper still on their desks, houses full of furniture. Undoubtedly, they wondered how a city that had once held so much promise could fade so quickly.

The *Herald* reported the town's demise:

April 1910: The street lights were turned off, and there were no longer funds available to pay for water.

May 1910: There were no more banking facilities; H. D. and L. D. Porter sold out their entire stock of merchandise at everything-must-go prices; the Commercial Hotel was sold to a D. Pecetto, who moved the entire structure, furnishings and all, to Las Vegas.

March 1911: The Montgomery-Shoshone closed down; two issues later *Herald* editor Earle R. Clements published his "Goodbye, Dear Old Rhyolite" editorial and fled for the coast. His newspaper died that May.

By 1920 there were only 14 residents left in Rhyolite. Some stayed until they were so poor they couldn't afford to move their belongings when they left.

In 1922 a visiting motor tour from the *Los Angeles Times* found only one remaining inhabitant, a 92-year-old Frenchman, J. D. Lorraine.

What was once Nevada's biggest city is now the biggest ghost town, creaking—and, somehow, noble—in the wail of the desert winds.

PIOCHE: Want to visit the site of the wildest, baddest shoot-'em-up boomcamp in the West? It's Pioche, 175 miles northeast of Las Vegas via U.S. 93.

Discovered in 1863 by William Hamblin (friendly Paiute Indians led the lucky prospector right to the ore-laden hills), the area was developed by a Frenchman from San Francisco named F. L. A. Pioche, who bought Hamblin's claim.

By 1870 the camp was well on its notorious way, with the first 75 deaths a result of shootings! During 1871–1872 over half the killings in the state of Nevada took place in or around Pioche. A murderer's row, fenced off from the more respectable dead, was started in the town's Boot Hill; it eventually became the resting place for about 100 killers. You can still see some of the graves today, and above them the remnants of a tramline that was used to carry ore buckets from the hills.

Though the camp produced over $40 million in ore, it is best remembered for myriad tales of violence. For example, there was the bartender named Faddiman whom everyone warned not to take a job in Pioche (no bartender had ever survived more than a year there). But he needed a job desperately, even one in a barely civilized town. His second week on the job he refused to serve a drunk another round. The drunk bounded over the bar, killed Faddiman with a six-shooter, stepped over the body, and helped himself to the contents of the till. Then continuing his rampage, he stepped next door, slit the throat of the buxom proprietress of the butcher shop, and emptied her till. The sheriff arrived and shot him full of holes. And so the graveyard grew.

Today you won't get shot at in Pioche, but you will see some interesting relics, among them the old Lincoln Courthouse. A museum and library are provided to acquaint visitors with Pioche history.

THE GRAND CANYON

There's really no way to describe the Grand Canyon, and oft-used phrases like "awesome panorama," "Seventh Wonder of the World," "timeless spectacle," "nature's finest monument," etc., cannot begin to evoke the reality.

More interesting is the story of the earth-building erosion that formed it, a story that spans two billion years of the earth's history.

The Grand Canyon is indeed *grand*. It spans 280 miles of the reddish-brown Colorado River, a powerful body of water that begins in the Rocky Mountains of Colorado and travels down 1,450 miles to the Gulf of California, with many canyons along its course.

Spaniards searching for gold discovered the Grand Canyon as early as 1540, but no attempts were made to comprehend its origin until the 1850s, when geologist John Strong Newberry explored the region. The subject is still a matter of debate, but all agree that it was carved by the dramatic upheavals of earth and the erosions caused by the powerful river.

The earliest rocks, dark and vertically layered, date from the early Precambrian era. During this era these rocks, sediments, and volcanic lavas were metamorphosed into mountains (as high as any in the world today), then eroded, bit by bit, to a plain near sea level. This stage began about 2 billion years ago and came to an end about 1.2 billion years ago. Though no fossil traces have been found in rocks dating to this period, scientists have uncovered signs of organisms and single-celled plants believed to have existed here. Perhaps the titanic forces of mountain building and erosion erased fossil evidence.

In the next stage of development, the late Precambrian era, sediments began to build in the shallow water that covered the eroded mountain remnants. The first layer was of algae-formed limestone reefs, and next came a brilliant vermilion rock, above which came deposits of a hard quartz-sand rock. Other layers accumulated until the thickness of rocks created in this era was over 12,000 feet. Approximately 600 million years ago this second stage, which also included the formation and erosion of another mountain range, was completed. Late Precambrian rocks can be seen today along the South and North Kaibab trails, in the

Shinumo amphitheater to the west of Grand Canyon Village, and on the floor at the eastern end of the canyon.

During the Paleozoic era that followed (it ended about 230 million years ago), the upper two-thirds of the canyon walls were formed, only to be covered in Mesozoic times (those were the days when dinosaurs roamed the earth) with sediments of 4,000 and 8,000 feet.

Then in the present era, the Cenozoic (it began about 65 million years ago), the Mesozoic rocks were eroded; you can still see the remnants of them at Cedar Mountain, the Painted Desert, and Zion Canyon. It was in this final period that the most widespread erosion took place and the earth was sculpted as we see it today. The last series of violent changes took place over a million years ago, when molten rock from deep within the earth spewed forth, creating volcanoes.

And of course, geology never comes to a standstill, even at America's major tourist attraction. Ultimately, after millions of years have passed, the Grand Canyon may one day be a level plain with the tired remains of the Colorado River flowing across it.

TO THE GRAND CANYON'S SOUTH RIM BY AIR: You
can fly to the South Rim of the Grand Canyon from Las Vegas, spend the day sightseeing, souvenir hunting, and enjoying lunch with a view, and be back in your Las Vegas hotel by early evening. What's more, the flights in twin-engine, nine-passenger Cessnas dip hundreds of feet below the canyon's rim—for the ultimate in spectacular views.

Scenic Airlines, 241 E. Reno Ave., Las Vegas, NV 89119 (tel. 739-5611), runs deluxe, full-day, air-ground tours for $181 per person, that price including lunch at the Grand Canyon, plus all air and ground transportation with guides. For children aged 2 to 11 the cost is $141. A four-hour air tour (basically a round-trip flight, to and from the South Rim airport) is $156, and a deluxe overnight tour, including lodging at the Canyon Squire Motor Inn, is pegged at $156 per person, based on double occupancy (single occupancy is $176; triple occupancy, $146).

The Freedom Tour gives you the round-trip flight and a three-hour stopover at the Grand Canyon South Rim to enjoy walking along the rim, hiking into the Canyon, or a variety of optional activities, for $156 per person.

In addition to the standard nine-passenger planes used by most Grand Canyon tour operators (every seat is by a window), Scenic Airlines features deluxe Vista Liners. The wings of these planes are above the oversize windows so the view is completely unobstructed. Six of the Vista Liners' 19 seats are on the aisle, but the windows are large enough that even views from these seats are terrific. The unique individual narration system translates to eight languages simultaneously. It costs an extra $10 each way to take the Vista Liner; it's well worth the price to try it at least one way.

Note: Both the nine-seaters and Vista Liners are very small planes, so they are much more at the mercy of air currents than larger craft. If you are susceptible to air sickness, it would be wise to take an air-sickness preventive before your flights. (But don't let this minor inconvenience prevent you from experiencing this trip of a lifetime!)

Several other companies offer similar excursions to the Grand Canyon from Las Vegas, and **Republic Airlines** (tel. 739-5784) has daily DC-9 service between the two (without the same spectacular close-up views of the canyon, of course).

The South Rim of the Grand Canyon is 225 miles from Las Vegas on the route flown east; the westbound return flight, more direct, is 185 air miles. Flying time to Grand Canyon Airport—an hour and 15 minutes.

Hues of the cliffs and slopes along the canyon's walls, mostly red sandstone, change with the passing day, painted by the sun and varied weather conditions. Its lowest points are a mile deep, a distance from which the mighty Colorado River appears no bigger than a thin stream. Boulders, rocks, and sediment are the grinding tools of the Colorado, employed for eons to cut deeper and deeper into the chasm.

From your first glimpse of the Colorado River, you're flying mostly over federal lands, "high desert" in local parlance, which means mountainous territory, as barren and dramatically sparse as the lower deserts you'll see around Las Vegas. The Colorado River and its contributing sources flow through the high-plateau country and on to the Gulf of California, 1,450 miles from their beginnings. The Grand Canyon was hewn from the southern slopes of the Kaibab Plateau. Its North Rim is about 8,200 feet above sea level; the South Rim, about 7,000.

The plateau reaches an elevation of 9,000 feet to the north. In width, the canyon averages 9 miles, with various distances measuring from 4 to 18 miles. The total area of the Grand Canyon, administered by the National Park Service, is 1,052 square miles (673,575 acres).

The South Rim of the canyon is open all year. Most visitors are concerned only with the South Rim, where hotels, dining, and shopping multifacilities are run by the Fred Harvey Company under a sort of grandfather-clause contract that's guaranteed him almost-exclusive commercial rights since 1904.

The Fred Harvey Company

Many of us who hail from east of Chicago first encountered the Fred Harvey name in the Judy Garland movie *The Harvey Girls,* which was famous for the tune, "The Atchison, Topeka, and the Santa Fe." The film romanticized history about how Harvey moved groups of chaperoned young ladies west, to work in his restaurants in such places as railroad junctions. That's where the action used to be, in the century before air travel. Not surprisingly, many of the Harvey girls married and settled down to help populate the American West.

Harvey made several fortunes with his concessions, eventually settling into a good number of the great national parks, building hotels and stores, lucrative operations that have outstripped gold mining for income by far. It appears that the empire he built in the West will go forever. He moved into the South Rim of the Grand Canyon in 1904. The Fred Harvey Company now is owned by Amfac, Inc. (canyon address: Grand Canyon National Park Lodges, P.O. Box 699, Grand Canyon, AZ 86023).

When you consider that the Harvey folks have practically no competition, they do a very good job. If you plan to stay over for a couple of days at the canyon, you'll snuggle into one of the Harvey hotels. And if you take a two-day mule trip down into the canyon, you'll ride one of the Harvey-trained mules.

Rooms at the canyon are as scarce as hen's teeth during the summer. You must—repeat, *must!*—make reservations in advance of your visit. Off-season, rooms are plentiful.

The hotel and lodges described below are part of the Grand Canyon National Park Lodges organization. For reservations at any one, call 602/638-2631.

The 70-room **El Tovar Hotel** is the classic lodge, spacious and rambling, with broad porches. Open year round, it's built of native boulders and great pine logs. All accommodations here were renovated a few years back. The better rooms offer views across the canyon. All rooms have bath with tub and shower, TV, and a switchboard phone. There's a big lobby with a fireplace. Nightly rate is $100 to $120, single or double occupancy; $7 for an extra person in a room. A few suites and posher digs run $140 to $225 a night.

The El Tovar's dining room serves both table d'hôte and à la carte meals. The food is hearty, all-American fare. Breakfasts are whooping affairs, dished out with the gusto of ranchhand informality. A cocktail lounge adjoins.

The **Bright Angel Lodge** offers a wide range of rustic accommodations year round. Rim cabins with bath, sleeping up to four people, are $55 to $70 for single or double occupancy; the same with fireplace are $70 a night. An extra person pays $7. A coffeeshop and cocktail lounge are on the premises.

The **Kachina Lodge,** adjacent to El Tovar, is a modern two-story facility. All rooms are equipped with bath/shower, TV, and phone, and some are canyonside. Single or double rooms rent for $84 to $91. The adjoining **Thunderbird Lodge** offers identical rates and facilities.

The **Yavapai Lodge East and West,** situated in pine and juniper woodlands, is a two-story facility offering rooms with bath, TV, and phone; it's open from Easter to November only. It is approximately three-quarters of a mile from the main village area, but is adjacent to the Mather Shopping Center. Rates are $62 to $71, single or double; $7 for each additional person.

In the southwest corner of the village area, just minutes from the canyon rim, the **Maswik Lodge** offers rooms with two double beds, bath, TV, and phone for $57 to $82, single or double; $7 for each additional person. It's open year round.

At the very bottom of the canyon, a vertical mile down, the **Phantom Ranch** offers a central lodge, rustic cabins, and a night of rest on a dozen acres. Dormitory facilities are $20 per person per night. Since cabin facilities are limited, it is neccessary to call the main number given above for rates and availability.

Outside the park boundary, six miles from Grand Canyon Village, is **Moqui Lodge,** a rustic accommodation offering rooms with two double beds and bath, but no phone. It's open from March to December. Rates are $58 to $63, single or double; $7 for each additional person.

Mule Trains

Long-eared mules have been used for visitor descents into the canyon since 1912. Unbroken stock is purchased in Tennessee and Missouri mainly, and the mules are trained at the canyon. They're big animals, bigger than most horses, and strong.

Some mules never measure up to carrying people, and they're used for packing supplies only. When a mule starts carrying riders, he's been trained as a pack animal for at least a year. Mules are considered to be the only animals sure-footed enough and fit for the strenuous work of descending into and climbing back up out of the canyon.

The two-day trail trip by mule (tel. 602/638-2631) includes guide, mule, box lunch, two meals, and overnight accommodations for $210 single, $360 for a couple. One-day rides to Plateau Point are also available at $70 per person, including box lunch.

This trip isn't for the faint of heart. The minimum height for descent into the canyon is 4 feet 7 inches. And you must weigh under 200 pounds, and be of good physical condition and sufficient stamina to take the heat and the saddlesore seating that you get on a mule. I suggest you make reservations six to nine months in advance for in-season (April 1 to October 31) trips.

For Your Information

In Grand Canyon Village, illustrated and informal talks are given by Park Service lecturers every summer evening. Talks are scheduled at specific times, which are posted on bulletin boards at the lodges.

Material covering geology, biology, prehistory, and other features of the canyon is exhibited at the **Park Headquarters and Visitor Center,** the **Yavapai Museum,** and the **Tusayan Ruin and Museum** (farther out on the East Rim Drive).

INDEX

NOW, SAVE MONEY ON ALL YOUR TRAVELS!
Join Frommer's™ Dollarwise® Travel Club

Saving money while traveling is never a simple matter, which is why, over 27 years ago, the **Dollarwise Travel Club** was formed. Actually, the idea came from readers of the Frommer publications who felt that such an organization could bring financial benefits, continuing travel information, and a sense of community to economy-minded travelers all over the world.

In keeping with the money-saving concept, the annual membership fee is low—$18 (U.S. residents) or $20 U.S. (Canadian, Mexican, and foreign residents)—and is immediately exceeded by the value of your benefits which include:

1. The latest edition of any TWO of the books listed on the following pages.

2. A copy of any Frommer City Guide.

3. An annual subscription to an 8-page quarterly newspaper *The Dollarwise Traveler* which keeps you up-to-date on fastbreaking developments in good-value travel in all parts of the world—bringing you the kind of information you'd have to pay over $35 a year to obtain elsewhere. This consumer-conscious publication also includes the following columns:

> **Hospitality Exchange**—members all over the world who are willing to provide hospitality to other members as they pass through their home cities.
>
> **Share-a-Trip**—requests from members for travel companions who can share costs and help avoid the burdensome single supplement.
>
> **Readers Ask . . . Readers Reply**—travel questions from members to which other members reply with authentic firsthand information.

4. Your personal membership card which entitles you to purchase through the club all Frommer publications for a third to a half off their regular retail prices during the term of your membership.

So why not join this hardy band of international Dollarwise travelers now and participate in its exchange of information and hospitality? Simply send $18 (U.S. residents) or $20 U.S. (Canadian, Mexican, and other foreign residents) along with your name and address to: Frommer's Dollarwise Travel Club, Inc., Gulf + Western Building, One Gulf + Western Plaza, New York, NY 10023. Remember to specify which *two* of the books in section (1) and which *one* in section (2) above you wish to receive in your initial package of member's benefits. Or tear out the next page, check off your choices, and send the page to us with your membership fee.

FROMMER BOOKS
PRENTICE HALL PRESS
ONE GULF + WESTERN PLAZA
NEW YORK, NY 10023

Date_____

Friends:
Please send me the books checked below:

FROMMER'S™ $-A-DAY® GUIDES

(In-depth guides to sightseeing and low-cost tourist accommodations and facilities.)

☐ Europe on $30 a Day	$14.95	☐ New Zealand on $40 a Day	$12.95
☐ Australia on $30 a Day	$12.95	☐ New York on $50 a Day	$12.95
☐ Eastern Europe on $25 a Day	$12.95	☐ Scandinavia on $50 a Day	$12.95
☐ England on $40 a Day	$12.95	☐ Scotland and Wales on $40 a Day	$12.95
☐ Greece on $30 a Day	$12.95	☐ South America on $30 a Day	$12.95
☐ Hawaii on $50 a Day	$13.95	☐ Spain and Morocco (plus the Canary Is.)	
☐ India on $25 a Day	$12.95	on $40 a Day	$13.95
☐ Ireland on $30 a Day	$12.95	☐ Turkey on $25 a Day	$12.95
☐ Israel on $30 & $35 a Day	$12.95	☐ Washington, D.C., & Historic Va. on	
☐ Mexico (plus Belize & Guatemala)		$40 a Day	$12.95
on $25 a Day	$13.95		

FROMMER'S™ DOLLARWISE® GUIDES

(Guides to sightseeing and tourist accommodations and facilities from budget to deluxe, with emphasis on the medium-priced.)

☐ Alaska	$13.95	☐ Cruises (incl. Alask, Carib, Mex, Hawaii,	
☐ Austria & Hungary	$14.95	Panama, Canada, & US)	$14.95
☐ Belgium, Holland, Luxembourg	$13.95	☐ California & Las Vegas	$14.95
☐ Brazil (avail. Nov. 1988)	$14.95	☐ Florida	$13.95
☐ Egypt	$13.95	☐ Mid-Atlantic States	$13.95
☐ France	$14.95	☐ New England	$13.95
☐ England & Scotland	$14.95	☐ New York State	$13.95
☐ Germany	$13.95	☐ Northwest	$13.95
☐ Italy	$14.95	☐ Skiing in Europe	$14.95
☐ Japan & Hong Kong	$13.95	☐ Skiing USA—East	$13.95
☐ Portugal, Madeira, & the Azores	$13.95	☐ Skiing USA—West	$13.95
☐ South Pacific	$13.95	☐ Southeast & New Orleans	$13.95
☐ Switzerland & Liechtenstein	$13.95	☐ Southwest	$14.95
☐ Bermuda & The Bahamas	$13.95	☐ Texas	$13.95
☐ Canada	$13.95	☐ USA (avail. Feb. 1989)	$15.95
☐ Caribbean	$13.95		

FROMMER'S™ TOURING GUIDES

(Color illustrated guides that include walking tours, cultural & historic sites, and other vital travel information.)

☐ Australia	$9.95	☐ Paris	$8.95
☐ Egypt	$8.95	☐ Thailand	$9.95
☐ Florence	$8.95	☐ Venice	$8.95
☐ London	$8.95		

TURN PAGE FOR ADDITIONAL BOOKS AND ORDER FORM.

FROMMER'S™ CITY GUIDES

(Pocket-size guides to sightseeing and tourist accommodations and facilities in all price ranges.)

☐ Amsterdam/Holland	$5.95	☐ Montreal/Quebec City	$5.95
☐ Athens	$5.95	☐ New Orleans	$5.95
☐ Atlantic City/Cape May	$5.95	☐ New York	$5.95
☐ Boston	$5.95	☐ Orlando/Disney World/EPCOT	$5.95
☐ Cancún/Cozumel/Yucatán	$5.95	☐ Paris	$5.95
☐ Dublin/Ireland	$5.95	☐ Philadelphia	$5.95
☐ Hawaii	$5.95	☐ Rio (avail. Nov. 1988)	$5.95
☐ Las Vegas	$5.95	☐ Rome	$5.95
☐ Lisbon/Madrid/Costa del Sol	$5.95	☐ San Francisco	$5.95
☐ London	$5.95	☐ Santa Fe/Taos (avail. Mar. 1989)	$5.95
☐ Los Angeles	$5.95	☐ Sydney	$5.95
☐ Mexico City/Acapulco	$5.95	☐ Washington, D.C.	$5.95
☐ Minneapolis/St. Paul	$5.95		

SPECIAL EDITIONS

☐ A Shopper's Guide to the Caribbean	$12.95	☐ Motorist's Phrase Book (Fr/Ger/Sp)	$4.95
☐ Beat the High Cost of Travel	$6.95	☐ Paris Rendez-Vous	$10.95
☐ Bed & Breakfast—N. America	$8.95	☐ Swap and Go (Home Exchanging)	$10.95
☐ Guide to Honeymoon Destinations		☐ The Candy Apple (NY for Kids)	$11.95
(US, Canada, Mexico, & Carib.)	$12.95	☐ Travel Diary and Record Book	$5.95
☐ Manhattan's Outdoor Sculpture	$15.95	☐ Where to Stay USA (Lodging from $3	
		to $30 a night)	$10.95

☐ Marilyn Wood's Wonderful Weekends (NY, Conn, Mass, RI, Vt, NH, NJ, Del, Pa) ... $11.95
☐ The New World of Travel (Annual sourcebook by Arthur Frommer previewing: new travel trends, new modes of travel, and the latest cost-cutting strategies for savvy travelers) ... $12.95

SERIOUS SHOPPER'S GUIDES

(Illustrated guides listing hundreds of stores, conveniently organized alphabetically by category)

☐ Italy	$15.95	☐ Los Angeles	$14.95
☐ London	$15.95	☐ Paris	$15.95

GAULT MILLAU

(The only guides that distinguish the truly superlative from the merely overrated.)

☐ The Best of Chicago (avail. Feb. 1989)	$15.95	☐ The Best of New England (avail. Feb.	
☐ The Best of France (avail. Feb. 1989)	$15.95	1989)	$15.95
☐ The Best of Italy (avail. Feb. 1989)	$15.95	☐ The Best of New York	$15.95
☐ The Best of Los Angeles	$15.95	☐ The Best of San Francisco	$15.95
		☐ The Best of Washington, D.C.	$15.95

ORDER NOW!

In U.S. include $1.50 shipping UPS for 1st book; 50¢ ea. add'l book. Outside U.S. $2 and 50¢, respectively. Allow four to six weeks for delivery in U.S., longer outside U.S.

Enclosed is my check or money order for $_____

NAME _____

ADDRESS _____

CITY _____ STATE _____ ZIP _____